Effective Evangelism:

The Greatest Work in the World

Effective Evangelism:

The Greatest Work in the World

by GEORGE E. SWEAZEY

1817

HARPER & ROW, PUBLISHERS
New York, Hagerstown, San Francisco, London

To Mary Handy Sweazey

Who Practices What I Preach

FIRST HARPER & ROW PAPERBACK EDITION PUBLISHED IN 1976.

ISBN: 0-06-067771-6

LIBRARY OF CONGRESS CATALOG CARD NUMBER: 53-5990

79 80 10 9 8 7 6 5 4 3 2

Contents

Preface to the Paperback Edition

This new edition contains a good many revisions. Some of them are required by our rapidly changing vocabulary. The increasingly important contribution made by women ministers makes a reference to "a brother minister" inappropriate. "Councils" have become "task-forces." "Personal" evangelism can now be called "relational." Some revisions are required by the change in mood. The past few years have been up-and-down ones for some church functions—for stewardship, Christian education, church attendance, evangelism. There are encouraging signs, but there is now not so much the exultation of a revival as a seeking of the sources from which revivals spring.

Every generation is right in thinking that it is living through a situation that is unlike any that was ever on the earth before. So in every generation there has been a demand for wholly new methods of evangelism because it is assumed that what has been successful in the past must be unsuited to the unprecedented species of humanity that has appeared. And in every age there has been a disappointing inability to discover any brand new evangelistic methods.

Surprisingly, perhaps, the ways by which the gospel can be communicated and people can be brought to faith in Christ have all been used, off and on, since the first century. One limitation on possible new ways of evangelism is the requirement that it must be personal. It is rare for anyone to become a Christian wtihout a contact with another person. Jeannie in Sir Walter Scott's novel *The Heart of Midlothian* flatly refuses to write to the king to beg for Effie's life. She insists that she has to go to London to make her plea in person because "a letter canna look, and pray, and beg, and beseech, as the human voice can do to the human heart." There are a limited number of human relationships through which a love for Christ can be conveyed. The contact may be person-to-person, or through the intimacy of small groups, or with one person speaking to a crowd. The means might be friendship, teaching, preaching, church fellowship, or the relationships within a home. There can be endless varieties of scene and manner. But it is unlikely that any new ways of relating people to each other for evangelism will be discovered.

Our generation has its special reasons for questioning the old ways of evangelism. Technology is explosively changing the conditions in which we exist. It has added outer space to human habitation, and it has caused the crowding of the space that is available for habitation on the earth. New means of preventing and prolonging life and of altering human character have introduced theological uncertainties. We might suppose that the vast extension of the human organs of sight and sound would produce new forms of consciousness that would require a new evangelism. From creation until my father's lifetime, the normal maximum distance for projecting intelligible speech in still air was about two hundred yards. I, with no strain, can project my voice to Tokyo. By satellite relays I can see almost instantly what is happening on the opposite side of the planet. But what I have to say to Tokyo is still confined to the very narrow limits of my personality. And what I get from that view from twelve thousand miles away depends on my hometown attitudes and sensitivity. The limits are still personal. In some ways technology inhibits an expansive consciousness. Contact with reality makes imagination less luxuriant. The awesomely diverse human family is becoming more homogenized. McLuhan's global village may give village states of mind a larger scale.

Putting astronauts on the moon simply moved the same old human drama to a larger stage. Miraculously, for a first-century Galilean, Jesus gave evangelism a worldwide scope. Indeed, the New Testament Greek says that Jesus sent his messengers "into all the *kosmos*." The Bible has always been more advanced than most of us in its reference to other spiritual beings who are not human. If future astronauts discover on some distant planet children of God who are not like us, it will affect the budgets of our ecumenical or mission agencies, but not their theology. Technological advances now require the evangelist to speak of compassion on a global scale. He has to point out that it is now a nuclear device, not a horse, that is "a vain thing for safety." But who we are and why God made us does not change. "Earth changes, but thy soul and God stand sure." The reasons for evangelism, and its message, and the essentials of how we have to go about it are not altered by external changes.

Goethe said, "Mankind is always advancing, but man remains always the same." Modern missionaries go out by jet, but they do not have to invent any jet-age methods of evangelism. The human situation when they are trying to share their faith with someone is just about what it was for those who went by sailing ship. The invention that would have seemed most likely to make the old evangelism out-of-date was not television or the computer but the printing press. Gutenberg made it possible for people everywhere to get the gospel. He let the most glowing evangelists of all time plead Christ's cause through words that can be read and pondered. This, as with all the other tools for communication, can be of great help when there is a human contact. But without that contact, the successful pleading of Christ's cause is not likely to take place.

The evangelism the modern world is needing will come from recovery and adaptation. Methods the Church has always had must be adapted to situations it has never had before. Vocabularies and moods and interests change so fast that the evangelist must move at top speed just to stay in touch. But once he gets in touch, he is on familiar ground.

The ways of getting the tried methods into use must keep changing. These better approaches are almost never rationally designed. When a denominational committee devises a scheme that is sent out to the churches, there may be every reason to expect it to succeed. But if it is the product of astute planning, with no sources in experience, it will probably fail. Progress in evangelism comes through what is tried out by individuals and congregations. Church executives and authors give their best help, not by recommending what ought to work, but by reporting what is working.

I have to admit that the program for "Evangelism Through Fellowship" (pages 186–89) demonstrates this. It had been thought out by denominational and ecumenical experts and was widely promoted when this book was originally written. It had been used successfully by youth groups, but not yet by other fellowship organizations. I am not sure that any of these others have ever tried it. I believe this is the only program recommended in this book which did not grow up out of practical experience, and which is not still being widely and successfully used. I have left it in because it illustrates how important fellowship groups are for evangelism. It may stimulate adult groups to lay out more explicit plans for the essential part they can play in their churches' efforts to draw people toward faith in Christ.

A book seems so long to the reader and so short to the writer! A good deal had to be cut from the original manuscript of this book to get it into a volume of reasonable size. A chapter on a church's spiritual preparation for evangelism was omitted in the hope that such preparation might be assumed. A chapter on the evangelism of special economic and cultural groups was left out. Many Bible references were omitted—the connections may be obvious. Stories of what has happened to people and to churches were regretfully removed; they were heartwarming but do not add much practical information and it should be plain that what this book recommends has been tested by much experience.

In this book, I have conformed to the custom in our language of using a capital C when referring to the Christian Church and the denomination and a lower case c when referring to the congregation and the building that houses it.

Effective Evangelism:

The Greatest Work in the World

I

The Walk with God

EVANGELISM IS A CONNECTED SERIES OF STEPS, EACH DEPENDING ON THE OTHERS.
"Can mass meetings bring people to Christ?" "Is lay visitation real evangelism?" "Is educational evangelism the right way?" "Does it do any good to 'bear witness' at every opportunity?" The answer to each of these questions can be "yes" if what is done is joined to something before and after it; the answer must be "no" if what is done is an isolated act.

This step-by-step process of evangelism can be seen through a beautiful Bible image. Repeatedly the Bible pictures the purpose of the earthly life as learning to walk with God. "Enoch walked with God: and he was not; for God took him" (Genesis 5:24). "As ye have therefore received Christ Jesus the Lord, so walk ye in him" (Colossians 2:6). "They shall walk with me" (Revelation 3:4). As each year we walk more closely with God, in our doing and our thinking, we become ready, like Enoch, to go on with Him into the Unknown—as with a friend whom we have come to love and trust. *The goal of evangelism is to bring people, through Jesus Christ, to walk with God.*

1. Contact

The first step is to turn toward the Church some of the feet which have been passing by its doors.

The Church has been put on earth by God to bring people to walk with Him. If it is to save men and society, it must have some way of making a contact with the secular masses beyond its doors. Most of those who pass it by do not dislike the Church, they do not like it—they simply do not think about it. It has no relevance for them. They regard it as the romantic but unnecessary hobby of the few who seem to need it. Evangelism has to find a way of breaking into this closed state of mind. It starts by arousing some sort of personal feeling for the Church.

The great weakness of much evangelism has been that it was addressed "To whom it may concern." That sort of invitation is not often accepted. Evangelism cannot commence until the Church has made a definite contact with individual people to whom it can give a direct appeal.

It is at this stage that evangelism uses a neighborhood religious census. Advertising, bowling teams and social events can make contacts for the Church. Community service and everything which builds good public relationships are important for evangelism at this level. Perhaps all of these should be called "pre-evangelism"; they make the situation in which evangelism can take place.

2. Cultivation

The second step is to get those who have turned toward the Church to put one foot inside the door.

Most of those outside the Church are not mentally or spiritually able to commit their lives to Jesus Christ. They must be held by some connection which will prepare them for the great day on which they can rightly join the Christian fellowship. It is at this stage that educational evangelism is needed. Church attendance is important. Evangelism through fellowship—drawing people from outside the Church into its organizations and activities—can make them ready for Church membership. Inquirers' Groups serve splendidly in this. Christian radio programs and gospel tracts and books can be of great value in preparing people to commit their lives to Christ.

The great danger is that this step will be a byway instead of a highway for the Lord. Religious education can produce those who have the facts and lack the feelings. Church organizations can become stops instead of steps into the Church. Religious broadcasts can encourage people to try to get all their spiritual nourishment from the air; they may create radio Christians—a class which the New Testament would not have recognized.

In this we can see clearly why evangelism must be a connected series of steps, each depending on the others. Contact and Cultivation lose their value without Commitment. But if a church neglects those first two steps, it soon ceases to get commitments. Its list of prospective members plays out. Its visitors come back disheartened by impossible calls. Its evangelistic preaching begins to falter because no one who is not a member is within earshot of it. Its whole evangelistic program grinds to a stop and stays stopped until another supply of possible new members slowly accumulates—which may take years if the church waits for them to drift in.

If a church is to be continuously evangelistic—which is to say, if a church is to be continuously a church in the full sense of its Lord's intention—it must work at all the stages in evangelism. It is this which distinguishes truly evangelistic churches from those which have only enough zeal for quick successes and spasmodic efforts.

3. Commitment

The next step is to get both feet in the Church, as people come all the way into membership and become acknowledged followers of Christ.

All experience confirms the Bible's repeated statements that the full benefits of the Christian life can be known only by those who have made up their minds—and said so (Matthew 10:32, Romans 10:9, I John 4:15). The state of "maybe" or "I suppose so" must be ended by the taking of a definite stand for Christ. A conviction never controls until it is consciously and clearly accepted. Some people come into the Christian life gradually and others abruptly, but all need a landmark which makes it clear that they have come. Vagueness specially threatens those who have always been surrounded by Christian influences and so have never seen a sharp boundary line between faith and unbelief. Jesus Christ cannot be taken for granted, even by those who have known of Him from their earliest childhood.

The Church must offer ways by which people can say—to the world and to themselves—"From this hour I know that I have accepted Christ as my Saviour and the Lord of all my life." The form of expression may be a written covenant, a handclasp, a spoken statement. The opportunity may be given in a church service, by callers in a home, at a youth conference, in a class. From the human side, all of the methods look inadequate; but there are many which God can use to work His miracle in human hearts.

Much of the Church's inefficiency comes from its neglect of this step. Of every one hundred pupils reached by the Sunday schools, sixty will disappear into the secular community; they have had the preliminaries of evangelism but have never been brought to a decisive experience with Christ. Church colleges have missed much of their function of producing strong members for the Church and Christian leaders for the community because their good Christian influences have been fixed by nothing. The impressions made by chapel services and Christian teachers resulted in no permanent decisions, so they soon became faded memories.

Commitment is only one part of the evangelistic process. Here again we see why there must be a connected series of steps. The whole value of a "decision" depends on what comes before and after it. Getting decisions—by evangelistic meetings or visitation campaigns—has too typically been all that people think of as "evangelism."

There must be preparation for Commitment. When the Church asks people to use words they do not understand—words like "profess my faith," "become a disciple," "be a Christian"—it does them grave spiritual damage. It is our modern form of the old error of unknown tongues—words with great emotional impact and no content. People are not necessarily accepting Christ when, perhaps with deep feeling, they accept a slogan in which the letters which spell His name appear. It is not a phantom Christ the Church is offering; there must be some knowledge of Who He is—immature though it may be.

On the other hand, Commitments depend on what comes next. The sawdust trail is too often a blind alley. This has been the unforgivable failure of evangelism; new Church members have been left to sink or swim and, as might have been expected, a tragically large and unnecessary proportion of them sank—about half, according to most church statistics.

4. Conservation

When both feet are inside the Church, the essential next step is to start them to walking.

Many who have come inside the door stand stock-still until they fall back out again. The Church must put loving hands on the shoulders of its new members and guide and propel them until they have learned to walk in the Way.

"Conversion," from the Latin *convertere*, "to rotate," is not a leap, it is a turning. It leaves a person about where he was before, but now aimed in a different direction. Change depends on what happens next. Two laymen by an evangelistic visit, or a preacher from the pulpit, can turn a person who has been facing in the wrong direction or in no particular direction until that person is facing directly toward Jesus Christ. That is important; it is life's great turning point. But the question still remains, "Is that person who has faced toward Jesus Christ now going to walk toward Him?"

Theologians may argue about whether or not Christians can backslide, but there is no doubt that Church members can. That implies no slight on Church members. We have here again the inevitable paradox—we are to trust as though everything were in God's hands, and we are to work as though great destinies depended on us. It is an abuse of theology which encourages churches to neglect their duty to their new members in the belief that " 'tis done, the great transaction's done." Even by the strictest Calvinistic doctrine, the Church must unceasingly labor to help its members make their calling and election sure. God has commissioned His Church to do everything it can to bring its new and old members constantly nearer to Christ.

The most important part of evangelism comes after people join the Church. There is an introductory period during which they need special instruction and oversight. They must be helped to catch up, in knowledge and attitudes, with those who have been in the Church before them. They are teachable in this opening period, as they will never be again. It is at this stage that evangelism needs special classes and reading programs and sponsors and training in Christian habits and induction into church friendships.

After how long a time does the care of new members cease to be an evangelistic responsibility? Any definite answer to that question will be arbitrary; but, without some limits, evangelism becomes everything and therefore nothing. The Church's distinct duty to reach outside itself to bring people into Christian faith and living has to be kept distinct. It may be well to think of evangelism as continuing for the first twelve or eighteen months after people join the Church. Beyond that, their care becomes a part of the normal "nurture of the saints."

Contact, Cultivation, Commitment, Conservation—all are essential for evangelism. Church people are sometimes inclined to specialize on just one of these, saying, "This is the sort of evangelism in which we believe." That temperamental preference is the clue to a one-sidedness which will cripple everything that a church does.

The view of evangelism as a connected series of steps makes it plain that it must be the work of the whole church. Evangelism failed when it came to be regarded as a special activity for special people at special times. It is succeeding when it is made a normal activity for all the church people all the time. Today's evangelism must be a regular part of the church program; no follower of the Saviour can dismiss it as someone else's duty; there are no closed seasons for the fishers of men.

When evangelism is seen to be a linked process it becomes obvious that the Church is the only adequate evangelistic agency. Only an organized congregation is able to care for all the steps by which people become Christians. Unattached evangelism can be colorful and wide ranging. Billboards, broadcasts, street meetings, talks to luncheon clubs—these may have some introductory value. But unless they start from the Church and lead back to the Church, their results are likely to be temporary.

There are churches in every town and in almost every neighborhood in America, and these offer the best chance to bring men's lives to Christ. The great hope for making this a more Christian nation lies in making its churches more effective in evangelism. The Church has been divinely established and equipped to bring people, through Jesus Christ, to walk with God.

II

Getting Our Bearings

1. What Evangelism Is

EVANGELISM IS EVERY POSSIBLE WAY OF REACHING OUTSIDE THE
CHURCH TO BRING PEOPLE TO FAITH IN CHRIST AND MEMBERSHIP
IN HIS CHURCH.

Words are fragile things, easily damaged. The word "evangelism"
has been spoiled for many church people. They associate it with
the shouter who makes a career of cheapening religion, or with
the zealot who demands, "Brother, are you a Christian?" They
may have the uneasy feeling that it is something they ought to be
doing, but their very flesh recoils from the thought.

This word is really one of the most beautiful in the vocabulary
of religion. It has a rich heritage of Bible association and a precious
tradition which the Church cannot spare. As art experts restore
an old master, we must take away the accumulations which have
obscured this word so that its glory can be seen and loved.

That is just what the modern Church is doing. It is taking
evangelism from the realm of the queer and the flamboyant and
showing it to be something which the ordinary Church member
likes and wants to try. As a denominational leader said, "A few
years ago, whenever in a meeting there was a discussion of
evangelism, people all over the room would get up to talk about
the sort of evangelism that would not work any more; but if the
Chairman said, 'Let's talk about what we *can* be doing,' a great
silence would fall upon the room. Today such groups are likely
to plunge immediately into discussions of what they themselves
have done, and how they can do it better."

The Church has been redefining evangelism in terms which

bring it straight into everyday living. Here are some of these modern definitions:

The Madras Foreign Missions Council—*Evangelism is so to "present Jesus Christ to the world in the power of the Holy Spirit that men shall come to put their trust in God through Him, accept Him as their Savior and serve Him as their Lord in the fellowship of His Church."*

The World Council of Churches at Amsterdam—*Evangelism is "so making Christ known to men that each is confronted with the necessity of a personal decision, Yes or No."*

Toyohiko Kagawa—*"Evangelism means the conversion of people from worldliness to Christlike godliness."*

Albert W. Beaven—*"Evangelism is simply the contagion of enthusiasm for Jesus Christ. The methods which we employ are only channels through which this enthusiasm flows."*

Archbishop Temple—*"Evangelism is the winning of men to acknowledge Christ as their Saviour and King, so that they may give themselves to His service in the fellowship of His Church."*

Samuel Boon-Itt of Siam—*"Evangelism means living, doing and talking for Christ."*

The Bible gives some rich insights into the meaning of the word. Before Christian times a joyful proclamation from the Roman Emperor was called, in the Greek-speaking provinces, an *"evangel"*—a "good-message." The New Testament took that word and made it sublime. The angel Gabriel told the awed Zacharias that he had come to show him the *evangel* (Luke 1:19). The glory-filled skies over Bethlehem rang with "the *evangel* of great joy which shall be to all people" (Luke 2:10). Jesus went among men "showing the *evangel* of the kingdom of God" (Luke 8:1). Paul is reminded of how beautiful are the feet of them that "bring the *evangel* of good things!" (Romans 10:15.)

The Church must jealously guard this word "evangelism." It can be stolen, not only by those who would limit it to what is too narrow, but by those who would waste it on what is too broad. The task of REACHING OUTSIDE THE CHURCH TO BRING PEOPLE TO FAITH IN CHRIST AND MEMBERSHIP IN HIS CHURCH is a distinct and specific duty. The word "evangelism" is the one which has traditionally been used for this duty. When the word is obscured, the duty is obscured.

The word and the duty are commonly obscured by forgetting that evangelism is: (a) directed to those *outside the Church,* (b) intended to bring them to a *definite and acknowledged faith.*

2. What Evangelism Is Not

"Why, everything we do is evangelism!" Beware of that often-heard plea. It is a sure sign that nothing that is done is evangelism. It is the defense of an inbred congregation which hopes to justify the devoting of all its energies to itself. It is the excuse of the program chairman when there has been no reference to evangelism in a Church convention. It is the honest bewilderment of the person who has never found out what evangelism really is. It is the rationalization of the church member whose faith is too unclear to seem worth sharing. It is the plea of the minister who has never learned to talk with people about their faith, and of the Church college which has forgotten why it was founded.

"A good Christian life is the best evangelism." No—it is pre-evangelism, but it is not evangelism. Such a life will produce admiring observers; it will make people receptive to an evangelistic approach. But until such an approach is made, the most beautiful Christian life in the community will bring no one to an experience with Christ or to prayer or to Bible reading or to Church membership. Christianity cannot be radiated. It is not only an attitude and a spirit—it is also a body of truth; and Christian attitudes have support only when those truths—about God and His Son and man—have been accepted. Knowledge of this truth can no more be radiated than can a knowledge of arithmetic. Evangelism must be definite. It is this old necessity which modern theologians have rediscovered as "confrontation." Evangelism might be made more popular in some circles by calling it *Begegnung*—which is just what it is.

"The witness of our church's life and ministry is our evangelism —we don't have to go out after people." This is the church form of the old fallacy that if a man builds a better mousetrap the world will beat a path to his door. It was never true of mousetraps, and it is not true of churches. A church's good influence in a community will produce well-disposed outsiders who will remain outsiders until someone says, "This is for you." Oscar Wilde wrote of his Aunt Jane, who died of mortification when no one came to her grand ball. She died without knowing that she had failed to mail the invitations. That is the story of many a fine church which has wonderful worship services, a splendid program—has everything, in fact, save a way of making some connection with those outside, who always assume that what the Church has is for someone else.

"The evangelizing of the Church membership is our first duty." This ignores the distinction which the New Testament always clearly makes between the nurture of those already in the Church, and *kerygma*—the appeal to the unsaved. Theology distinguishes between sanctifying—the care of the converted, and saving—the winning of converts. Practical experience shows that the improvement of those who consider themselves to be a part of the Church requires a psychology and methods quite different from those needed to bring those outside the Church into the Christian life. Moreover, a church which puts its own spiritual welfare ahead of its concern for others is pursuing a receding goal. Evangelism and revival always go together.

"Our officers' retreat was real evangelism." "The every-member canvass is evangelism in action." "If feeding those starving Europeans isn't evangelism, then I don't know what evangelism is!" Such statements reveal the confusion which blunts the evangelistic mission. "Evangelism" is not just a catchword to be used for ornament. Unless the Church has a special word for the special duty of *bringing those outside its membership to faith* that duty will never be clear. From the World Council of Churches and our great denominational agencies to our smallest local church committees, we will be wise to save the word "evangelism" for that specific meaning which the Bible and the historic Church have given it.

3. Conservative and Liberal Misunderstandings

Evangelism is spoiled equally by attempts to change its message and reluctance to change its methods. It has to be as up-to-date as the morning paper and as old as the ways of God with men. There has been no really new discovery in evangelism in the past nineteen hundred years. Every revival has been a recovery of what Christians already knew. But what is changeless must be fitted into a perpetually changing scene. It must be directed to new situations, new moods, new points of view. Thus a vital evangelism will be under criticism from both sides.

A true conservative mistakes the moss on his shoulder blades for wing buds. He will oppose any change from the ways of the past with the emotional intensity of one who believes that he is fighting for the angels. He will be hurt by an attempt to state Christian truth in terms which were not used in his youth.

The self-conscious progressive is likely to be dubious about anything as old-fashioned as evangelism. As nearly as can be learned, through a vocabulary which bristles with terms from all the new sciences and none of the arts, he expects Christianity to be propagated through the subconscious. Beliefs are to be given to people while they are not looking.

Evangelism can learn from both sorts of critics; but it is done for when it is dominated by either.

4. Evaluating the Techniques

A great many modern Christians are in the peculiar position of believing in evangelism in general without believing in any sort of evangelism in particular. They find reason to mistrust all the methods. Every evangelistic method the Church has ever used can do great harm; it may therefore easily be discredited by calling attention to its misuse. Evangelism is always dangerous—though not so dangerous as the lack of evangelism. Any evangelistic method must be taught to a church as a boy is taught to use a gun —the first lessons must be on its safe handling.

A part of the scorn of methods comes from the illusion that there is something unspiritual about committee meetings and mimeograph machines and filing cards. This may derive from a misplaced mysticism or from plain weariness. Finney used to say, "Revivals have to be worked up as well as prayed down." While it is true that a church can be overmechanized, it is just as true that no great thing can be done without mechanics. Machinery does not have to kill the spirit. Ezekiel saw God in a vision of wheels, and wheels within wheels—but the divine Spirit was shining through the wheels. That is the test for all church machinery—there is not too much of it as long as the Spirit still dominates the machine.

New evangelistic techniques are often not added tasks but more efficient ways of doing something on which effort has been wasted. By requiring hours they save years.

Methods are often rejected on the plea, "We cannot do that—we are different." There is no such thing as a normal church. Every congregation applies to itself the text, "The Lord hath chosen thee to be a peculiar people." New Englanders are sure that if something succeeds in other parts of the country it is certain to fail in New England—a sentiment which is more than echoed by Californians. This mistrust of standardization is usually unrealistic. People sing the same songs and sin the same sins in Florida and Oregon. Attempts to prepare manuals on rural evangelism have discovered that the rural churches which are most successful are using the same methods that city churches use, with minor differences in terminology and timing. Elaborate and simple churches need the same advice and make the same mistakes and find the same blessings.

A method does not have to be perfect to be infinitely better than none at all. One is often reminded of Dwight L. Moody's famous answer to a critic, "At least, I like my way of doing it better than your way of not doing it."

5. Pedantry

Those towering intellects which, like weather-breeding mountain peaks, determine our ecclesiastical climate are likely to devote much intricate thought to such matters as, "The Re-Christianizing of Modern Man in a Depersonalized Culture"; but on such a subject as "The Christianizing of My Next-door Neighbor" they tend to be vague. Those who deliver the pronouncements on evangelism are often those who themselves never discuss religion with any but the clergy. Too many seminary courses on evangelism are full of information about Ambrose and the Welsh Revival without ever getting to a study of how modern churches are winning modern people—which is what prospective pastors need to know. Studies on the emergency presented to the Church by urbanization or the tyranny of technology make too few suggestions of what the congregations—which are the Church—can do about it. A great deal more would be accomplished if a larger proportion of the publications and conferences on evangelism were devoted to reports on who is really bringing people to the Christian faith—and how.

Youth projects in evangelism are likely to begin—and end—with an investigation of such questions as, "What has the Gospel to say to modern minds?" "Is the Church necessary for Christian living?" "What is the relationship of evangelism to areas of racial tension?" Having thus laid a sound basis for evangelistic action, the young people turn to something else—without having done anything which would bring anyone but themselves any nearer to the Kingdom.

6. The Illusion of Short Cuts

SHORT CUTS IN EVANGELISM NEVER WORK. That invariable rule must be learned soon and remembered often! There is no easy way to bring people to the Christian faith. Only those who are willing to do the most important work in the world in a conscientious, painstaking way will have—or deserve to have—success.

Churches keep hoping that they can hire a revivalist to do their evangelism for them. Or they send out half-trained members to ring doorbells and call it "evangelistic visitation." This always ends in disillusionment.

The new evangelism has discovered some labor-saving methods, but no easy ones. God grants effects which are far beyond the human causes—but miracles in evangelism are never a substitute for the stern demands which are imposed on the evangelists.

III

The Motives for Evangelism

Evangelism is never the line of least resistance. A church always tends to drift away from evangelism, never toward it. The coal bill has to be paid; the bulletin must be mimeographed; next Sunday's sermon must be prepared; the church school must be staffed. If the present church members are neglected, it can bring embarrassments; but those whom a church has not yet reached are in no position to complain of being slighted. A pastor never finds time to do all he should be doing for the members he already has. Church people never catch up with a church's domestic tasks. Therefore the tendency is to put evangelism in a file marked, "Important . . . for the first free moment"—a moment which in church life never comes. Unless a church, in sermons and meetings, is kept continually reminded of the urgent motives for evangelism, it will inevitably drift away from it.

Church people have to be shown how the great motives for evangelism, which stand out so starkly in the Bible, fit the realities of daily living. The secular-minded often seem to get on very well. The distinction between their pagan and Christian neighbors may not seem to church members to be as sharp as theology says it is.

In part this indistinctness comes because we live in a culture which for generations has been influenced by the Church. A good deal of spilled-over Christianity gets to people who never come near the fountain source—though it loses its freshness and picks up impurities as it drains to them. Americans cannot help getting scraps of the gospel at Christmas and Easter time. Christian thought has colored the worldly man's ideas of decency and sportsmanship and good manners and right living. This blurs the contrast between Christian and non-Christian. The Church must make clear the vital distinction which Jeremiah shows between "the fountain of living waters" and "cisterns" (Jeremiah 2:13).

In part, the present force of the motives for evangelism is obscured because they are expressed in words which do not seem to apply to daily experience. We must learn to put the changeless truths into vivid American terms. Every period of religious stagnation tries to get along on the stale vocabulary of the last revival. And every period of religious awakening puts the timeless truths in words and illustrations which are close to daily life.

Here are some of the motives which make evangelism a perpetual emergency:

1. God's Intention for Human Life

"God is love" (I John 4:8). Love cannot exist in loneliness; love wants to share good things. Therefore, God created human beings to have fellowship with Him and to enjoy His blessings. Away from Him man is off center, like a flywheel that is pounding itself to pieces. As Augustine put it, God has made us for Himself, so that our hearts are restless until they rest in Him.

God has put some knowledge of Himself and how to live in every man. "He left not himself without witness" (Acts 14:17). "What the law requires is written on their hearts" (Romans 2:15, R.S.V.). But far beyond that is the entrance to God's presence and to great living which He has provided through Jesus Christ. Jesus Christ came to the earth and gave Himself on the cross to open up possibilities of living so glorious that entering into them is like being born again.

Those who have not found the daily presence of God and the sort of life which Christ makes possible are spending their time on earth without ever knowing why they were born. They are missing the greatest good that life can have.

If we literally believe that we are living among those who are missing so much, then all our love and pity will drive us with a desperate urgency to do something about it. Christians who have found in their own experience how much difference Christ makes cannot help but feel a passionate sympathy for those who are missing it. That is the motive for evangelism which has carried the gospel over oceans and mountains and centuries—all the way to us. It is compounded of gratitude plus love plus sympathy. We dare not break the faith and the succession.

"The Gospel is true always and everywhere, or it is not a Gospel at all, or true at all." In that, William Temple states the unshakable optimism of the evangelist. There is no one whom he is not supposed to win; the Christian life is for everyone on earth. Your banker and your bootblack, the scholar and the coolie, were all born with the capacity and the need to come to God through Jesus Christ.

2. Jesus' Clear Commandment

If it hurts us to see people who are spending their lives without knowing Jesus Christ—think of what it means to Him! We can begin to guess how much He cares when we think of the cross on Calvary. It was for these neighbors of ours that Jesus died. He was telling of Himself when He told of the shepherd who could give himself no rest as long as one sheep was lost from the hundred who belonged in the fold and who greatly rejoiced when the one lost sheep was found. If 1 per cent was so important to Him, how much He must want us to care about the 50 per cent of our neighbors who are outside His fold.

The one commandment which Jesus repeated in all of His final meetings with His disciples was the commandment to go out and tell others about Him. He made us His channels of salvation. We are the instruments of His love. If we fail, to that extent "the cross of Christ should be made of none effect" (I Corinthians 1:17).

3. The Situation in Our Communities

More than half of the people in the United States make no profession of any faith in Christ. (In 1950 approximately 55 per cent of the population belonged to some religious body; more than 5 per cent are in non-Christian groups.) Seventeen million boys and girls are growing up in this country with no sort of religious training. These are not people remote from most of us—in some backwoods area or miserable slum; they are the people with whom we are associating every day—at business, in school, in our clubs, over the back fence. They are suffering what, if we believe our faith, is the most tragic loss a life can have. They grope and strive and hope without ever turning to Him Who came to earth that they might have life, and have it more abundantly.

We like to think of our churches as established institutions, like banks or post offices—but they are not. They are mission stations, out on the frontiers of faith. They are outposts of Christianity, surrounded by the unbelieving masses. Church members in America are native Christians, living under constant pressure from those who do not share their faith and cannot understand their point of view. When they cross the streets outside their churches, they go over into Macedonia.

The need to evangelize is the most pressing emergency for every generation of Christians. Those who reproach the Church with not having converted the world after twenty centuries of trying, forget that the task must start over every morning. The steady succession of death and birth is constantly removing Christians from the world and replacing them with unbelievers. The kindergarten is the perpetual mission field. Humanly speaking, the Christian faith is just one generation from being lost from the earth. The most Christian nation in the world can, in a few years, become the most heathen. When a church stands still, it slips backward.

4. Sin and Salvation

Fair-minded church people know that most of their nonreligious neighbors are not scandalously evil. If Christians are to get a powerful motive for evangelism from the thought of salvation from sin, they must glimpse the awesome difference it can make to people whom they know and care about.

Modern man has dropped the word "sin" from his vocabulary —and so the world is perishing of a disease without a name. Sin is man's frustration and lovelessness, his enmity and worry and feverish materialism. Many people are dogged by futility and boredom. Many are disappointed in themselves, harried by memories they cannot change, ashamed of habits they cannot break. Minds are battlefields of contrary impulses and crossed up emotions. Sin is not only wrongdoing but a wrong inward state, though each produces the other.

"Lost" means having missed the way. It means waking in the morning without any great purposes to make the day worth while. It means being lost from certainties. That man is lost in sin who has lost his enthusiasm, who has lost his joy in living, who has lost his sense of God. Who can doubt that in such ways "all have sinned and come short of the glory of God"—missing a glory God intended for their lives to have?

When church people see sin as everything which keeps a person from his best—and when they see that there is a power which can lift their neighbors to glorious possibilities of living they had never even guessed were there—then there will be an eagerness to help that come to pass.

The Church must know, not as poetry nor as a theological word game but as a current event, that Jesus Christ really does take men to God. He heals their sick souls and satisfies their hungers. Right in our towns and villages He is giving beauty in place of ugliness and joy instead of discontent and peace for troubled minds and light through darkness. He is freeing people from their mind-distorting worries over past misdeeds and mistakes. Through faith in Him and His atoning death people like the postman and the grocer are finding power to rise into newness of life.

Christians must be shown that what Christ and the Church have done for them can be done for anyone. A Church member who is not sure of any great benefits from his faith will not have much interest in evangelism. But most can recognize quite clearly that their lives and homes are far different from what they would have been without the Christian faith. When they see that, they have their motive for evangelism—and they have their message.

5. Homes

In their sociological study, *Predicting Success or Failure in Marriage,* Professors Burgess and Cottrell reported, among other things, on the effect of church participation on marriage. They found that one-fifth of all marriages end in divorce; but only one-fiftieth of the couples which have an active church connection are divorced.

Bringing people into the Church means saving homes. Christians do not think of their marriage as an agreement between two parties, but as a covenant among three. Their love for each other is strengthened by their love of God. In their religious faith they are united by the deepest interest that can join two human beings. The very act of going to a church and sitting together through worship softens resentments and bickerings.

No one can fail to be troubled by the appalling number of broken homes and broken hearts and broken lives. Anyone with an ounce of pity must be eager to do something to prevent this. In evangelism we have the thing that we can do.

6. Practical Guidance

What a pity it is that we cannot wait for the wisdom of three-score years and ten before deciding some of the great questions which rush at us early! It is in youth that we decide what sort of schooling to have, whom to marry, what our life work will be. Young people desperately need some guidance which can save them from damaging their whole lives. They need fixed principles to which these choices can be referred. That is what a definite Christian faith can give them. A sailor who sets out with no compass or landmarks is courting shipwreck. The evangelization of youth is urgently important.

That same need remains through every age. As long as life lasts it is shaped by its choices. Its success or failure depends on its guiding principles—on how right they are and how firm they are. If there is a God whose laws govern life, then everything depends on whether we are living in harmony with those laws or are crossed up with them. Evangelism brings into daily living the guidance of the Maker of all laws.

7. Temptation

The well-behaved person, who seems to get along pretty well with no definite religious faith, may be unprepared for the violent onslaught of unusual temptation. In the time of moral storm and stress, when judgment is distorted and the whisper of conscience is drowned out, evil can temporarily appear to be almost a virtue. Then it is that one needs a hold on something definite. A person who has lived in a culture which for centuries has been influenced by Christianity may have a personal code which in many points matches Christian ethics. But the difference between a personal code and a Christian faith is the difference between subjective intuitions and a revealed gospel, between unsupported opinions and the clear teachings of a Church, between abstract ideals and a living Lord.

8. Trouble

In the even routine of uneventful days your neighbors may not show, or feel, great need of faith. But eventually trouble comes crashing into every life. Loved ones die; plans go to pieces. The day when the rain descends and the floods come and the wind twists the joists is the day when foundations—and evangelism—are seen to be important. It is the certainty of trouble tomorrow which makes evangelism so urgent today. Christian people are amazingly tough. A wonder which church life constantly reveals is the way in which the members can come through terrific disasters, not crushed, but smiling and triumphant. When we see that, we know the practical urgency of a hold on Jesus Christ—and we know why evangelism is a pressing matter.

9. A Purpose for Living

Human beings can drift for a while, taking things for granted. But everyone finally has to have an answer for such questions as "What is life for?" "What is worth while?" "What is it all about?" Those who find no answers are headed for futility and melancholy and frustration.

Many respectable people, who by no means appear to be candidates for the mourners' bench, are none the less wasting their days in tedium, with no clear incentives.

It is such incentives which Christian faith puts into a life. It shows every life to be a fascinating romance with a plot whose clue is found in God's love. The service of God and of one's fellow men gives every day an absorbing purpose. Jesus breaks into our solitude and ties us by our heart strings to the joys and sorrows of those around us. Faith makes us rise every morning with eager anticipation of what the day will bring. The knowledge that God has called us to our daily work makes its dullest tasks exciting. The gospel gives a working philosophy of life for children and philosopliers, for housewives and Senators. Until people have found such a faith they begin at no beginning and they end at no end.

10. Loyalties

Those who adhere to no Church or creed are dangerous—to themselves and to the world. They are the ones who are most susceptible to the wild political and religious faiths which curse the world. Fascism, communism and fanatic nationalism have a rank growth among the sort of people whose hearts are barren of any commanding loyalty. It is often the highly intelligent who are most susceptible to outlandish cults. Repeatedly there is the astonishing spectacle of people who are otherwise well balanced embracing some fantastic faith.

A human spirit cannot long be satisfied without some loyalty. If it does not have one that is high and noble, it will give itself to one that is tawdry. There is an incurable tendency to religion, to the worship of something greater than oneself—presumably because God is, and the need for God is always there. Jesus' parable about the empty heart taking in seven evil spirits is still sadly true.

Men who will not make God their Ruler will make a ruler their God. A country in which the strength of religion deteriorates will be taken over by some frantic messiah. When we see the worst that has happened in other lands we must say, "There, but for the grace of God, goes the United States in one more generation."

Christianity today is fighting for the souls of men. It is competing against fiercely organized rivals which have surpassed it in a dozen lands. For the Church, this is no time for "just a little bit more of the same as before." Unless Christians can match the hard-driving evangelism of modern pagan movements, they will be driven backward across the earth.

11. Social Righteousness

In our eagerness to put Christian principles into the social order we may have thought of ourselves as thrusting something into something. By main strength and agitation we may hope to force principles into society as raisins are stuffed into a bun.

But the only way Christian principles can be put into the social order is to put them into the hearts of one member of society after another. There will finally be no safe regard for the principles of Jesus Christ without a regard for Christ Himself, as Lord and Master. Without a social gospel, evangelism heads toward superstition; but without evangelism, the social gospel is a sowing of the sand.

There is no hope for racial justice among people in whom the vicious pack impulses of the human animal are still untamed. World peace cannot be kept among nations whose citizens have no peace in their hearts. There will never be a fair division of profits and wages among materialists. A righteous society cannot be built from unregenerate human beings.

Christians are not able to bring order and decency on earth because there are too few of them. Society is not saved by the Christian principles of honesty, justice, brotherhood and love, because there are not enough people—in the United States or in the world—who believe in them.

Democracy will not be supported by props if it is cut from the gospel roots from which it sprang. Thomas Mann said, "Democracy is a polite name for the ideals Christianity brought into the world." It is only on a Christian basis that our country can survive the tensions which threaten it. To bring more Americans to the Christian faith is the basic national defense.

When we see signs of weakness in the American character, in college athletic scandals, in the tie between gambling and government, in legalized corruption at Washington—and in the failure of many people to be shocked by such disclosures—then we are seeing the reasons for redoubled intensity in evangelism. A spiritual sickness demands a spiritual cure. As Herbert Hoover said, commenting in the late summer of 1951 on the national security, "Our strength is not in politics, in prices, or in production, or price controls. Our strength lies in spiritual concepts. It lies in public sensitiveness to evil."

Atomic power has not made the winning of men to Christ an iota more urgent than it was before—but it has dramatized the urgency. We have always known that the world was lost without Christ, but never before has a time limit been set. Power has so far outrun control that modern man seems like a child playing on a nursery floor with a box of dynamite and a hammer. Scientists join generals in warning that the only final defense must be spiritual. As the UNESCO charter puts it, "Since wars begin in the minds of men, it is in the minds of men that the defenses of peace must be constructed." Church study commissions are essential—but we are not going to inactivate the atom bomb by burying it under mimeographed pronouncements on world order. Evangelism is the only answer.

Church people do not need to wring their hands and wish that there were something they could do. They can put their hands to the thing that can save the world. As the Church throws the switches in men's souls it is controlling the destiny of nations. Everyone's home town is one of the crisis spots of modern history. Evangelism is the basic patriotism. It is the essential service to the country. It is the root of all reform.

12. Death

Each life is overshadowed by the knowledge of approaching death. Whether as a dread we vainly try to shut from our minds or as a joyful prospect, this thought increasingly colors every day. Though we could remain indifferent to the prospect of our own dying, when those we love are taken we are forced to confront what we think of human destiny and God. If we can see nothing beyond the shabby and painful and wasteful way good lives sometimes seem to end, we are forced to the bitter conclusion that that is a poor way to run a universe.

Every human being desperately needs a way of facing death. In that we see the urgency of evangelism. In the very core of thinking it can make the difference between cynicism and confidence, between resignation and hope, between fear and glad expectancy.

This is a matter of immediately practical importance because the view of death governs the view of life. When men drop the idea of a future life they tend to play fast and loose with this one. History shows that cultures which lose the belief in immortality tend to tyranny and social evils—because temporary creatures get less respect than do immortal souls. An evangelism which can lift people to the dignity and permanence of the children of God is an essential for social reform.

The thought of what will happen to people after they die gives an overpowering motive for evangelism. We have so recoiled from an evangelism which is concerned only with Heaven and Hell that we have tended to overlook the plain implications of our faith. We believe that death is not the end of life. We believe that life is continuous, so that it goes on after death in the same direction it was pointed in this world. When we think of how much is being missed by those who are not turned to Jesus Christ, we know that the tragedy goes clear beyond this world. Our forefathers dwelt on the horror of dying without Christ; we are more likely to think of the awfulness of living without Him. But if we believe in immortality we cannot fail to be horrified by both.

13. Men's Need of the Church.

Every human being needs the Church. One man and a god could have a religion, but it takes at least two men and God to have Christianity. Christianity, whose key word is "love," requires fellowship. It requires the company of others who share the faith. The Bible makes it plain that one cannot be obedient to Christ and remain aloof from the fellowship of His followers. If a Christian could not find a congregation which could satisfy this need, he would have to start a new one.

We need never apologize for saying that the purpose of evangelism is to bring people into the Church. Evangelism fails unless it does that. We must, of course, perpetually guard against making the adding of names to a church roll an end in itself. But that danger should not frighten us from trying to make the number of those who can be soundly brought into the membership as great as possible.

Every period of Christian history has had its characteristic heresy. The future may record that the peculiar heresy of our generation is the belief that there are Christians, and among them there are a special sort who also belong to a Church. The faith which has been delivered to the saints and confirmed by nineteen centuries of experience is that there are Christians, and among them there may be an abnormal and crippled and defrauded few who do not belong to a Church. And these must be an occasion for pity and concern.

That deficient evaluation of the Church is accepted by many of its members. They therefore have no great zeal to win their neighbors to what is, after all, merely a matter of taste. They must be shown that the Church is God's appointed means for giving blessings which every life needs. They must be made to see that the Church is not a human institution at all—it is something let down from God out of heaven, not for one sort of people but for all mankind.

There is an experience of God which we never have by ourselves. Religious solitude and religious fellowship are both necessary because of our dual nature as separate individuals and as social creatures. A church service by radio is as welcome and as unsatisfying as a courtship by telephone. When we worship with others, God does something miraculous in us. It does not come just from the music or the sermon or the prayers. It is an effect which is greater than all the causes we can trace.

Well-mannered Church people rightly shrink from implying that they are Christians and others are not. But do those words have any meaning? Northwestern University made a survey of the religious knowledge of junior high school pupils. It was found that 52 per cent did not know in what part of the Bible the life of Jesus is found; 62 per cent did not know that He had taught the Lord's Prayer; 51 per cent could not recognize His most familiar parables. Are the churches of that community entitled to believe that they have something which those boys and girls need, and lack? Is it presumptuous to assume that most of those outside the Church do not understand the Bible as well or pray as often or refer to Christ's guidance as definitely as they would if they were faithful members of the Church? It is simple realism for grateful Christians to recognize that they have found blessings through the Church which multitudes around them are missing.

Our broad-minded readiness to admit that a person may be a Christian outside the Church should not make us forget that he cannot be a Christian without knowing about Christ. Knowledge of Christianity does not always make a Christian, but one cannot be a Christian without it. A follower has to know who or what he is following. A church is a place where people come to learn Who Christ is and what He taught. A Church member must never imply to those outside, "I am a better Christian than you are." But he must know that he has a better chance to be a Christian than they have. Men need the Church because it is divinely appointed and equipped to show them Jesus Christ.

Amid all the stifling pressure of material cares, men need the Church's reminders of God. They need the habit of church attendance as a dependable framework for existence. They need the physical act of walking into the doors to reimpress on their minds the reality of spiritual things. Men need the Church's teachings and its promptings to virtue and duty. They need the opportunities for service to God and to men which it affords. In a world where bewildered people are groping for a faith, Christians need their Church membership as a way of letting their neighbors know what they have found.

Many of the members of our old established Churches have missed the wonder and gratitude which first-generation Christians have. They have taken the Church's benefits for granted. If they can be made to see the Church as it really is, and to recognize what it has done for them, they may get a consuming eagerness to bring their neighbors to it.

14. The Church's Need for Men

Everyone who loves the Church and believes in it will work to make it stronger. We do not try to enlarge the Church just to build a more flourishing institution, but to make a more powerful instrument for God's hand.

The Church's work is always partly undone because it needs more workers. It needs more man power for all its tasks—for giving ideals to the young, fighting for righteousness, teaching the gospel, helping the distressed.

The health of a local congregation depends on its bringing in a constant stream of new life. As its members die and move away, it slips toward extinction. Without a constant infusion of new members a congregation becomes stagnant, complacent—a perversion of what a church should be.

15. Our Own Soul's Good

These old sayings are still true: "There are only two things

you can do with the Christian faith—give it away, or give it up."
"What you keep to yourself, you lose; what you give away, you
keep forever."

The evangelistic visitor who loses courage before ringing a
doorbell, and walks around the block desperately asking God for
help, is finding a new reality in prayer. One whose poor, stumbling
efforts have been used to bring someone into the Christian faith
has learned the meaning of partnership with God. One who on
Sunday sees in church those whom he has brought into the Christian life has discovered one of the greatest happinesses anyone can
have.

The unending responsibility to evangelize is God's provision for
keeping life and soul in His Church. It is essential for the Christian's spiritual growth and vigor. History shows that those periods
in which the Church has been most vital are those in which it has
been most intent on reaching outside itself. Present experience
shows that churches which are least intent on winning others are
those which do least for the members they already have. A church
of the saving Christ must be a saving church.

A pastor may be so trapped by parish concerns that he has
no time for evangelism. When this happens he knows that he is
a kept man—the private chaplain to a few self-centered families—
and something within him dies. But let him take time from undone
domestic tasks to seek those who are outside the Church, and
a new freshness and power come into his ministry.

Members of a church whose energies are all devoted to itself
become deeply conscious of a broken tie. They are shamed by
the gospel's plain calls to a wider discipleship and frustrated by
their knowledge of what a church was meant to be. The inevitable
result is that they turn dull and cold and formal. The glow is gone.
The church, seeking its life, has lost it. But the promised miracle
of finding self by serving others has been amazingly demonstrated
by many congregations. When, with much of the church work
still undone, they give themselves to an effort to bring others to
Christ and to the Church, a new vision and sense of mission flow
through everything they do. "Whosoever will lose his life for my
sake shall find it."

IV

The Invisible and the Visible Goals
of Evangelism

Evangelism, because it aspires to what is infinitely high, readily gets lost in the clouds. Because it must have external results, it readily becomes mundane. In order to escape the twin dangers of vagueness and externality it must keep two sorts of goals in view—the invisible and the visible.

A. The Invisible Goals

If evangelism loses sight of the spiritual goals, it will do great damage to the Church and to those who have been led to think that they have become Christians when they have merely become church members.

1. Belief in Basic Truths

Faith must have a content. There are certain views by which Christians are distinguished. People are not kept waiting outside the Church door until they settle all of their religious questions; they spend a lifetime doing that within the Church. But Church membership would have no meaning if it did not require some basic convictions.

A Christian must believe that there is a God, and that God is good and all powerful. He must believe that Jesus Christ came to the earth as the revelation of the nature of God, as the teacher of righteousness and the Saviour from sin. He must believe that Jesus is not dead, but a living friend and Lord. Such basic beliefs are what evangelism is trying to bring people to accept. They distinguish the Christian point of view.

This requires more than an assent to words. A person may say in all earnestness, "I accept Christ as my Lord and Saviour," without the slightest idea of what those words mean. "I want to be a Christian" may signify only, "I want to be decent" or "I do not want to be a heathen."

Christianity is not scholarship. In its wonderful democracy the ash collector may be a better Christian than the greatest scholar in the land. But both the ash collector and the scholar must have some definite idea what it is that they believe. Theology is simply the dictionary which defines the words we use when we talk about religion. The scorn of theology often springs from the desire to be unencumbered by anything very definite. The plea for a simple faith is often the plea for words without meanings. The names "God" and "Christ" can be attached to monstrous misconceptions. In its evangelism the Church must take care lest it receive those who are using the right words in the wrong way.

It is true that Christian knowledge by itself will not save people. Caiaphas knew more *about* Christ than Paul did. A person may understand and accept every word of the creed and still be a complete pagan. "The devils also believe, and tremble" (James 2:19). But there must be some clear beliefs as a framework to support the Christian life.

2. Conversion

Immanuel Kant said that every personality is like a pyramid resting on its apex. There is one basic choice which supports every other choice in life. To change that primary decision will alter the whole structure of a personality. Such a change is what religion means by "conversion" or being "born again." That basic choice, at the point of the pyramid, is what is meant by "faith."

All living is choosing. It is shaped, from one instant to the next, by the choices we are making. What we say and read and buy—and are—is selected from the stream of possibilities which constantly pass before us. But these momentary choices are settled by reference to the basic ones. Once you have decided what you most want—money, pleasure, love, power—you will choose from instant to instant whatever seems most likely to get it for you. A stable character is one in which the key desires are fixed; the unstable change from day to day.

Paul said that when this key choice is changed to faith in Christ, a person becomes "a new creature: old things are passed away; behold, all things are become new" (II Corinthians 5:17). He told how, when that happened to him, it was as though the old Paul had died and a new man moved into his body. John said it is like passing "from death unto life" (I John 3:14).

Evangelism tries to bring that key decision for faith in Jesus Christ. Some people may become conscious suddenly that they have made the choice. For others it may come as a gradual realization. For either it will be a great deal safer if there is some definite evidence that the choice has been made—some visible sign to mark the direction one intends to travel.

3. A Personal Relationship with God through Jesus Christ

Christianity at its heart is not a creed or a ritual or ethics—it is a personal relationship with Jesus Christ; everything in the Church gets its significance from that connection. Children can be deeply religious because personal relationships are the first thing that they understand. The message of the early disciples as they went flaming out from Jerusalem and Antioch was, "Let me introduce you to Jesus, the Christ."

"God is love"; He made the human race that there might be beings in loving communication with Himself. Jesus Christ came to earth to make that communication possible. He is the Mediator Who brought the Infinite and Eternal Being within range of human hearts. He is the Word, which translates the language of Heaven into terms which we can understand. He makes the mysterious knowable and says, "He that hath seen me hath seen the Father." In Him the love and friendship of God become very real.

Evangelism must bring people to the experience of God's presence, so that they will start each day in the glad sense of partnership with Him, and go to sleep each night secure in the knowledge of His love. It ends the abnormality of going through a world which is filled with God without knowing He is there. It takes people from their isolation and turns them to Him Who has been trying to get their attention all along.

Evangelism can easily fail in this. It may bring people to an intellectual acceptance of truths about God and His law and His Church without ever bringing them to God Himself. We may be like the geese in Kierkegaard's parable; they regularly assembled to praise the glories of wide, soaring flights—though they themselves never left the barnyard. It is not enough to talk about prayer without showing how to pray and arranging for great experiences of praying.

After Father Ronald Knox had been with the tourists who were taken through St. Paul's in London he reported, "Never have I been so conscious of the real absence." But the real presence of the Lord can be known in our churches. It can be felt in that awed sense of the beauty of holiness which sometimes comes over a congregation while it worships, or in that special awareness that God is there which often kindles from heart to heart when small groups pray together. In the midst of some church task there is often the feeling that God is right at one's shoulder. The Church can hand on the practical methods which Christians through the centuries have discovered best help private worship to go from immature fumblings to great experiences with God.

Evangelism must bring people, not only to know about God, but to know Him.

4. Self-Dedication

The Christian has accepted Christ as the Lord of all of life. He has found his freedom by coming under the Divine control. The person with whom evangelism has been successful has said to God, "Take me, and all that I am, and use me for Thy loving purposes." He will regard his daily work as a sacred service to which God has called him. He will see all his possessions as God's property which he has been trusted to administer.

B. The Visible Goals

Christ and the Bible and all Christian history have set certain outward signs to mark spiritual realities. Though there is constant danger that the sign may become a substitute for the reality, the risk must be taken because human minds have to have something tangible by which the intangible can be revealed. Love needs weddings and education needs diplomas and patriotism needs a flag—and Christianity needs sacraments and open professions of faith and religious practices.

Evangelism's good work is likely to be lost if it takes the outward signs too casually. A church may comfort itself for its failure to add many members by the thought that it is making Christ real to people in other ways. But it must ask itself whether it would not be making Him more real more permanently if it made better use of the outward tokens of discipleship. Today's strongest purpose may be growing vague by tomorrow unless there is some tangible reminder of it. Intentions have a way of becoming indistinct unless they are connected with something which remains as evidence that "I made up my mind—I took my stand and it is settled."

1. The Act of Decision

Our days are not equal. Most are lost in level uneventfulness—but there are some which tower up like mountain peaks to dominate forever after the landscape of a life. It is the business of a church to bring such days to pass.

As we look back, we find that our decisive days have been marked by some act which has kept them uneroded in our memories. Something happens at such times which fixes them as landmarks by which we can find our way.

Every community is filled with Sunday-school alumni who never go near a church because they were supposed to develop gradually. Many churches with elaborate educational programs fail because no catalyst is ever introduced to make definite patterns of thought crystallize out of the amorphous mass of information and emotional experiences they supply. Most church adult groups have adherents who have been with them for years without ever being confronted with a time and a way to make clear to themselves what they believe.

This is more than just sound psychology. It was theology which first taught that there is a special grace of God which is available only to those who have made their commitment definite. The new life is first known when one comes out of the shadow land and consciously and clearly says "yes" to Christ.

When an inclination to faith has begun, it still is not faith until something happens to make it clear. Until then there is always an element of maybe-and-maybe-not about it. Life needs points of reference.

An astonished evangelistic caller said, "I thought that I had to talk people into being Christians, but I found out that God had been talking to them for years; all I did was raise the question." But if the question had not been raised, it is likely that those people would have gone on and on without any definite attitude to Jesus Christ. People are naturally inclined to put off making up their minds until some crisis forces them to do it. Evangelism arranges for the crisis.

Is it possible that a conversation in a home or a single sermon or a youth decision service can make a Christian of an unbeliever? It cannot by itself, of course. Much depends on what comes before and after. But the astounding truth is that in half an hour something can happen which will make the whole direction of a life forever different. There are millions of Christians whose lives are evidence that in some brief time of decision a tremendous thing can happen. This is the Church's ageless miracle.

Children who have always thought of themselves as Christians still need some act of decision which they can remember as marking the time when they pledged themselves to Christ. They will be robbed of an experience which might have influenced their whole lives if they are brought into the Christian fellowship by the casual advice, "You are old enough now, so you had better join the Church."

"If thou shalt confess with thy mouth the Lord Jesus, and shalt believe in thine heart that God hath raised him from the dead, thou shalt be saved" (Romans 10:9). There is a natural need for a physical act, confession with the mouth, to identify what has happened in the heart. Whatever act is used to symbolize a decision —a spoken statement, a signature, a handclasp, a coming down the church aisle—it must require an exercise of the will. It must be definite. It must be clearly connected with the inward state which it expresses. It must have consequences—religious responses which are isolated from the rest of life do more harm than good.

Improper decisions are injurious. The person who expresses a faith which is not real, simply to go along with the crowd or to avoid embarrassment or because of high pressure, has suffered a grave spiritual hurt. The cheapening of religion, or the sense of shame and resentment, will make a genuine faith less likely.

The act of decision must be safeguarded. People are sometimes very glad to make decisions on improper grounds: "After all that the church has done for my children, it is the least that I can do." "I want to support any institution that is for the public good." "I want to line up with the right sort of people." Those who are accepted into Church membership at a low level are very hard to raise above that source. A church which has filled its rolls with those who have never really understood its purpose is disabled and discredited.

2. Public Acknowledgment of Faith

"Whosoever therefore shall confess me before men, him will I confess also before my Father which is in heaven" (Matthew 10:32). The act of decision must lead to an acknowledgment of faith in the presence of the congregation or to some other way of letting the stand for Christ be publicly known.

There are many reasons for this: (a) Declaring a faith strengthens it. (b) A person is more likely to remain true to a purpose when he has told about it. (c) A willingness to speak up and be counted for what is believed is necessary to discipleship. (d) A Christian must express his gratitude to Christ. (e) The unashamed profession of faith is a sound start in witness bearing. (f) The faith of the audience is renewed and strengthened. (g) One who is publicly identified as a Christian is saying to all the bewildered people who are groping for moorings or tempted by false faiths, "I have found the way, and the truth, and the life."

Giving assent in a church service to questions which have not been considered in advance has little meaning. People may justly resent being forced in public to say things they are not sure that they believe. There should be a chance to know what will be asked, and to think and pray about it.

3. Baptism

Baptism is an essential evangelistic goal for denominations which baptize only adults. Denominations which baptize infants must make the "confirmation" of that sacrament a goal of their evangelism. In a sense, infant baptism has not been completed until the person comes into full Church membership and says, in effect, "What my parents promised for me has really come to pass."

4. Church Membership

There need be no embarrassment about making evangelism a "join-the-Church" program. It was that in the New Testament. The presence of the Lord in the early Church was felt to be demonstrated by the fact that there were "added to the church daily such as should be saved" (Acts 2:47). The success of Paul's missionary efforts was reported in terms of how many were brought into the Church. A church is entitled to be happy when it is adding many to its membership, and troubled when it is adding few.

The Church is not just a tool for building the Kingdom—it is a part of the Kingdom. Membership in it is one of the promises of the Covenant.

What we have to fear is not the delight in adding members to the Church but the temptation to take short cuts in doing so. The tendency to see the symbol and miss what it should symbolize, to let what is easy be a substitute for what is difficult, is a perpetual danger in evangelism. But we do not make ourselves more able to bring people into membership properly by being less interested in bringing them into membership at all.

Is it right to set numerical goals for evangelism? It can be. It was not considered irreverent to report the results of the Day of Pentecost statistically. To say "Let us see whether we can win fifty people by Christmas Sunday" will send workers to the task with more vigor than if the appeal is "Let us try to win all we can as soon as possible." It is a tiresome road that has no milestones. There is not much incentive in a formless duty. Goals put dimensions to a task. They are the adjectives which describe a great endeavor. It is no sacrilegious limiting of God's power to specify the number of people we hope to win within a stated time. It is

God's will that we win seventy-five million Americans by to-morrow; but we are likely to come nearer to doing our part if we have a definite aim. A church which has taken the risk of setting numerical goals must be very careful to describe them always in spiritual terms. When it does, they are safe.

Jesus in the parable of the sons distinguished three levels of obedience (Matthew 21:28-31). The lowest was that of the son who said, "I go, sir," and went not. He is the Church member who does not live up to his profession. Better than he was his brother who said, "I will not," but he did. He is the person outside the Church who lives a faith he does not profess. But neither son had the right relationship with his father. Jesus always makes it plain that His true followers are those who both profess and practice their faith. The greater sin of the professing son must not make us forget the wrong his brother did in his recalcitrance.

The Church is a school whose teachings the world needs above all—and evangelism enrolls the pupils. The Church is an army which fights through the centuries against wickedness and tyranny —and evangelism is its recruiting agency. The Church is a channel of power from on high—and evangelism makes the connections. The Church is a home where love is learned—and evangelism gathers the family.

Bringing people into the visible Church is a goal which the Head of the Church has set before us. We never dare forget how impor-tant that definite connection is.

5. Christian Practices

The earliest creed which Church historians have found was simply "Jesus Christ is Lord." To become a Christian is to accept Jesus Christ as the ruler of all life. It will result in the adoption of a distinctive pattern of living and thinking.

What that pattern is will not be dictated by outward rules; it is determined by the inner compulsion of the love of Christ. But the Bible and the centuries of Christian experience give some very clear indications of what that pattern should be. Being honest and pure and loving are a part of it. Millions of Christians have found that it needs to include such habits as prayer and Bible reading and public worship and generous giving and regard for the

Sabbath day. It embraces good citizenship and family religion and a practice of brotherhood which breaks through the barriers of class and race and nation.

All of these are visible goals for evangelism. The Church must avoid giving invitations which will permit a response which leaves some areas of life unchanged. Its appeals must never be so one-sided that people will accept Christ as Saviour without accepting Him as Lord—and as Lord not only of the home and worship but also of business and politics.

What are the right methods for evangelism? How well are we doing? The answer to such questions may be determined by observing the sort of behavior which results.

V

The Personal Requirements for
Evangelism

1. Beliefs

A powerful hold on faith produces powerful evangelism—a fumbling hold on faith produces fumbling evangelism.

A person does not have to have a complete grasp of all Christian doctrine to be an enthusiastic evangelist. In India as soon as a peasant has learned just one Bible story he is sent out to tell that story; then he comes back and gets another one to tell. In America a Christian who has hold of two or three or four great convictions has something to share. Often the beginner in the faith is a more ardent evangelist than are those whose familiarity with the wide range of Christian truth has blurred its distinctness. Like the man who had been healed of blindness, all their uncertainties cannot lessen the force of the "one thing I know" (John 9:25).

There will be little keenness for evangelism among Church members who have assumed the faith of their fathers without ever bothering to think about just what it is—among those who feel that the open mind should be open at both top and bottom—among those who love to quote the old incongruity, "I don't care what a man believes, all that matters is how he lives." A church which proclaims "the Jesus way of life" without much idea who Jesus is, which is intent on a morality that is left hanging in mid-air, will not be warmly evangelistic.

All Christians are plagued by problems of belief, from the cradle to the grave. It is a part of that good fight of faith by which we gain strength. As Browning said:

With me faith means perpetual unbelief
Kept quiet like the snake 'neath Michael's foot
Who stands calm just because he feels it writhe.

Everyone's faith has a central core of firm conviction surrounded by an area of uncertainties. If we work out from the center, faith grows and life has moorings and evangelism has great reasons. If we start from the outside, we are likely to get lost among the uncertainties and lose touch with the things we could believe. And we will never be ready for evangelism.

Some shrink from evangelism because they do not understand it—and others because they do. Those who have always run away from the grueling ordeal of deciding what they believe are likely to have a sense of inadequacy which makes them extremely sensitive. Their immediate response to any suggestion of evangelism is likely to be that they have no patience with this "come to Jesus stuff." This determination to think of evangelism in terms of a caricature does not come entirely from a lack of opportunity to know what modern evangelism really is. It is a desperate attempt to flee from something which puts one religiously on the spot. It is the hope of hiding a deficiency behind a superior pose.

When we are thinking chiefly about our own unclarity as Christians, there is a natural discomfort and uneasiness in the thought of sharing beliefs with someone else. The minister who is waiting for a golden summer of study and reverie when he will settle his religious questions is likely to postpone evangelism. Meanwhile, there are important things to do—making pastoral calls, polishing and preaching helpful sermons, working for social justice. But that golden summer never comes and, while he waits, these other things remain a little tentative. The shrinking from evangelism may be the shrinking from the ordeal of coming to terms with our own souls. God's call to us to evangelize is His call of us back to Himself. When we start to share our faith we will be the first to sing, "Lord, I'm coming home!"

An attorney told some of his friends about an experience which had deeply troubled him. A business acquaintance had made a luncheon engagement in order to talk about his state of deep discouragement. He was prospering, but he had lost interest in his work. His marriage was not happy. He was depressed about the state of the world. He was so sunk in despondency that it was becoming impossible for him to go on. He said, "I know that you are a church man, and I never have been. I thought there might be something you could say to help me." The attorney, in telling about the incident, said, "The thing I can't get over is that I have been going to church every Sunday for years, and I couldn't think of anything to say."

It was not that he is not a Christian. The Christian faith is woven into the fabric of his thinking and attitudes. He has it in his bones but he does not have it clearly in his mind. He has never bothered to make it explicit to himself—and so he could not tell anyone else about it. This unexplicit faith is a common weakness of second- and third- and fourth-generation Church members. They tend to take their faith for granted. The harm in that is not only that they cannot tell others. But, never having told themselves plainly what they believe, they miss the sharp impact and distinctive power of belief. That is why members of the older denominations are likely to lack the generosity in giving and the evangelistic eagerness and the grateful joy in their Church which is typical of members of the newer sects.

2. Ability to Pray

In evangelism we are working for effects which are greater than the sum of their causes, in other words—for miracles. The apparent inadequacy of the causes makes people see no possibility of the evangelistic effects. It is not reasonable to suppose that the sort of artless, hesitant appeal an inexperienced pair of lay visitors can make will turn hearts to Jesus Christ. There is nothing in the combination of hymns, a reading, prayers and a sermon in a church service which seems likely to transform anyone's life. The Sunday morning collection of restless, inattentive children does not look much like souls finding a Saviour. All of the evangelistic methods would have to be dismissed as impractical, save for the fact that they succeed. Obviously, something which we cannot see is added to the factors we can see. The effect of this invisible factor is so well established in common church experience that we can base our calculations on it. To devise ways to make the greatest use of it is simply sound spiritual engineering. Prayer is the most important element in our success.

The results which come from our apparently inadequate efforts in evangelism are a convincing demonstration that the age of miracles has continued into our matter-of-fact twentieth century. The human part is important. There must be committees and plans and organization. But in it all there must be the sense that "we are labourers together with God" (I Corinthians 3:9). The keeping of this sense of the divine partnership—of the humble dependence on a Greater Power—is the clearest essential for evangelism.

There is a special danger which comes to those who have done well in evangelism. They are likely to grow less dependent on the sort of anxious prayer which comes from fear and the knowledge of inadequacy. The members begin to feel, "I am getting good at this; I have mastered the techniques." The minister counts the flattering number of those who have come into Church membership and gets to believing that he has brought them. That is the point at which evangelism begins to fail in a church. The Lord rewards only the humble. When evangelism becomes merely a matter of well-polished methods, it is finished. Prayer is the basic evangelistic method, upon which all other methods depend.

"Ye shall receive power, after that the Holy Ghost is come upon you: and ye shall be witnesses unto me. . . ." is the promise to us (Acts 1:8). People sometimes wonder whether they do not have to wait for some special spiritual fitness—some sign that God is ready to work through them. But ours is the post-Pentecost Church, to which the power of the Holy Spirit is always promised when the conditions are fulfilled. We know what those conditions are—earnest prayer, a sense of need, dedication to a work about which we greatly care. "Try and see" is God's way for evangelism. Our willingness is the Holy Spirit's signal. We cannot say that we are waiting for God's good time; God's time for evangelism is always now.

3. Attitudes

Genuine liking for people—really caring about what happens to them—is an essential attitude. The people we approach will feel it if our motive is simply to do a duty or to build up the church. What is needed, of course, is Christian love. But Christian love has to be recognized as just plain friendliness. A warm-hearted friendliness is not the whole of evangelism, but it opens the way for the rest. It is the credential which people instinctively look for in those who wish to talk to them about the Christian faith.

Modesty is a saving quality. Christians are embarrassed by the necessity of implying that other people ought to be as they are. We know that in our faith we have something our friends need, but we shrink from saying so. We remain dumb about the greatest thing we have ever found for fear of implying our superiority.

Remember that Paul, as a prisoner, could say to a king without blushing, "I wish that you were as I am." But he added, "except for my limitations" (Acts 26:29). That addition can take any hint of offensiveness from our witness. Our attitude must be, "Even with all my limitations, I know the wonderful things the Christian faith can do." Our invitation is never, "Come up where I am"; it is, "Let us together try to go where Jesus leads." We ask others to be like us only in our faith. We point to Someone else Who is above us.

The prisoner's cry to the king, "I wish that you were as I am," is in the heart of every Christian as he looks at those who are missing the greatest thing in life. Every impulse to love, to unselfishness, to consideration—all the sources of real manners and courtesy—are in the Christian's longing to help another find what he has found. As Daniel Niles of Ceylon puts it, "Evangelism is one beggar telling another beggar where to get food."

There is a possible impulse for evangelism in a sort of sanctified conceit. It can be detected in a subtle condescension. Cockiness or censoriousness convince others only that it is well to avoid the company of church people.

Tact is essential. "Always be ready with a reply for anyone who calls you to account for the hope you cherish, but answer gently and with a sense of reverence" (I Peter 3:15, Moffatt).

Goodness is important. "Maintain good conduct among the Gentiles, so that in case they speak against you as wrongdoers, they may see your good deeds and glorify God" (I Peter 2:12, R.S.V.).

Enthusiasm for our church and for our faith will be more convincing than any arguments we can use. This cannot be pretended; it must well up from deep inside. But if we really feel it, letting it be seen has a powerful influence on others. As the Psalmist put it, "Restore unto me the joy of thy salvation. . . . Then will I teach transgressors thy ways; and sinners shall be converted unto thee" (Psalm 51:12, 13). Our joy makes us convincing.

Patience is necessary. Results from our work are sometimes discouragingly hard to see. But a human soul has a marvelous and mysterious filing system. Ideas we give may be hidden for years before anything comes of them. How many hours can we afford to spend in changing someone's whole lifetime? We can always trust that no good work for God is ever thrown away (I Corinthians 15:58).

4. Becoming Qualified

In a suburb of one of our great cities is a church which could fairly have been described as above the average in education and income and below the average in fervor and spiritual warmth. If the minister had tried to revive the prayer meeting, which had been given up a generation ago, he would have met only disapproval and empty chairs. A few of this church's members were induced to go with members of other churches in the district in a program of evangelistic visiting. To their surprise, they were so pleased with it that they persuaded their church to have its own visitation program. The visitors discovered two things—first, how eager people are to have someone come to talk to them about religion, and second, how much they themselves needed to know about it. They asked their minister to meet with them for a series of evenings on Christian belief and on prayer. These became general meetings for the whole church, and they continued far beyond the date announced for their termination. They were so valuable that they were recommenced after the summer holidays as neighborhood gatherings.

The evangelist is always his own first convert. The layman who tries to tell someone about Christianity, and spends the next day thinking of the things he wishes he had said, will be learning more practical theology than in a year of pew warming. The minister who prepares a special series of evangelistic sermons must preach them first of all to himself. They will require a systematic rethinking of his own certainties, something which the constant preoccupations of a minister's life may have made overdue.

The ne'er-do-well may explain that he cannot take a job because he is so full of aches and pains. And he is so plagued with aches and pains because he does not have a job. Churches often explain that they are "not yet" doing much about evangelism because of their ailments; and they fail to see that they have those ailments just because they neglect evangelism.

The psychological order in which things should be done is not always the logical order. It is logical to get spiritually fit before commencing a task. But the church which says, "We will first get ready and then we will start our evangelism," is likely never to start. When for this purpose it undertakes prayer groups and retreats and devotional studies, they may soon go dead because they have ignored the first law of the spirit which says that inspiration can never be divorced from expression.

The heartbeat does not pick up until after exercise has started. The power of the Holy Spirit does not come to those who with folded hands are looking toward heaven waiting for a visitation, but to those whose hands have taken up some work that is too big for them. Apparently His power only flows in where there is some chance for it to flow out. Our souls do not grow through spiritual exercises alone, but through spiritual exercises made necessary by the urgency of some great task. Jesus may have meant the order to be significant when He said, "Take my yoke upon you, and learn of me" (Matthew 11:29).

Prayer meetings always go better when people know what they are praying about. After a congregation has started its evangelism and is keenly concerned about it, then, when the officers or the Sabbath worshipers or special groups pray, there is an earnestness and intensity in it which routine prayer never knows.

When Jesus prayed, "For their sakes I sanctify myself," He expressed a timeless spiritual principle (John 17:19). When we attempt to improve ourselves spiritually for our own benefit, we are far less successful than when we yearn for better prayer and faith and living because we need them to help someone else.

By ourselves, our thoughts tend to wander endlessly among our doubts. We may travel a hesitant and fogged-in course because most of our attention is on the things we have not yet settled. But when we try to help others to believe, we are forced to keep in mind the great things of which we are sure. By this we build in ourselves a firm foundation from which we can move on to more truth. The best way to help a new Christian to grow in faith is to send him out to share what he has already found.

Callers who come back glowing with what they declare has been the greatest experience of their lives are often chilled by settling into business as usual at the church. A church will miss a strategic chance if it does not take advantage of the receptiveness which evangelistic work produces in its own people. The opportunity soon passes. Every sort of evangelism rouses a new spiritual enthusiasm in a church. It creates the state of mind in which study groups and prayer fellowships and devotional reading will be most eagerly welcomed.

VI

The Evangelistic Appeal

The basic assumption of evangelism is always this: IT IS NORMAL TO BE A CHRISTIAN; IT IS ABNORMAL TO BE AWAY FROM CHRIST. Because so many people are abnormal, and because Christians "are not of the world," we are likely to feel that in trying to get people to be Christians we are trying to get them to do something strange. We need perpetually to encourage ourselves by the knowledge that the unnatural person is the one who is living apart from God; such a person is a distortion of nature, a caricature of what he was born to be. Evangelism makes normal personalities out of distorted ones. "Nature," most deeply understood, is on its side.

The universe is not neutral on evangelism any more than it is neutral on the question of the shape of the world. The best encouragement in the difficult task of bringing people to the, at first thought unreasonable, view that the world is round is the fact that the world *is* round. There are difficulties in persuading people that there is a God Who loves them and wants them to love Him; but more important than all the difficulties is the fact that it is true. In our evangelism, the stars in their courses are with us.

Access to a human soul is like access to a mountain peak. Some, including very lofty ones, offer many easy approaches. Others are craggy and difficult. Like Alpinists who circle a peak to find the least forbidding path, so the evangelist must often go all around a person, looking for the point of access.

There are no sure approaches. The appeal which will reach one person will miss another completely. If we assume on philosophical grounds that every human being has a conscious hunger for God, we will meet some people who, by this rule, will not seem human. It was a believer who said that "God put salt in our mouths to make us thirst for Him"; most unbelievers would be amused by that idea. They have the thirst of which Augustine spoke, but they do not yet connect it with the thought of God. It is unrealistic to expect people to feel the lack of something they have never had; an approach on that line may well get the complacent response that nothing more is needed. An evangelist will be doomed to disappointments if he assumes that everyone is oppressed by a sense of sin, or appreciates Christian fellowship, or is dissatisfied with secular living. The only assumption the evangelist can make is that God has provided some way to approach every human being. When one way fails he must try another.

That is why a church cannot specialize—in its preaching or its program. Paul talked like a legalist to those who were legalistic and forgot about the law with those who took no interest in it, and appealed on their level to those who were weak. Like him, the Church must be all things to all men that it may, by all means, save some (I Corinthians 9:20-22). It may offer the social gospel, peace of mind, a philosophy of death—any fragment of the truth which can make a first appeal. Faith often makes its entry through a very narrow beachhead.

The beachhead can be expanded. The person who has been awakened to the need for just one small part of Christianity is likely to begin to appreciate the rest of it. Once Christ makes contact with a human soul, slumbering faculties are roused. Fishermen, who left their nets to be with a fascinating man, before many months were calling Him their Lord. Those who today come to Christ only as a prophet can learn to adore Him as priest and king. There is a strong pull toward wholeness. The self-centered person, who comes to church only to find peace of mind, may soon discover the joy of fellowship. One who has never felt the least need for worship, having found God through the moral grandeur of the gospel, may then discover the value of prayer. A one-verse Bible tends to grow until it includes whole chapters and books.

This does not happen inevitably. A one-sided church will make one-sided converts. But churches which are "good stewards of the manifold grace of God," and which try to help those they reach to grow in the knowledge of that many-sided grace, can safely make their first appeal through just one aspect of the gospel.

1. The Sense of Sin

Saints are keenly conscious of their sins and grateful for a saviour—sinners are not. Evangelism cannot always go with the good news of salvation to those who know that they are lost; it must often go with the bad news that they are lost to those who think that they are doing very well.

There are some who have a deep sense of guilt from which they are longing to be free. The unworthy son, the father who has neglected his family, those whose bad habits have wrecked their own and others' lives may be ashamed of themselves and eager for salvation. But the typical secularist is likely to believe that he is doing as well as could be expected.

When Bishop Linton, who was called the most successful evangelist to Moslems in the Church of England, was asked what he found to be the element in Christianity which appealed most to Mohammedans, he answered that "it was the Person and Character of Christ, *not* conviction of sin. The sense of sin developed in converts, but played no part in their conversion." He believed that the same thing was true in England.

There is no question that there can be an evangelistic appeal through the sense of sin, if it is understood in realistic terms. There are many who are cringing under a sense of failure, dogged by guilt, frustrated, discouraged by weaknesses. The offer of the chance to be a new person and to find a new quality of living will have a wide appeal. Most people have some sort of belief in God and will be interested in a chance to "get right" with Him.

Human nature has not changed, and neither has the gospel. The evangel's joyful message is still the offer of salvation from sin. The problem is how to state it so that people outside the Church will connect it with their needs and desires.

2. Dread of Impersonal Forces

Modern man still cringes before the principalities and powers of darkness, though he does not personify them as did his ancestors. Economic and governmental pressures have mounted until they seem to be vast, dire forces against which the individual has no defense. He fears that the problems of an increasingly industrialized age have become so complex that no one, even with the best of will, can cope with them. A closely integrated, mechanized world seems to him to be doomed to lurch on through wars and depressions and oppressive bureaucracies because human beings cannot know enough to make it run right. As the worried citizen scurries through his daily affairs, with an anxious look over his shoulder for the dreaded portents of disaster, he will listen to anything which offers to rescue him from this state of foreboding.

This is an offer which evangelism can make. It can give the assurance that the world's destinies are still in God's hands, and that He is the God of the future as He has been of the past. It can point to a more than human wisdom by which the world can be run right, if men will follow it. It can offer the security on which the followers of Christ can rely, regardless of external happenings —"In the world ye shall have tribulation, but be of good cheer; I have overcome the world" (John 16:33). It can promise that "neither death, nor life, nor angels, nor principalities, nor powers . . . shall be able to separate us from the love of God, which is in Christ Jesus our Lord" (Romans 8:38-39). As Emerson said to the woman who warned him that the world was about to come to an end, "We can get along without it."

3. Lost Assurances

Ultimate assurances are being shaken. Americans for generations have thought of wars which lay cities waste and annihilate whole peoples as belonging to other lands and times. Now we expect the next world war to annihilate our cities and kill millions of Americans. Until the Vietnam War we assumed that our country always won its wars because it was always in the right. We are facing the possibility that the sort of life we had always assumed was normal may not be lived in this generation. There is the apocalyptic feel of nations in commotion and mountains toppling and abysses opening up. With all that seemed fundamental being shaken, people are wondering whether there is something still more elemental in which to trust. They are wondering about the sort of certainty that led Chesterton to say,

Though giant rains put out the sun,
  Here stand I for a sign.
Though Earth be filled with waters dark,
  My cup is filled with wine.
Tell to the trembling priests that here
  Under the deluge rod,
One nameless, tattered, broken man
  Stood up and drank to God.*

Into this mood the Church can bring its assurance that the essential things have never changed, and never will. "Heaven and earth shall pass away, but my words shall not pass away" (Luke 21:33). It can point to the certainties which have been the reliance of all generations because they are anchored on eternity.

4. Anxiety

Anxiety is an endemic disease in modern life. Many are harassed by insecurity. They are fearful of losing their jobs, worried about falling below the economic standard their families and friends expect of them. They are afraid of not being loved, of losing the love of husband or wife. They cringe at the thought of illness and death for those they love and for themselves. The Church can offer salvation from fear, which is one phase of salvation from sin. It will find many who are interested.

5. Boredom

Plain boredom is a prevalent malaise. Many people rise from their beds with nothing ahead which gives much interest to the day. They do their work without a great deal of confidence that it is really worth the trouble. They have no pleasures in which they find much fun. With no clear aim in life and no enthusiasms which give a meaning to it, they are oppressed by a sense of triviality and missed purpose. This is the New Testament's *hamartia*, the missed aim—a meaning which many people do not recognize in the translation of that word as "sin." That is the state from

* From *The Collected Poems of G. K. Chesterton.* Copyright, 1932, by Dodd, Mead & Co., Inc. Reprinted with permission of Dodd, Mead & Co., Inc. and A. P. Watt & Son.

which Christianity, with its exciting purposes and commanding loyalties and vivid interests, can promise salvation.

6. Self-Perplexity

Man is perplexed and embarrassed by himself. Every morning as he looks into his mirror he confronts the troubling riddle of existence. When he stops to think, he is discomfited by his self-consciousness. Evangelism will find a ready hearing if it can give an answer to such questions as "Who am I?" "Why did I happen?" "What is it all about?"

7. Death

The question, "If a man die, shall he live again?" is still one which people are achingly anxious to have answered. There is not now the obsession with the fear of dying which seems to have oppressed many in the past. The focus has shifted. It is not the thought of their own death, but of the death of those they love, which sets our contemporaries to staring bleakly into the darkness and longing for some light. Only the very young would be unconcerned if they thought the Church could give that light.

8. Loneliness

Many a person is lonely because no one has found him. It is a loneliness which runs from tea table to cosmos. There is the failure to find in constant social contacts any meaningful communication with other human beings, and the feel of being a lost waif in an indifferent universe. The Church has a double answer to loneliness. It offers a real fellowship in which people know and love each other. And it brings together the waif and the Father Who has been searching for him with a solicitude which makes the universe a home.

9. The Sense of Something Lacking

People are wanting to hear a voice which comes from beyond human affairs; they want contact with something which is outside this world. To call this a hunger for God would be misleading; it is too vague to be identified so definitely. But one of the clearest indications of the existence of God is the fact that on the purely human level there is always the sense of something lacking. If the Church can supply that lack, people will come to it.

That is the only appeal the Church really has. Those of us who love the Church cannot understand why people will not come to it for its good times and its wholesome influence on youth and its cultural advantages. But the fact is, as some of us have discovered to our chagrin, most will not come for those reasons. Secular organizations can outbid the Church in everything except its specialty. Not all the kindly charm of its minister or its well-planned programs will attract people to a church. But if a church can bring a message from beyond the world, if it can really connect people with something which is greater than themselves, they will come.

10. Hunger for Truth

Modern seekers are asking in a more desperate tone than Pilate's, "What is truth?" TRUTH is the first attraction the Church offers. It is the one on which the other inducements depend. Until people are persuaded that what the Church teaches is really true, they will not have much confidence in all the good it is supposed to do for the individual and the family and the community. Unless there is such a God as Christianity describes, there are no good enough reasons for going to church; if there is such a God, there are no good enough reasons for staying away. As Lord Halifax said, "Men will not be brought to embrace the Christian religion because it is recommended as expedient, or necessary, or full of moral values. But they will go on their knees if they can come to feel that it is true." Evangelism will find an audience when it makes it plain that it is offering solid facts about God and man and the universe.

11. The Missing Significance of God

Many who think that they believe in God actually have no confidence in His being of much practical help and influence. They assess their problems and compute their chances without making the fact of God a very important part of their calculations. It is no redundancy when the Bible speaks of "the living God." Psychologically there are two sorts of God—just plain God and the living God. In our wrongdoing we could stand the thought of falling into the hands of God—but to fall into the hands of the living God, that, for the writer to the Hebrews, was the fearful thing (Hebrews 10:31). It can be pretty flat comfort to be told that God is with us. But when we can discover, like Hagar in the wilderness, that our place of trouble is *Beerlahairoi,* "the well of the living One who sees me"—that makes everything different (Genesis 16:14). Evangelism can go to those whose God is not doing them much good with the promise that He can be the LIVING God.

12. Mistrust of Life

G. A. Studdert-Kennedy described a night when he was a sentry at a lonely post which he knew was exposed to enemy patrols. In the darkness he heard stealthy movements. It was his duty to call out a challenge. If an enemy were moving there, the answer might be a burst of machine-gun fire. With terror almost choking him he forced his voice to call, "Who goes there?"; and the answer came back, "Friend." He recalled that experience a long while after on a night when he was alone on the cliffs above the English Channel. He was wrestling with his doubts, and oppressed by the sense of a vast and mysterious universe. Into the darkness his questioning called out, "Who goes there?" and with a rush of relief he felt that Something answered, "Friend!"

That is the answer which evangelism can let people hear. Many are wondering whether their ideals are realistic, whether the universe is hostile or indifferent to human values. To them the Church can bring the knowledge that the Ultimate Power is on their side; that what Christ was in time, God is in eternity. It can proclaim to philosophers and children the profoundest and simplest fact of existence, "God is love."

13. Inner Conflict

Their own civil war is the problem of many minds. Conflicting desires and crossed-up emotions keep them in a turmoil. It is so general that A E. Housman ascribed it to the inherited enmity of the Saxon and the Dane who fought over England before they intermarried,

> *In my heart it has not died,*
> *The War that sleeps on Severn side;*
> *They cease not fighting, east and west,*
> *On the marches of my breast.**

Psychologists talk of the dissociation of personality, of disintegration and frustrations. Our forefathers thought of it in terms of the onslaughts of Satan or the persistence of the "old Adam." The terms may change but the problem persists. Its magnitude and seriousness are demonstrated by the rush for any formula for "peace of mind." A book by that title immediately became a best-seller. It would not have sold so well if it had been called, *Salvation from Sin*. But Christianity's offer of peace of mind is salvation from sin—with sin recognized as not only wrong conduct but a wrong inward state. The church must beware of offering peace too cheaply, or of promising that good people need never be disturbed. But it is Christ who says, "My peace I give unto you" (John 14:27). Evangelism can go to the many who are torn by mental conflict, driven to distraction by inner jangling and discord, and can tell them how to get the harmony and poise and serenity which come from faith. It can point them to the sources of quietness and confidence and help them find in God the peace which passes all understanding.

14. Resentment of Material Domination

People are ready to rebel against the tyranny of the material. They resent the increased strain of high-speed living. The necessity for a growing number of possessions and contraptions arouses a certain sense of being put upon. There is a reaction which makes even materialists a little wistful for the things the Church has to offer. Evangelism can make the most of this.

---

* From *A Shropshire Lad*. Reprinted with permission of Henry Holt and Company, Inc., The Society of Authors, London, as the Literary Representatives of the Estate of the late A. E. Housman, and Messrs. Jonathan Cape. Ltd.

15. Eagerness for a Better World

The passion for social reform gives the Church a point of contact with many high-minded people. It is already with them in their outraged sympathy and moral indignation and desire to build a better world. It has been said that Marxism took one page from the New Testament and threw the rest away. Many who are attracted to political radicalism by that one page could be attracted to the Church. They can find in the Church the power that has upset thrones and blasted tyrannies and forced open the doors to enlightenment and health and freedom for countless multitudes. The Church can show that it not only has the incentives and the laws for a just social order but that it also has the more than worldly support which those who struggle against evil have to have. Through their desire to serve human needs, evangelism can reach many who can then be shown what else the gospel has.

16. The Appeal of the Heroic

The gallant urge to give oneself to some heroic cause is one to which the Church can respond. The discontent with a useless, uneventful existence and the yearning for the greatness which comes through abandonment to some high undertaking are God-given. Their perversions have sent millions into the political fanaticisms which have cursed our generation. Evangelism can bring many, who are ready to follow a call to selfless devotion, into the service of the Kingdom and its King.

17. The Craving for Brotherhood

The thrill of brotherhood in a common undertaking has a powerful appeal. It rescues the individual from sterile isolation and joins him to a living whole. The brotherhood and sisterhood of those who are laboring together in the greatest cause of all, the Church of Christ, can supply this consciousness of belonging; it meets the need for group support. Evangelism responds to the urge to join something with the invitation to come into the Christian fellowship.

18. Love of Home and Family

Love of home and family offers a wide-open door for evangelism. Most people will do what they believe will bring happiness to those they love. Parents are anxious for whatever will benefit their children. It is not hard to demonstrate that religious faith is an important factor in the happiness of a marriage. Many people who never go to a church themselves are glad to have their children get Christian training, if only for its "character-building" qualities. The Church, with this contact made, can point out that it cannot succeed without religious practices and training in the home.

There is a danger here. This motive is sometimes urged in terms which suggest that church membership and religious forms are painful requirements to which parents must submit for the benefit of their children. Parents can be badgered into joining the Church with no motive save the determination to do their duty by their small sons and daughters. It must be shown that it is not just the common Church membership which holds a family together and gives foundations to young people—it is the shared love of Christ, the devotion to His teachings and the sense of His presence.

19. Admiration for Jesus Christ

By far the finest and most effective contact the Church has with the minds of modern men is through the attractiveness of Jesus Christ Himself. This is the appeal that, in some sense, is involved in all the others. Though there are many who are anxious to criticize the Church and Church members, there are few who will criticize Christ. As far as He is known, He is loved and admired. It is in this agreement about Christ that the Church finds its first common ground with many people.

A good many who are out of the Church could echo what Dostoevski wrote to his brother, "I want to say to you that I am a child of this age, a child of unbelief and skepticism. And yet . . . I believe that there is nothing lovelier, deeper, more sympathetic, more rational, more human and more perfect than the Saviour." Evangelism can start that far along with many. If it can get them to see more of Jesus Christ, they will grow in their love of Him until they are ready to give Him, not only their admiration, but their lives.

20. The Power of the Cross

What Jesus said of Himself is still true, "I, if I be lifted up from the earth, will draw all men unto me" (John 12:32). The figure of the loving Christ, crucified for men, has a powerful attraction. The strongest appeal that evangelism has is not the appeal of Christ as the hero, or as the beautiful character, or as the finest of all teachers—it is the appeal of the Son of God giving Himself on the cross. It is the print of the nails which brings modern skeptics to say, with Thomas, "My Lord, and my God."

There *is* power in the blood. Our aversion to the crude use of the expression "saved by the blood of Christ" as a sort of incantation may make us forget that it is true. It is because of His atoning death that Jesus is able to draw men from all that has captivated them, from their evil habits and lesser loyalties, and bring them to give their hearts to Him. We cannot trace the mechanics of something so far beyond our mental range, but we cannot doubt the fact. College professors and newsboys, Fiji Islanders and salesmen are shown that Jesus Christ died for them, and they find a strange power to break from whatever guilt and limitation may have held them back, and they go out into a new and glorious life.

21. Questionable Appeals

There are some other appeals which are unquestionably effective, but questionably Christian:

The use of *fear* in evangelism can be hotly debated. It can be argued that the Bible uses it. There are threats in the Ten Commandments and in the Sermon on the Mount. Fear of unhappy consequences must be implied in preaching. Preachers who would be horrified at the thought of frightening their congregations with the Divine justice and judgment frighten them instead with the atom bomb and economic disorder and neurasthenia. If we really believe that a person's condition after death has any connection with his actions and attitudes here, we can say so. As one minister has put it, "I would rather frighten them into Heaven than let them go to Hell unafraid."

The case against fear has been clearly put by Professor W. D. Chamberlain in his illuminating little book, *The Meaning of Repentance*.

> Jesus offered citizenship in the Kingdom, not the menace of Hell, as the motive for repentance. These two approaches represent radically different conceptions of religion. . . .

> The Christian is not a man driven to do right by fear of a scourge; the Christian is motivated by the Spirit of God within. When Jesus preached repentance, he offered opportunities for service; his followers have often coupled repentance with threats of damnation. . . . In Jesus' teaching, also, there are references to judgment, but they are made only after men have rejected an invitation.

All would agree that the reaction against the extreme use of fear is healthy. When a comet appeared over Boston, Increase Mather terrified his congregation by declaring, "The Lord hath fired his beacon in the heavens among the stars. . . . The warning piece of heaven is going off." Jonathan Edwards got results when he preached, "The bow of God's wrath is bent, and the arrow made ready on the string; and Justice points the arrow at your heart and strains the bow. . . . The God that holds you over the pit of Hell—much as one holds a spider or some loathsome insect over the fire—abhors you, and is dreadfully provoked." By such preaching four thousand people were brought into the Church in the "Great Awakening." But it was a distortion of the gospel. The fact that children can be easily manipulated by their terror of the supernatural does not justify the damage that it does. The attempt that some child-evangelism groups make to use this method discretely is a little like an attempt to discipline children by a discrete use of the garrote.

Social pressure can be improperly used. "We want every member of this class to join the church." "You know how happy it would make your wife." "Your brothers and sisters all joined the church when they were twelve years old." "Now with all these others standing, won't you who still are seated take your stand for Christ?" Example may properly have some influence. Group action may well furnish the occasion for decisions. But unless the church takes great care to keep this motive secondary, it will be receiving those who consent to call themselves Christians solely out of the desire to conform.

Worldly motives can be exploited successfully. "All of the best people in town are in our church." "There is no better place for a young doctor to get acquainted." "This community likes to have its school teachers interested in a church."

Superstition (i.e., pulling God down to man's purposes instead of lifting man up to God's) can creep in without being recognized. The difference between a covenant and a deal is sometimes not made clear. The suggestion that becoming a Christian makes an alliance with the forces which bring good luck can be given without intending it. The fact that many Church people can point to their conversion as the turning point in their material fortunes makes it hard to keep this motive from slipping in.

VII

Knowing Whom to Win

It is futile to dream of evangelizing people in general. There is no such thing as a person in general. Evangelism never begins until definite people are identified and kept in view.

There are five essential pieces of equipment for a church—a Bible, a pulpit, a communion table, a baptismal furnishing and a file of prospective members. That file is the church's evangelistic field. A church may be surrounded by countless numbers of those whom it might win; but the only ones it is likely to win are those whose names it knows. A church's whole evangelistic opportunity is measured by the size and quality of that file.

The keeping of the file is a sacred task. It cannot be dismissed as an avoidable detail. Each card represents a human being—a human being who is likely to be neglected if the card is treated carelessly.

The pastor is normally responsible for the file, though he may have lay help. Its cards are never taken away until they are permanently removed; calling assignments are copied onto other cards. Husbands, wives and minor children are listed on the same card. Other adults in a home have separate cards, with cross references to relationship. Every bit of personal information which might be useful in evangelism is noted on the cards. So is the report of every contact, with recommendations for future action. The cards should be clearly classified by urgency and likelihood. The whole list should be read over frequently to keep it up to date and freshly in mind.

The file of prospective members is also used as a prayer list, as a mailing list and as a source of prospective members for the church organizations.

Prospect or Assignment Card

Name_____

Address_____

_____Attends Church Service   _____Some of Family Members
_____Attends Sunday School   _____Child in Sunday School
_____Attends Youth Group   _____Baby on Cradle Roll
_____Attends Adult Group   _____Contributor
_____Member Elsewhere   _____Survey—Prefers Our Church

Other Reasons or Information_____

_____

Called on by_____ Date_____

Report and Follow-up Recommendations_____

_____

Some small-town or rural churches have let themselves believe that there are no prospective Church members in the whole community. Discouraged city churches, in neighborhoods where the population has changed, often assume that no one who might be brought into a Protestant church lives near them. These assumptions come from looking over people's heads instead of at them. When such a church makes a systematic check on the people in each block or on each farm or at each place of business, it almost always discovers numbers of excellent prospects whom everyone, for some reason, has overlooked. An Ohio pastor told how surprised his church was to win 53 people when a real effort was made in "an over-churched community in which there are 10 churches for 2,100 people." A church in an industrial section of New Jersey reported, "We are in an almost totally Roman Catholic community. But on Palm Sunday we had 33 new members—19 from Catholicism, without our proselyting."

We may not see the fields white unto the harvest until we get rid of the blinders which convention has fixed upon us. Descendants of immigrants from countries which are loosely considered non-Protestant are often completely outside any church and will eagerly welcome a friendly approach. Many with a Jewish background have no religious connection of any sort and are hungry for it. People with a limited education may become the best examples of what a Church member ought to be, once they are convinced that the church really wants them. Modern evangelism has to look beyond the too-limited sector which many churches have thought of as their field.

It is at the point of entrance that churches have to confront most directly the question of racial exclusiveness. In many towns there is no possible provision for the religious needs of racial minorities —even in separate churches. Or the only Negro churches will often be of a primitive sort in which educated and spiritually mature black people could not be at home. As a Negro professional man sadly told a Presbyterian conference in New York state, "When we black Scotchmen move up from the south, there is no church for us."

A committee which was arranging for the national convention of its denomination in a Missouri city had a meeting with the hotel men to try to persuade them to accept the Negro delegates. The chairman was saying something about democracy and Christianity when one of the hotel owners exploded, "How do you get this preaching to us? Your churches are just as segregated as our hotels are. Suppose you try practicing your Christianity before you tell other people what to do."

The minister of a New Jersey church reported, "Our evangelistic program brought a new vision of what the Christian Church is, and what it means to reach out in the name of Christ. As a result, we received our first Negroes into membership. Our people now take it as a matter of course to have these new members with them in all the activities of the church. They are pleased that people of a sensitive race should feel so welcome in our church that they want to come. And one of these new members told me, 'I decided long ago that if I had to have religion on a segregated basis, I wasn't having any. When I saw that this church was different, I wanted to be a member.' "

Those who keep the file of prospective members must be regularly drawing from all the sources in order to have a list that is alive and growing. Here are some of those sources:

1. Members of Organizations

The rolls of all the church organizations, including the school, should be regularly searched for the names of those who might be brought into Church membership.

2. Relatives

Relatives of members of the church or of its organizations should be on the list. Parents of those in the church school, including the Cradle Roll, have a high priority. Whenever a member is received by the church or an organization, the church status of all others in the home should be recorded. If this has not been done, the record can be made by giving or mailing census cards to all church and organization members, with the request that these cards be returned with the information about others in the family entered on them.

3. Pastoral Services

Those who have come to the pastor for weddings, funerals, counseling, etc., are likely to be favorably inclined to the church, and to have no other connection.

4. The "Prospect Consciousness" of Church Members

Church people can be trained to be alert in noticing and reporting those who might be brought into the Church. They are constantly meeting such people—in their business and clubs and schools and neighborhoods. They must also be urged to make the first approach themselves. Otherwise there will be too many such reports as, "He is in my lodge. I don't know whether he belongs to a church, but someone can find out."

When there is an every-member visitation, perhaps for the financial canvass, the callers can ask in each church home, "Do you have neighbors or friends whom we should be trying to interest in the church?" Ministers in their pastoral calling may ask that. Those who give such information may be encouraged to make the first attempt and to send a report of it to the church.

New members of the church can be the source of a whole set of new contacts, with their friends and relatives. Their fresh enthusiasm may make them eager to help bring others to the church. This should be urged upon them.

5. An "In-Church Survey"

Cards can be given out on which members of the church and its organizations are to report within a set time the names of those whom the church might be reaching, together with all useful information. This can be dramatized by having an "In-Church Survey Sunday." Such a specific program helps to develop a habitual prospect consciousness.

6. New Arrivals in the Community

"When you see a moving van, let it suggest e-VAN-gelism," is the wise suggestion of a Lutheran publication. Many a church has been built by following the moving vans. People who are approached soon after their arrival in a community are often grateful and impressed. The longer this is delayed the less effect it has. Church members living in each block or section can be appointed to call on all families which move into their areas. Public school records, if they give church preference, can be checked. In some cities there is a commercial greeting service, such as the "Welcome Wagons," which will collect information about the church interest of newcomers and will sell or give it to the churches. One minister gets from the electric-light company the list of all new connections, and he telephones these homes with a welcome in the name of the churches of the community, learning at the same time who might be prospects. Another minister checks each new telephone directory against the old one and calls the new numbers.

7. Visitors to the Sabbath Services

Alert ushers and the pastor at the door and church members who are assigned to strategic points can try to become acquainted with visitors to the services, and to learn about the possibility of their continuing interest. Those who fear that they may greet some rarely seen member as a stranger (which might be a good thing) can say, "I am still trying to know everyone in the church—are you a member?" Names and addresses may be tactfully requested by saying, "We would like to send you ——— (mentioning something the church will soon be mailing)."

A guest book at the door or guest cards in the pews will be

signed only when a visitor is given a direct and personal invitation to do so.

The best way to get the names and addresses of visitors is to have a registration of the whole congregation. Visitors will register only when everyone does. It can be made as meaningful a part of the service as the signing of communion tokens. The minister may say, "As a part of your worship, will you identify yourself now with your fellow worshipers by filling in a card and putting it on the offering plate (or leaving it in the pew)." Some call this "The Ritual of Friendship" or have "Here Am I, Lord" on the registration slips. There may be a space to note church membership and length of stay in the community. Most churches have their own attendance slips printed or mimeographed or have them torn from the bottom of the Sunday bulletin; in a few weeks they are used in such quantities that it is not economical to purchase them by mail. Some churches have a registration every Sunday, some through a season, others on one Sunday a month throughout the year. This tells who the visitors have been and how often they return. This also reveals the attendance habits of church members. This may be marked on the church roll. A list of those who need rewinning can be made.

A better designed plan uses sheets about nine inches wide. Down the left side are as many spaces for names and addresses as there are seats in a pew. Vertical columns to be checked have such headings as, "Member This Church," "Member Another Local Church," "Visitor to City," "New Resident," "Desire a Call," "Wish to Join Church." A wider column is headed "Denomination Or Other Information." These sheets are bound into pads with a cardboard back. During the "Ritual of Friendship" the minister asks each person at the end of a pew, where the pads have been placed, to fill out a line and pass the pad on. After it is filled out each one is asked to look at it, as it is passed back, so they may be introduced to each other in writing and greet each other after the close of the service.

The custom of inviting everyone to come after the service to another room for refreshments and fellowship is a valuable aid to evangelism in many churches.

8. Lapsed Church Members

Those with whom the church has failed should be specially on its conscience and its heart. They should not easily be given up as hopeless. Often, through some development in their lives or thought, they complete the circle and can be brought back to the church again.

9. A Neighborhood Religious Census

God has given every church a parish and has made it directly responsible for taking the good news to a certain section of the human race. The only way a church can discover those it should be reaching is for it to go out and find them. A census saves a church from working in the dark.

Almost half of the people living around our churches have no religious affiliation. Moreover, a giant mixmaster keeps stirring the American population so that in every decade more than half of the church members are uprooted and moved too far to be within reach of their former churches. The only way many of these will be discovered is through a census.

This same shifting of the population has built up sections which are underchurched. A community-wide census can determine where new churches ought to be.

A census is indispensable as a source of prospects for the *first stage* of evangelism. Two warnings, however, must be sounded with a foghorn's monotonous insistence:

First—NEVER TAKE A CENSUS BEFORE THERE ARE DEFINITE PLANS FOR USING ITS RESULTS!

A religious census is one of the easiest of all evangelistic maneuvers, and one of the most spectacular. It is therefore one of the most popular of all ways of wasting time. A census can readily be taken by a church which has neither the morale nor the stamina for serious evangelism. An exhilarating adventure of ringing doorbells ends in a glow of satisfaction over an impressive stack of cards. For the first week the cards are right on the minister's desk. The next week they are moved to his bookcase, and from there to the closet shelf. He may finally save himself the shame of throwing the cards away by turning them over to a committee which will do it for him.

This surprisingly common procedure is a source of endless spiritual damage. It injures the unchurched, who have been led to expect some sort of attention from the church. An interest which has been disappointed will be harder to arouse again. It deludes the church with the false feeling of accomplishment. It burns over the ground, for householders do not like to answer the same questions too often. It wastes precious energy which has been given for the Kingdom.

The first step in a census must always be to lay definite plans to cultivate those whom it discovers. Only after this has been assured should the rest of it be undertaken.

The second warning is this—THE GREATEST BENEFITS OF A CENSUS CANNOT BE KNOWN FOR MONTHS!

Without this warning, those who make calls following a census are likely to decide that the whole thing was a waste of time. They may not win one person in ten calls, while in visitation evangelism they have been used to the excitement of frequent success. They will come back from this slower sort of work discouraged and resentful unless they have been told in advance that in most cases they are simply starting a long process which will sometime lead to decisions for Christ's Church.

Those who tell the census takers that they prefer the Baptist Church usually mean no more than that they recognize the Baptist as the Church they stay away from, or that their grandfather's farm was nearer to a Baptist church than to any other.

A census is the first stage in evangelism—Contact. It must be followed by the second stage—Cultivation—before many will be ready for the third stage—Commitment. A church must surround those weakly interested people with its friendships, it must follow them by mail and by calls, it must bring them into its organizations and services and activities—until they begin to understand and to love the Church and its Lord. A church which is not enough in earnest about evangelism to do all that had better stay away from a census. But those who persevere can find a census to be endlessly rewarding.

a. When a census is needed. Census information is needed unless a church already has more prospects than it can possibly follow. Such information gets out of date about every three years, so that another census should be made. A rapidly changing community may need a census every year. Rural populations change less rapidly than do those in cities and do not need a census as often.

b. Time of year. In most cases, late summer or early fall is the best time for a census. There is less moving after that time, and a church needs its full operating year to cultivate those a census discovers. However, some churches find they can do better work with a census in the less rushing period soon after Christmas. A farm census may better be taken in the early spring. A census should come within a month before a Visitation Evangelism or Evangelism through Fellowship project which is to use it.

c. Who does it. A census may be taken: (1) by all the churches, for an entire city or county, (2) by the neighbor churches, for one area, (3) by a single church, for its immediate neighborhood.

The first way is by far the best. It gets to more people. It reaches places no one church would survey. It discovers prospects for a church outside its immediate neighborhood. It is less work for any one church. It spares householders the annoyance of repeated doorbell ringing by separate churches. It gives the community an impressive demonstration of church co-operation. It promotes fellowship among the churches. It gives the callers a better entree. It secures better newspaper publicity, which prepares homes to receive the callers. Co-operating churches are more eager in following up their prospects than a church will be which has been generously presented with its prospect cards by another church which has made the census.

However, if other churches are too distant or disinterested, a church can have a very valuable census by itself.

d. Organization. There must be a Census Committee, under a chairman who is energetic and proficient with details. This Committee may appoint subcommittees to be responsible for: (1) enlisting the workers, (2) training the workers, (3) ordering supplies, (4) division and assignment of the territory, (5) publicity, (6) distribution of the results, with directions on how to use them, (7) finance. In a co-operative census this committee is selected from the participating churches. Each participating church also has its own census leader who arranges for getting supplies, preparing assignments, enlisting and training workers, having the lunch, sorting and organizing the returns.

e. Schedule. Two months before the census date, the Committee meets and assigns responsibilities. Two weeks later it meets again to have a report on the plans of all its subcommittees. One month before the census, all the materials should be distributed to those who will use them. Before two weeks in advance, all the workers are enlisted and their names reported.

On the census Sunday:

12:30 P.M.—A light lunch for all the workers. In a co-operative census the workers go to the headquarters church in each area.

1:00 P.M.—Instructions

1:30 P.M.—Assignments and dismissal with prayer

Sunday afternoon—Census taking

Sunday evening, Monday and Tuesday—return calls made at the addresses where no one was at home.

Wednesday evening—the filled-in cards are returned to the room in which the assignments were made.

Thursday—the returned cards are assembled and then sorted. They are then distributed with explicit instructions on how to use them.

f. Area. A co-operative census can take in a whole city or an entire county. A small-town census should include the adjacent rural areas. A single church census should take in as large an area as it can cover with its workers, going farthest in directions where other churches are scarcer. It can then take another census in another area, allowing enough time between to get the cultivation started. In two hours, churches can, on an average, survey an area whose population is seven times their total membership, if they use 15 per cent of their members as workers.

g. Preparing the assignments. A large map of the area to be covered is needed. The number of addresses for each side of the street in every block or country road is written on the map and the total for all four sides is written in the center of each block. A city directory or voters' list will give this information. Without such a directory, the number of houses and flats on each street can be counted from a car. Divide the whole map into units of fifteen to twenty calls each in a city and fewer in a rural area. Put the units in groups of six, for a captain and his five workers. Each unit should be numbered, with the number and the exact location copied on an assignment envelope. A rough map showing the assignment may be drawn on the envelope, or a printed map may be cut up, with the piece for each worker put with his envelope. In each envelope are put one and a half times as many census cards as there are addresses, and a pencil.

In a co-operative census, units around each church are assigned to it in proportion to its membership. If this requires more than 15 per cent of a church's membership as workers, the area must be reduced or more churches brought in to help. A downtown church, with few calls to be made in its neighborhood, may be given also a residential section where some of its members live.

h. Supplies. These materials are needed: One or more maps of the census area (city engineers' or real-estate maps are excellent), one and a half times as many census cards as there are addresses, one-fifteenth that number of assignment envelopes and pencils, printed or mimeographed instructions for each worker, instructions for each captain, two cards containing a written agreement to serve for each worker. Each church will also need prospect file cards on which to copy the information from the census. Some denominations supply the cards, envelopes, and instructions; or a church can readily design its own.

i. Enlisting the workers. A church enlists the number of census takers it will need by their written agreement to give the time required, with one copy of this for the worker and one for the church. No skill is required beyond tact and the ability to make a good impression for the church. Women and men are equally competent. Census takers usually go alone, though there is some advantage when they work in pairs. A church will also need a few clerical workers, to prepare assignments and to classify and distribute the returned cards.

j. The use of captains. Every sixth worker is the captain of the five whose assignments are next to his. He sees that these have transportation from the training meeting to the place where they will work. He is responsible for seeing that each worker completes the calls as soon as possible. Some churches appoint the captains and get them to enlist their five workers. The captains' instructions should be mailed to them in advance. (Captains are useful—not necessary.)

k. Publicity. The callers will be better received if the newspapers have given good publicity to the census in advance. This is especially valuable in the papers on the Sunday of the census. It may help if it is said that information about Roman Catholics will be given to their churches. Radio announcements or a dramatization of an interview may sometimes be arranged. Church bulletins should announce the census. Church people on the census Sunday may be told, if they are to be away from home, to pick up a census card and fill it out and leave it under the door. Newspapers may print a census card, with directions for filling it out, and a request that those who will be away when the census is taken tear it out of the paper and leave it, filled out, where it can be picked up outside the door.

l. Training the workers. For a half hour before the census takers are sent out, they are instructed. They should also be given a printed or mimeographed summary of the instructions. The right way to make a call may be dramatized. Census cards are passed out before their use is explained. Each worker then fills out this card for his own home and, if possible, gives it to the one who will be calling on his street. An inspirational statement about the great importance of the work should be made.

The work of the captains is explained to all. There should be a chance for questions. The importance of finishing the calls completely and soon must be reemphasized. Then the assignments are passed out and the workers are dismissed with prayer. A record of the workers who are with each captain, and their assignments, must be kept.

A census can do serious harm if it leads people to expect further attention from a church which fails to follow through. A church which has not already prepared for its second round of calls must never make the first one.

CENSUS CARD	Caller(s)		Date	
Family name			Not at home	
		How long at	Vacant house	
			Declined in-	
Address		this address	formation	

First name	Age if under 21	Church membership	Church preference	Sunday school attending
Single				
Husband				
Wife				
Children				
Others—give connection				

Write more information on the other side

The instructions to the workers cover these points:

1. Keep carefully to your assignment, so there will be no duplicate calls and no omissions.

2. Write the address on a census card before ringing the doorbell.

3. Call at every apartment, flat or separate dwelling. When no one is at home, do not ask neighbors for the information—call back. Do not fill out a card without calling, even though you know a family.

4. Complete the call as quickly as possible at the door, unless the weather is bad or the person who answers the door is infirm. You may give a cordial invitation to a church, when it is suitable, but do not linger for conversation.

5. Be smiling and pleasant. Make friends for the church.

6. Start by explaining your purpose and asking for help. Then ask, in this order, for the family name, the names and relationship

of all who live there (write "Mrs. John Smith" for a wife, "Miss" for an unmarried woman), the length of time at that address, the ages of those under twenty-one, the membership or church preference of each one (the name and town of a specific church if possible, if not, the denomination; if the preference is unclear, ask what church was attended in youth or what minister would be called for a wedding or funeral) the Sunday-school connections. Fill out a separate card for every roomer who is not a member of the family. Express real gratitude for the help, then leave.

7. Write plainly without abbreviations. Recheck each card to be sure the notations are clear. If there is no church preference or Sunday school, write "None." Record any additional information such as transiency, church attitude, race, nationality, occupation, need for a pastor, interests—but do not ask about these. Put your name on every card. Make out a card marked "vacant" with the address of every vacant dwelling. When more than one church or denomination is mentioned on a card, make out an exact copy of the whole card for every church or denomination which is mentioned. Mark each copy at the top with a different one of these so the cards will get into different piles in the sorting.

8. A missed call spoils the census. It may be a spiritual disaster for someone who could have been brought to the Church. At about a fourth of the addresses there will be no one at home. The sooner you go back for these calls, the better chance you have of making them all. Try again Sunday evening and Monday and Tuesday. Have all your reports back at the church by 7:30 Wednesday evening.

m. Distribution. The returned census cards are sorted in piles marked for each major denomination, or marked "Combination" (religiously divided households), "Miscellaneous" (denominations with no local church), "No Preference" and "Declined to Give Information." Complete copies of the "Combination" cards must be made, and one put in the pile of each denomination mentioned. Merely nominal non-Protestants should be classified as " No Preference" prospects.

Denominational cards which mention a local church are assigned to it. The others are divided geographically among the churches of that denomination, with some from residential areas assigned to downtown churches. "Miscellaneous" and "No Preference" cards are divided among the participating churches.

n. Follow-up by local churches. The first big task a census brings is clerical. Do not regard this as an anticlimax. It will save hours of future time and prevent the defeat of evangelism by vagueness. A corps of volunteer workers in one evening can change a disordered mass of census information into a clear guide for action.

Cards from the homes of members of the church are checked for new information and then put aside.

Then a prospect card is made out for every person or couple who might be a prospect for Church membership. These are classified as: good (Church members new in the community, young couples, teen-agers), fair (long inactive Church members, parents of older children, single people up to middle age), poor (those indifferent to Church, childless people past middle age.)

The names of all children whose parents are not actively opposed are entered in the church-school prospect list for immediate attention.

An organization or class prospect card is made out for each person who might be interested in such a group—a separate card for each group.

From all this information, mailing lists and calling lists are made out. Special projects in Visitation Evangelism and Evangelism through Fellowship are undertaken. Invitations to the Sabbath services or to special evangelistic meetings are given. Every part of the church has someone to reach and something to do.

o. Apartment Houses. Permission to call in an apartment where a doorman blocks the access may be gained if the caller has a letter from the minister or a Church Federation official. The way may be prepared if a minister talks to the doorman in advance. In a co-operative census a minister and a rabbi—perhaps also a priest—may go together to ask permission for the callers to be admitted from the superintendent or owner of an apartment. Some apartment officials will give a minister information about all families who move in. Riverside Church, in New York, has developed a highly successful plan for churches surrounded by apartment houses; a church family in each apartment house learns the names of new tenants and periodically invites all who might be interested for a neighborly evening—with dessert. The conversation turns to the church and an offer to take the new friend is given.

VIII

Lay Evangelistic Visiting

The darkness of these times has been slashed by rays of light. One of the brightest of these is the rise of a new sense of lay vocation. Something fresh and powerful is stirring among lay Christians. This can be seen in recent theology. Traditional theology defined the Church by the clergy. Catholics saw the Church passed down across the centuries by an apostolic succession of the hierarchy. Protestants defined the Church by what the clergy do, as they preach and administer the Sacraments. The tendency now is to identify the true Church through its laity. The apostolic succession belongs, not to the clergy, but to the laity, who are the successors of the Apostles. The Church is known through what it does, but this mission is performed by the whole people of God.

This theology is seen in the writings of Professor J. C. Hoekendijk of Holland. In *The Church Inside Out* (1966) he says it is the whole congregation that makes "the apostolate credible through her existence and life, through word and deed" (p. 66). The laity are to become "articulate Christians" as they present the gospel out in the world. The clergy are not in the world but they can "equip the laity for their service" (p. 86). A clergyman can share the apostolate only as he "behaves like a layman." Prof. Hoekendijk's choice between "centrifugal" and "centripetal" evangelism seems unnecessary, but he speaks for much of the newer theology when he insists that the Church exists when the laity make Christ's redemption known to those outside the Church. Our generation's rediscovery of lay evangelism is one of the brightest signs of hope.

1. The Reasons for Lay Evangelistic Visiting

a. It Is Biblical

Evangelism by private conversations was a method Jesus used. He spoke to crowds—but a great part of the Gospels is the record of the conversations Jesus had in private, as with Nicodemus and the woman of Samaria and Zacchaeus.

Not only did Jesus use this method, but He trained His disciples to use it. And, like His disciples today, they were amazed and joyful at their success (Luke 10:1-20).

The apostolic Church relied on evangelism in homes. There are repeated references to it. "Daily in the temple, *and in every house,* they ceased not to teach and preach Jesus Christ" (Acts 5:42). Paul reminds the Elders from Ephesus, "I have shewed you, and have taught you publickly, and from *house to house*" (Acts 20:20). The Bible's commandments to evangelize are addressed to all believers. The Great Commission strikes the pulpit and the pew at the same angle.

In the Hebrew temple only the high priest was allowed to go behind the veil into the symbolic presence of God, and only the priest could come back from the Holy of Holies, bearing God's mercies to those who waited outside. But at the moment of Jesus' death "Behold, the veil of the temple was rent in twain from the top to the bottom." (Matthew 27:51). In that instant the priestly monopoly was ended. The barrier which shut the unordained from the holiest place was torn away. Because of Christ, the humblest believer can go into the very presence of God, and can come from there to minister to a needy world.

b. It Is Normal

We need to put historical foundations under our recovery of lay evangelism. It is no novelty. In Christianity, revolution is always return. The hour of the layman struck nineteen centuries ago.

Jerome in the fourth century said, "Baptism is the ordination of the laity." *(Sacerdotium laici, id est baptisma.)* In other words, everyone who has been baptized or confirmed has been ordained as an evangelist. (In the United Church of South India every convert when he is baptized is required to place his hand upon his head and repeat solemnly Paul's words, "Woe is unto me, if I preach not the gospel!") A publication of the Church of England says, "Confirmation, from earliest times, has been considered the Ordination of the Laity, when they are commissioned and empowered to exercise their apostleship of evangelism."

It worked out that way in the early Church. As Adolph Harnack put it, "The most numerous and successful missionaries of the Christian religion were not the regular teachers but the Christians themselves, by dint of their loyalty and courage." A pagan philosopher, walking by the seashore, fell into conversation with an old man of gentle face and grave demeanor. Because of that conversation the pagan philosopher became Justin Martyr, one of the most convincing defenders of the faith—for which he died. That was evangelism in the early Church—and that is evangelism, at its best, today.

As late as the thirteenth century Thomas Aquinas taught that in joining the Church a person is given "power and responsibility, not only to effect his own salvation, but also, by sharing in the priesthood of Christ, to act as His apostle in the salvation of the world."

During the Middle Ages the Church became priest ridden. The laity lost the office Christ had given them. Resentment of this dispossession of the laity was one of the strongest forces behind the Reformation. We may misunderstand the Reformation. Its effect, as has been well said, was not to destroy the priesthood and leave a Church of laymen; but to destroy the laity and leave a Church of priests. Convent and monastery walls were broken down, not to let out those who were under holy orders, but to let all believers in.

The Protestant Church has had lapses into clericalism. There was such a lapse in the period when evangelism was thought of as something the Church members could hire an expert to come in and do for them once a year. When evangelism is seen as the prerogative of specialists, though they be all the clergy, it is done for—and the Church members are defrauded of a function Christ intended them to have. Elton Trueblood traces the sickness of the modern Church to the tendency of the members "to occupy the rear seats in the synagogue," "to play the easy and comfortable roll of spectator." "It is on a level with our commercial sports in which the multitude watch and the experts perform."

A discouraged young minister recently wrote of his three years of uselessly trying to get his officers interested in lay evangelism. Their invariable answer is, "Preacher, that is what we are paying you to do." That is clericalism, in its deadly Protestant form. It seems to assume that the minister is paid to be good and the laymen are good for nothing.

During the Civil War it was possible for a man who had been drafted to hire a substitute to take his place. Our government does not allow that now—and Jesus Christ never has.

The modern development of lay evangelistic visiting is a sign that the lay members are reclaiming their intended role. The last three and a half decades have seen a highly practical adaptation of this ancient method to the psychology and circumstances of our time. It has been worked out through trial and error. Criticism has helped to correct some of the weakness which came with the first Visitation Evangelism crusades. The result is that Protestantism now has in this a highly spiritual and effective way of evangelism which every congregation can use. It has proven to be very successful in some of the younger Churches overseas.

c. It Can Be Soundly Spiritual

Lay evangelistic visiting has a built-in safety device—when it is wrongly used it fails. It falls flat as a mere membership drive. Americans are not interested in joining another organization; their lives are already overorganized. If the message of the visitors is "We have a wonderful minister and the best choir in town, and you should get lined up with the right sort of people," they will come back deeply discouraged by their lack of success—and they deserve to be. But when the visitors tell what Christ can do for a life, when they talk of the possibility of connection with a higher power, when they speak of the church as a place where one may hear a voice from outside—then people will be interested.

Those who say, "I can live and die all right without the Church," will not say that about Jesus Christ. When they decide to take Him as Lord, then coming into the Church often seems the natural result of the desire to know and serve Him.

Evangelistic visiting is simply a ready channel by which a church can deliver whatever message it has. If it has no gospel the method will, of course, have little spiritual importance. But if a church has something real to say about faith in Christ, its laymen can be trained to say it.

The question whether laymen will really talk about religion has been well answered by experience. The fact is that many laymen are far less embarrassed in talking about faith than are their ministers. Ministers are afraid of sounding preacherish; laymen talk about religion because it is interesting.

New callers are invariably astonished at how ready those they visit are to talk about spiritual things. Often such questions have been pent up with no chance to discuss them. When the visitors offer the opportunity, a flood of needs and problems pours out. People will readily talk to church callers about things they have never before discussed with anyone.

Married couples, surprisingly, will often tell visitors what they have never told each other. The written report of one visit said, "The husband of one of our church women had not been baptized, and so the subject of Christ and His Church was rarely mentioned. Two of our men called and, to the amazement of all, the husband stated right away that he had been giving the Christian life and Church membership considerable thought. He had decided that he wanted to be baptized and received as a professing Christian. The Holy Spirit had been at work and all the men had to do was to open the way. Most people are more willing than we usually realize!"

That explains the cordial welcome visitors receive when it is found that they have come to talk about religion. They go out terrified of rebuffs, and come back amazed at how happy people are to have them come. A South Dakota pastor wrote, "This town never had so many scared people in it at one time before. But when they came back they were laughing and beaming. They had won people to Christ for the first time in their lives, and they were amazed at their reception." Dr. John Timothy Stone, who was famous for his ability to engage in conversations about Christ, with anyone at anytime, has said, "Some interviews were not successful, but I never met with a rebuff."

Among the thousands of calls reported in a nationwide denominational program there was only one report of a gruff reception. In this case the assignment had been made by mistake. The minister had found the man to have such a bad-tempered attitude toward the church that he had put aside as "hopeless" the card which bore his name. By some error that card was put back with the assignments. When the unsuspecting callers arrived at the door the man brusquely told them, "I'm busy. I'll give you five minutes; then you have to go." At the end of five minutes, they offered to go, but his interest had been roused and he begged them to stay. Over an hour later he had given his heart to Christ and they had all prayed about the resentments which had been barring his way.

Like every form of evangelism the Church has ever used, this one can be abused. Insufficiently trained visitors are likely to do all sorts of harmful and improper things. The untrained, in spite of good advice, almost never get beyond superficial conversations. But with a very little help they can learn to make these calls deeply spiritual experiences.

The directness of this sort of evangelism more than compensates for whatever it may lose in emotional force. While expressions of deep feeling and tears of joy are not infrequently reported, decisions made in a home may not always have the intensity of emotion which is associated with other sorts of evangelism. But there is a great spiritual advantage in presenting the claims of Christ face to face, in terms of the thinking and needs of the person approached, and in the surroundings of the daily life.

d. It Strengthens the Ministry

For most ministers, stage fright is in inverse proportion to the size of the audience. They can pour out their hearts before a congregation with little embarrassment; but talking to one or two people about personal religion may be blocked by an unendurable nervousness. There is nothing in a minister's work which forces this practice on him. One who is deeply dedicated to his calling may take his seminary training and be ordained and go through years of a pastorate without ever talking face to face with anyone about the deepest things of life. But because of that he will have a frustrating sense of inadequacy and guilt.

The pastor is the natural teacher and leader of lay evangelism. It forces him to learn and it forces him to practice. A program of lay visitation is likely to bring to the pastor something essential which he may never get in any other way.

A preacher cannot be sure that his public messages are not missing the mark unless in intimate talk with people he has learned what that mark really is. The best preaching is simply conversation continued. Its mood is "—as I was saying." It has a high exhilaration when it gives the preacher a chance to say those right things he was not quick enough to think of when a conversation called for them. If he has not been talking of such matters in private, he misses the flying start, the eager sense of unfinished business, which good sermon preparation has to have.

e. It Is Peculiarly Well Suited to Our Time

What A. W. Hopkinson said of England is as true of America, "The fisher of men in a modern parish is not one who casts his net into the sea and gathers in of every kind. He is more like a dry-fly man on an over-fished river; the fish are sophisticated, and he must watch for a 'rise'; sermons may be tried . . . but the striking and landing are done by interviews."

If the Church is to reach people with its message today, it must take its message to where the people are. They no longer flock to an evangelistic service because it is the most exciting thing in town. It cannot compete with moving pictures and the radio and television for the attention of those who do not already have a religious interest.

There are some hopeful signs that large evangelistic meetings are regaining their usefulness. But crowd evangelism rarely leads to lasting results unless it is joined with person-to-person contacts. Dwight L. Moody and Billy Sunday laid great stress on the teams of personal workers who labored diligently between and after their meetings. One of the most widely heralded of the new generation of mass evangelists tells the committees which bring him to their cities that the chief value of his meetings will be in producing a situation in which innumerable private evangelistic conversations will be taking place.

Our contemporaries have discovered the timeliness of person-to-person evangelism. The Jehovah's Witnesses, relying largely on home-visitation evangelism, increased their membership from 44,000 to 425,000 in six years. One of the best-known Roman Catholic evangelistic leaders writes, "It can be taken almost as an axiom that all recruiting must be done by personal contact. All other methods are not very productive. Lay apostles must be used." Any church which fails to use this method has not read the signs of the times.

f. It Mobilizes the Church's Greatest Power for the Church's Greatest Task

Seeing people in their homes requires a vast number of hours and workers. All of the pastors of America, spending every free minute at it, could only make a small beginning in the task. Most such visits must be made in the evening, and many of a pastor's evenings are claimed by church affairs.

There is approximately one pastor for every five-hundred members in the major denominations of America. That one pastor cannot possibly do what God wants all those five-hundred members to be doing. The power of the laity has been called "the greatest untapped force in the Christian Church." The country's worst unemployment problem is its spiritual unemployment. It is a sad thing that many a church has found no better use for the religious abilities of its fine, spiritually-minded members than to ask them to hand out bulletins or to take tickets at the bazaar.

There is grim point to the story of the minister who preached so movingly on "Christian Service" that one of the congregation came to him and said, "You have made me ashamed of myself. What is there I can do for the Kingdom?" "Gracious, I don't know," the embarrassed preacher said, "We already have sixty ushers!"

Modern evangelism—in Contact, Cultivation, Commitment and Conservation—has an endless number of very definite and highly important tasks for lay Church members. It depends very largely on the laity. Evangelistic visiting restores to lay disciples their intended function—and it restores to the Church the only force by which it can fulfill its mission. The great reason for lay evangelistic visiting is not the overworked minister but the underworked field. A church which is not organized to use its laity will surely fail those whom it should be reaching.

g. It Gives Direction to a Duty

Many church members suffer from a peculiar frustration. They long to share their faith without knowing how to go about it. As they see with pity the trouble and heartbreak and colorless living which a faith in Christ might have prevented, they wish desperately that there were something they could do about it. They often wonder how they might let their friends know what Christ might do for them. They cannot believe that to confront someone with an abrupt, "My brother, are you a Christian?" would do much good. But just what they might be doing today or tomorrow eludes them—and keeps on eluding them for years.

A program of lay evangelistic visiting gives church members the immediate, practical things which they can do to share their faith. It turns a vague obligation into an immediate task. It shows how and when and who. That truism which all church members accept—"A Christian's duty is to witness"—quite suddenly ceases to be a platitude when a person finds himself on a doorstep and hears someone coming to the door.

h. It Uses the Special Power of Witness Which Laymen Have

When a minister tells someone that he finds great value in Christian living, it is not very striking news; that was already assumed to be his peculiarity. But when the grocer or mail carrier tells what his faith and church are doing for him—that is impressive evidence. As a lawyer put it bluntly to a group of visitors, "A jury always discounts a paid witness."

Professor John Baillie told the Amsterdam Conference,

> Formerly men listened more readily to ordained clergy, supposing them to be better instructed in faith, but in our time lay witness gets a much readier hearing. . . . In university circles in which my own life has been spent, I have remarked again and how a single teacher of science or philosophy or history who

testifies to Christian faith has a better chance of penetrating the hard crust of unbelief than the combined eloquence of the theological faculty.

People want to know how Christianity looks from the pews. The minister seems like a salesman, but the layman is the satisfied customer. When a minister calls there is always the thought that he is out to build up his church, which is his job; but when laymen come it is clear that their only motive is a disinterested desire to do good. The minister is under some inhibitions in describing the value of services which he conducts; lay members are free of that restraint. The minister can talk about the fine fellowship of the church, but a visit from lay members demonstrates it.

The minister has more chance to study the teachings of the Bible; the layman has more chance to apply those teachings to the world. Most of a minister's time is necessarily spent with Church people; it is through its lay members that a church is making most of its contact with the world. If people outside the Church are to see what Christianity is and what Christ might have for them, it is the lay Church members who must show and tell them. As William Temple, England's great Archbishop, said, "We must move nearer to a state of affairs where the minister stands for the things of God before the congregation while the congregation stands for the things of God before the outside world."

This does not mean that the minister can leave all of the evangelistic calling to the lay members. He must be in it with them—and he will find in it one of the finest sorts of fellowship a minister can have with his members. He is what major-league baseball calls a "playing coach"—but he is not the whole team!

i. It Is Successful

Lay evangelistic visiting is at present bringing more adults into Church membership in the United States than are all other methods combined. When Church work in general declines, evangelistic calling declines. Its use is the most common source of any marked increase in the reception of adults.

The statistical results are impressive; but statistics show only one dimension. They do not show height nor depth. Have the great numbers who have been added to church rolls also been added to the Christian fellowship? Judging by the accounts from many churches, the spiritual results have been impressive. These stories, selected from church reports, are typical:

"One family was on the verge of separation, with alcohol as the chief cause, when they were visited by two laymen. Now there is a really devoted Christian family who know what God can do for them."

"The physician was an atheist and his wife a backslid Catholic. Both are now happy in a new experience with God. All five in the family are now working full pace in the church."

"As a result of our visitation evangelism program we received the manager of one of our state's largest gambling establishments into our church. Now he is a new man, bringing some of the leaders of vice to our church and winning them to Christ. He will open a sporting goods store in order to foster clean athletics among the youth of our city."

"A middle-aged woman, who had lost her husband through an accident and her daughter through illness, had grown extremely bitter against the world and God. Her connection with the church had been inactive for years. She was brought back through our lay workers. Having rediscovered her faith in God she now possesses one of the most dynamic spiritual experiences I have seen."

"He had no interest in church at all. A team of our men called on him. It opened his eyes to the fact that he was really wanted and needed in the church. He has made a confession of faith and was baptized. He is now one of our most active members and generous contributors."

"Three of our trustees, three deacons and the president of the Women's Association were brought to the church by lay calling."

"We have kept a special check on those who were won for Christ and the Church through visitation evangelism and have noted that throughout the year they have been our most regular attenders and the most cooperative in the whole program."

A denominational Secretary for Evangelism has gathered from many churches reports on the present activity of those who were won by lay calling three or four years ago. Eighty to 85 per cent were found to be still active. "While that is not as good as it should be," he writes, "it is a better level of activity than that of the membership as a whole, and has improved our long time record of losing about half of those who joined the church."

The lasting results of evangelistic visiting depend on what happens next— as is the case with every form of evangelism the Church has ever used. It offers the Church a God-given opportunity. It can give a sound beginning in the Christian life. This may be wasted in churches whose evangelistic zeal ends when decisions have been gained. But in churches which go on from there, lay visiting can be the source of endless blessing.

j. It Is Suited to Every Sort of Church

The use of lay visitors for evangelism is equally successful in rural or city, in sophisticated or unpretentious churches. Country churches which feared that their people could not call on neighbors whom they have long known have found out that this turns out to be an advantage. Downtown churches which have hesitated because of the lack of a compact parish have discovered that lay calling is the long-sought solution to the problems of city life. Mission churches which wondered about their lack of well-educated lay workers have found that artless earnestness is what makes their callers successful. Suburban churches which feared that their prosperous commuter members could never go into homes to discuss religion have been reproved for their lack of faith by the simple directness with which their callers have talked about the Christian life.

Whenever a church—rich or poor, dignified or informal—says, "We are not a church which can do that sort of thing," it is possible to find another church which is its exact twin and is declaring that this is the greatest work that it has ever done.

There must be minor adaptations, of course. Laying out of calls is done in a different way for country sections and for city blocks. The vocabulary must be adjusted. But churches which try to change the method which has been worked out for congregations of every sort over a period of years are likely to run into disappointment. The "improvements" are often simply the repetition of mistakes which others have long since discovered. Those who are just commencing to use lay evangelistic callers can count on success only if they follow the methods which most other churches have been using.

k. It Prepares a Church for Other Forms of Evangelism

The spark which kindles a church's whole evangelistic program is most likely to come from lay visiting. Those who go out to talk in homes about the deepest things in life have a stimulating experience with practical religion which can radiate spiritual enthusiasm through a whole church. The satisfaction of winning new members may turn a church from indifference to eagerness for evangelism. A concentrated program of evangelistic visiting focuses attention on prayer and beliefs and the motives for sharing the faith; it brings the thrill of an exciting enterprise. All of this is a basis for every other sort of evangelistic activity.

Logically, all the ways of contact and cultivation come first. But psychologically, a church which has not been doing much about evangelism will be wise to start with lay visitation. Such a church will usually have a backlog of those who are ready to be approached for a commitment. After a church's evangelistic zeal has been stirred in this most direct way it is more likely to be successful with such things as evangelism through fellowship or a census or a series of special preaching services.

l. It Puts New Life into All a Church Is Doing

Here let the churches speak for themselves. These quotations are taken from replies to a questionnaire on the results of lay evangelistic visiting:

> Many have been brought into the church, but the best effect has been on the men and women who have made the calls. They are finer, more mature Christians; they have a clearer conception of what they believe and of the value of their faith; they are more loyal churchmen, more solidly interested in the whole program of the church than before. Life is richer, broader and more satisfying because they have learned the joy of a definite service to Christ in witnessing for Him and His Church.—from a large Kansas City church.
>
> It has brought a new reality into all we are saying and doing,

showing us the way to make Christianity a reality and not a theory.—from a tiny mission church in New Mexico.

It has transformed our church, which was a typical "dead" church, into a church that is alive and realizing its responsibility for the community and for reaching out to the unchurched. The spirit of defeatism is gone and indifference has been replaced by enthusiasm for the church and for bringing more people into the Kingdom of God. Our benevolence giving has almost doubled.—from the Midwest.

This church had to have it proved that evangelism could be done in a dignified way. It is changing a very formal church into an active, vital fellowship.—from a New York town.

It has given our church a sense of true purpose that it has not had before. It has given it more members by double and more budget by triple.—from a small rural church.

It has made it apparent that the church belongs to the members, and not to the minister. It has made the community aware that it is welcome to our church, the house of God. It has helped to tone up the whole atmosphere of the life of the church.—from California.

A new spirit of concern for the unchurched has come into our congregation. Members delight in informing the pastor of new or unchurched families. This spirit has overcome a former coldness. People tell us that a warm friendliness has come over the congregation.—from Harrisburg, Pennsylvania.

It has broken barriers of selfishness and indifference in a class-conscious church and opened the way to Kingdom building in this urban community which has made an impact upon the whole city.—from an East Coast city.

It has taken our church out of a slump which was due to the emergence of some old jealousies. These have been laid aside again in this larger interest in the unchurched folks of the community.—from the Southwest.

In the diocese of Dornakal, in India, most of the church members give up their work and pay for a week each year in order to spend all their time in witnessing to their Hindu fellow countrymen. The late Bishop Azariah stated that this annual week has not only brought the rapid expansion of Christianity in South India but is the source of a notable devotion and consistency of Christian life among the Church members.

2. The Preparation for Lay Evangelistic Visiting

a. Getting the Church Interested in It

"The only difficult door to get through was our own door!" was the surprised comment one church made. Many churches require a great deal of persuading before anyone will go calling. There does not have to be complete conviction at the outset. The skeptical are often convinced only by experience. But the more enthusiasm and prayer there is behind a program, the more likely it is to succeed.

The congregation can be persuaded by sermons, or by a lay chairman's address. Evangelism in the pulpit keeps a congregation reminded of a church's mission. Frequent public prayers for it reinforce evangelism. Programs in the church organizations can impress the urgency and the possibility of evangelism.

If a denominational or interdenominational body is back of the plan for lay visiting, it helps to persuade slow-moving churches.

Meetings of church officers must give a good deal of discussion to lay visiting. It may have to be patiently proposed several times. Conservative minds, like cold motors, often have to turn an idea over for a while before the spark catches. The proposal is more likely to be accepted if it is first brought to the officers or to the congregation through a committee, rather than through one person. If lay visiting is enthusiastically presented at some outside meeting which church officers attend as delegates, it will help persuade them.

If a church cannot be persuaded, the minister or some member who is interested can take just one person on evangelistic calls. That person, having caught the zeal for it, can take someone else. Thus, by multiplying from a single pair, a corps of workers can be formed.

b. The Organization

In some churches the pastor by himself proposes the plan, enlists and trains the workers, prepares the assignments and makes all the arrangements. It is better when a committee which represents the most concerned church groups takes charge of this—with a lay chairman as the leader; or an official board may be the directing body for the program. In these cases, too, the pastor is likely to be the moving spirit behind the scenes—though there have been successful programs in which the pastor did almost nothing.

c. Setting the Dates

The most common schedule, and probably the best one, is this:

Sunday—3:00-4:30 P.M. The basic instruction meeting
Monday, Tuesday, Wednesday, and Thursday evenings—

6:10- 6:40	Supper
6:30- 6:55	Instruction (starting during supper)
7:00	Dismissal with prayer
7:00- 9:00	The Visiting
9:30-10:15	Report and Review meeting (there can be Sunday afternoon and evening calling)

Calls are usually made during the evening, though housewives may be visited during the day and farmers sometimes prefer it.

Four or five consecutive evenings are better than one evening a week for several weeks. The enthusiasm is more intense in a concentrated program; what is learned one evening is better carried over to the next; the dates are more readily cleared; callers are less likely to drop out. Workers can be engaged for consecutive nights as readily as for consecutive weeks. An extended program has a tendency to fall apart.

The dates should be set far enough in advance to permit the callers and the church to be free of conflicting engagements.

There are several seasons with special advantages: The fall, long enough after Labor Day to allow for preparation, gives the largest part of the church year for the assimilation of new members. Before Christmas, the radio singing the name of Christ in every home makes it an easy time to have conversations about Him. The beauty of the star and the manger and the infant Saviour brings in the hearts of those outside the Church a glow which is close to wistfulness—a glow which may be kindled into the light of a clear Christian faith. January is sometimes the least crowded season for the church and church people. Before Easter there is an emotional reinforcement for evangelism, both in the church and outside. The Pentecost season is appropriate but it has the great disadvantage of not allowing much time for a sound start in the the church before vacations interrupt.

The calling should be aimed at a featured date—at a Church Membership Sunday or the first session of a New Members' Class. The callers can then refer to that date as a special reason for an immediate decision. It also reassures the timid who would prefer not to be alone when they join the Church.

d. Prayer

Many churches have discovered that prayer for the calls has much to do with their success. Sometimes the shut-ins are enlisted to pray while the calling is going on. Those who serve the church through their prayers may be given a special name—the "Guild of Intercessors" or the "Prayer Crusaders." Each caller may have a "prayer partner." There may be prayer for the calling at the regular church services and meetings. Some pastors have a special meeting for prayer while the calling is going on.

e. Enrolling the Visitors

The desired callers are listed. They are then engaged through personal interviews, not by telephone. Almost always the minister is the best one to do this, perhaps in company with a lay chairman. In the interview, the work and its importance are explained. Those who fear that they may not be capable are reassured. A definite promise to give the time specified for the training and the calling is requested. A card form is often used to make this promise definite and impressive. The promises should be secured a month or more before the calling is to be done.

Beginners who can give only one or two nights should ordinarily not be used. Their first attempts are likely to be the least effective and the least satisfying. Those who stop soon will not understand how fine the work can be.

Some believe that asking for volunteers secures those who are the most sincerely interested. The majority opinion, however, is that this is not wise. It will enlist some who are not qualified; it

---

I Will Help

I agree to help in the program of evangelistic visiting.

I will attend the instruction meetings unless prevented by circumstances beyond my control.

I will do my share of the work within the time assigned.

Name..Telephone................................

Address..

---

will fail to enlist others who are qualified but too humble to offer their services; it does not make the work seem as important as does an interview.

Train beginners by pairing them with the finest callers. Try not to put exceptionally shy callers together. Most callers prefer to stay together through successive evenings. One must have a car. A married couple may be an excellent calling team, though they find it difficult to keep their calls from being merely social visits. Young people do well in calling on other young people and they make good teammates for older callers.

The extrovert who can go into a home radiating friendliness, talk and ask questions with a disarming frankness and close the call with a hearty "This has been wonderful—let's pray about it!" has a gift that can be greatly used. But the simple earnestness of the person who finds words difficult is sometimes even more convincing. There is no one type for evangelistic calling. The able Christian salesman has a talent which qualifies him to visit and to teach others how to do it. The quiet and deep person who can listen sympathetically and say the tactful word at the right time can be wonderfully successful.

On this subject, John Timothy Stone has well said, "Is there a lass who would want a man to indulge in fine phrase-making while proposing, as if he knew how to propose? It is not a matter of experience or form. No one would be impressed by the mere word or manner of expression, unless the heart revealed itself."

One who can tell of anything which his faith has done for him does not need to be an expert in the finer points of doctrine. Hard questions on theology rarely come up, and when they do can well be postponed for the minister to answer, while the conversation returns to the simple essentials.

Callers must have a sincere enthusiasm for the Church and its Lord, a reliance upon prayer, a willingness to be taught and a manifest liking for people. The born tactless, those zealous ones who seem always to irritate others and those who are not respected in the community must be assigned to other tasks than calling.

The number of visitors needed can be estimated by assuming that under average circumstances twenty visitors can make one hundred calls in four evenings.

f. Preparing the Calling Assignments

Names, addresses and all personal information which will help callers to understand the situation are put on assignment cards. (See the sample of such a card in the chapter on "Knowing Whom to Win.") Such information also gives the callers a chance to show some friendly knowledge—"We are glad you have moved to our town," "We are enjoying having Charlotte in our Sunday school." Do not write notations which might be embarrassing if the cards are accidentally left in the home—"Queer character," "Wife a problem."

The accuracy of addresses is to be carefully checked. Directions for finding difficult addresses may be put on the card. The name and church status of everyone in the household should be given. This will help the callers win the entire family.

The assignments should be classified as: (1) Likely (recently active in other churches, church-school parents, young couples, teen-agers, members of church organizations, those with whom the pastor has had a close relationship). (2) Less likely (childless couples married more than ten years, single people twenty-five to forty-five years old, church members' relatives who show little interest, long inactive church members). (3) Least likely (alienated former members, those who have shown no sign of increased interest since other callers failed to win them, childless people past middle age.) Those most likely to respond are usually visited first.

Assignments are grouped by neighborhoods.

Assignments for one evening's calling, with decision cards for each prospect, are put in envelopes. Each envelope is marked with a team's names. An average of three calls can be made in an evening; each team should have five or six assignments, as some will not be at home. There should be a record of who has each assignment so that there may be an immediate check-up on any which are not returned with a report.

Callers are usually not given literature to leave in the homes. It distracts everyone from the chief purpose of the visit and makes the callers seem to be mere colporteurs. But if they save them until they are ready to leave, visitors may very usefully give printed invitations from their church or descriptions of what it offers or evangelistic leaflets or devotional aids.

The callers are arranged in pairs. The two-by-two method which Jesus used is still the best. Two make a better impression than does a lone visitor. They help each other and enjoy the companionship. They give each other confidence and are a double source of good ideas. More than two would appear to be an attempt to overpower by numbers.

Callers should be as much as possible like the people they visit —sending farmers to farmers, employed women to employed women, professional men to professional men. Specially qualified teams should be sent to see people with unusual problems or with unusual power for good.

Trading teammates or assignments may be allowed, but not encouraged.

A map on which callers can locate addresses just before they start will save their time.

There are two reasons for not notifying people by mail or telephone that callers are coming to see them: (1) Calls cannot be scheduled for definite times. A conversation about the Christian faith which is taking longer than usual cannot be abruptly ended so that the callers can get to their next appointment. (2) When people know that visitors are coming from the church, possibly to talk about membership, they decide what their answer will be before the visitors have a chance to be heard. They are most likely to decide to do what they have already been doing. The visit then starts with the great disadvantage of minds that are closed in advance. One pastor quit writing preparatory letters when more than half of the recipients telephoned to say that the visitors need not come; he believes that most of these could have been won.

In spite of this, some pastors insist that a warm, personal letter prepares the way for the visitors and makes their task easier, as well as making it likely that more people will be at home. There are other sorts of preparation by mail which unquestionably are helpful—friendly letters which say nothing about callers, messages about the Christian faith and the Church, advertising folders which describe the local church and its program, a parish periodical.

g. Training the Visitors

Anyone can take a few names and go out calling; therefore, the temptation to slight what other churches have found to be essential to evangelistic visiting is always present. A church may feel, "Since this is our first attempt, we will do only a part of what is supposed to be done, and be satisfied with a partial success." But, like installing three-fourths of a telephone line, the result is not a three-fourths success, but none at all. A poor attempt at evangelistic visiting does more harm than good.

The use of improperly trained visitors is one of the most common, and most disastrous, short cuts. As one church was discussing its plans a kindly officer said, "We know that our minister has too much to do, and if he wants some of us to help him with the calling we will be glad to. But he mustn't expect us to waste time coming to any classes. We have been around this church a long while and we do not have to be taught how to make a call."

That attitude is entirely natural and completely wrong. The greatest saint in the church will make his full share of the familiar mistakes. The most experienced caller will continue to omit many of the things he should be doing until these are shown to him. Even though there were any who needed no advice, they should be willing to come to training meetings because those who do need the instruction will not come unless the meetings are for all.

Personal evangelism is the most intimate and delicate work that a human being can possibly do. It deals with the emotions and habits of people—with their relation to their God. No one could ever get beyond needing more help for that. Moreover it is big business, by any measurement. It is the key task in the largest institution in America, and in the world. Armies and industries and universities, statesmen and scientists, are waiting on the evangelists. Evangelistic calling is a tremendous enterprise, and it is worth doing in a big way.

If the body is badly injured, nature throws it into shock to protect it from unendurable pain. The casualness, even the frivolity, with which we can do Church work may be a natural defense. God may veil the glory because of human weakness. Perhaps we are kept from seeing steadily just what we are doing in evangelism in order to shield us from realities which would upset our reason if we saw them as they are.

Someone who is asked to do evangelistic calling may wonder wearily whether he can spare the time required for the instruction and the calls. But think of the implications, on three levels. First, the most superficial—there will usually be at least one decision from an evening's calling. Such a decision will require of the one who makes it at least two hours a week. That is three thousand hours of the average remaining lifetime which is claimed by the caller—and he wonders whether he can spare one evening for it! Next, on a deeper level, if that decision for Christ is real, every hour and every minute of the remaining lifetime will be different because the caller came. Going still deeper—we believe that life continues after death and that it goes on in the direction it had before. Evangelistic visiting has implications which go clear beyond this world. If we saw all of that just as it is, it might unhinge our minds; we would be too appalled to get a conversation through our paralyzed throats. So God lets it look like just another call.

Evangelistic calling does not require complicated techniques. The skills are relatively simple; enough to start with can be taught in a short while. But there are matters of common sense which are obvious only after they have been pointed out. The same situations will be met repeatedly, and the callers can be prepared in advance. There is such a thing as salesmanship for Christ, and it can be learned. The wisdom which others have worked out through years of experience can be passed on. Mistakes can be warned against. Even veteran callers need to keep on learning.

There is another reason for bringing experienced callers to pre-liminary meetings. The danger time comes after a successful experience with evangelistic visiting. On the first round the callers are likely to be frightened and excited by the importance of what they are doing. They pray hard and have the visiting on their minds for many of their waking hours—and as a consequence do well. The next time they feel that they are expert. They go out, casual and confident—and come back deeply humiliated by their failure. Callers can deteriorate. They get used to trying to win people for Christ, and their enthusiasm plays out. Forgetting that this is a work about which no one ever knows enough, they have no interest in learning more, and even lose what they have learned. Before each effort the visitors must have a renewal of their vision of the greatness of what they are attempting, and of their inadequacy. The arrangements each time must dramatize how seriously the work is to be taken. The tendency to go stale is natural and must be overcome.

The familiar schedule gives an hour and a half of basic instruction on the Sunday afternoon before the calling starts, and a twenty-five-minute period each evening before going out. If the visitors have supper together, the evening instruction can be commenced while the meal is being finished and they can get their assignments and be on their way without losing calling time. It is a misfortune when any of this falls behind schedule so that time which should be spent in the homes is wasted in getting started.

Some rural churches, whose calling covers a wide area, have a second long instruction period instead of the shorter ones each evening. A downtown church assembles the visitors for coffee and doughnuts and an instruction session on Sunday mornings before the church school.

Usually the pastor of the church is the teacher, though a layman may be. Often a church which is just starting invites as teacher a minister or layman from a church which has had experience.

The teacher should beware of trying to make every caller a copy of himself. He can show what is to be said, but he cannot show just how to say it. The caller must put his free, spontaneous personality into the call. To try to say things in words that are not his own, or to do what is unnatural for him, will make him stiff and unappealing.

The training sessions require serious teaching. Impromptu pep talks will not do. Here is a possible content for the classes:

THE BASIC INSTRUCTION MEETING

The motives for evangelism (briefly). *See pages 26-39*
The reasons for lay evangelistic calling (briefly). *Pages 89-102*
The necessity of coming to all of the meetings for instruction
How to make a call (a concise preview, step by step). *Pages 113-30*
A commissioning of the visitors

THE FIRST EVENING

How to secure transfers of membership. *Pages 145-48*
How to secure decisions. *Pages 124-27*

THE SECOND EVENING

Encouragement for apparently unsuccessful callers
The reasons to be given for decisions. *Pages 136-44*
How to deal with excuses. *Pages 149-58*
Review of experiences and problems

THE THIRD EVENING

Dealing with former Roman Catholics. *Pages 148-49*
Mistakes to be avoided. *Pages 122-24*
Review of experiences and problems

THE FOURTH EVENING

The care of new members. *Pages 206-43*
Plans for keeping on with evangelistic visiting. *Pages 130-34*
Review of experiences and problems

The teacher needs to prepare with great care—there is much to be said and little time in which to say it. He should study one or two of the books on the subject. If he has had little experience with the methods they recommend, he will be greatly helped if he practices them by doing some calling before the main effort commences.

Printed instructions for visitors can reimpress what the teacher says and go beyond it. These can be gotten as leaflets or booklets from denominational or independent sources. A teacher may study the books on visiting and on evangelistic conversations and write out his own instructions, which can be mimeographed. A one-page typed summary can help the workers remember the important points about calling. (See pages 113–30.) Visitors specially need advice on how to bring religious matters into a social call.

A dramatized call is instructive; someone raises the difficulties which are most often encountered and the teacher or members of the class, in the role of callers, try to answer them. One pastor asks each prospective caller to tell of something that Christ and the Church have done for him or for her—having in advance requested two or three to be ready to start the response. Thus the visitors get practice in saying things they may say again on their calls; moreover, they supply each other with quotations which can be used in calling—"Why just this evening I heard one of our members say . . ."

The leader closes the instructions with very definite directions on how and when to report. Then the callers are sent out with prayer.

There is very great advantage in a review session each evening after the calling is finished—say at 9:30. This may not be possible for those who have traveled far from the church. But for those who can come, there are three important benefits: (1) It is a clinic —they discuss their experiences and problems, learning from each other and exchanging advice. (2) They report what they have found out about the people they visited while it is still fresh in their minds. (3) Those who have not been successful are kept from losing faith in the enterprise by hearing from those who have done better.

Visitors must be guarded against discouragement. They can be told that, even though there are no obvious results, the seed they have planted may bring a harvest later. Some who refuse invitations will reflect on them and later accept. No work sincerely done for Christ is ever thrown away—"your labour is not in vain in the Lord." Callers should not be contented with small results— or defeated by them. An insurance agent told a group of church callers, "In my business I think I have done well if from ten calls I get three good leads from which I make one sale."

3. How to Make an Evangelistic Visit

a. Pray

On the evening before they start out one frequently hears new visitors saying, "I can't do this sort of thing; it's just not in my line!" Two hours later these same visitors return declaring with amazement that it has been the most wonderful experience of their lives. They were right in the first place—bringing another person to the Christian faith is something no one can do—it is not in anybody's line. But something else enters in which cannot be explained on the human level.

There are actually three persons on these calling teams—and without the help of the Divine partner, the other two do not do well. What two callers in Cincinnati told about themselves is typical of a thousand others. The first evening they had done poorly, while all the others seemed to be enjoying the work. The second evening this team was the only one with no decisions to report. Before they went out on the third evening they checked over all of the instructions to find what they had been doing that was wrong. They could find only one recommendation that they had failed to follow—the advice to pray. So, before going to the car, they went into the church sanctuary and prayed. That evening, everything seemed different. They had a warmer feeling about the calls; people responded to them in a better way. They won some decisions but, even if they had not, they would have known that everything was different.

We unmystical moderns do not need to theorize about this. A very little experience, trying it both ways, shows that the difference is too plain to be doubted. The saying, "This is not man's work but God's," becomes an obvious matter of fact.

It is a good thing when the callers are frightened by the importance of what they are trying to do—they pray better then. For this reason they must be kept reminded of the awesome difference their calls can make; they must be kept aware of the risks they take in attempting to manipulate the most precious and sensitive thing there is—the souls of human beings (though the failure to make

that attempt is a great deal more dangerous). They must be kept
from getting used to evangelism.

Some churches dedicate their visitors at a Sunday morning
church service. Visitors may partake of the Lord's Supper before
they call; it has a special significance for them—the inner reinforcement by the spirit and power of Christ, the channeling of His
salvation to the world through the Church, the consecration of
His followers to be His earthly body. The preparatory meetings
should close with a prayer for God's presence and help in the
calling.

The advice to pray before they call is the most important part
of the instruction. The callers may have a prayer in the car before
they start the evening's work, or they may pray before they ring
each doorbell. Their prayer can be as brief and pointed as a blessing at the table—"God, use us to help these people," "Help us to
say what will bring Christ into this home." Some churches give
each new team a slip of paper with a prayer they can read before
they call.

Callers can pray during a visit, without seeming to. After a
difficult call, in which an embittered invalid was brought to see
his need for Christ, one of the visitors said, "I was certainly praying
while you talked." "You were?" the other one answered. "That
is just what I was doing while you were talking."

Sometimes, after a call appears to have failed, there is nothing
left to do save to pray long and hard about it afterward. That
prayer often seems to accomplish more than the conversation did.
Something happens in the mysterious channels of the spirit and
the person who said "No" is soon a grateful member of the
Church.

b. Review the Information

Just before ringing the doorbell the callers should review the
information on the assignment card so that it will be freshly in
mind. Then the card should be put out of sight.

c. Decide Who Takes the Lead

So that the callers will neither hang back nor collide with each
other, they must agree in advance who is to make the introductions

and start the conversation. The one with more experience or more contact with the people they are visiting may be the leader, or they may take turns. The other is by no means a silent partner—they help each other with the conversation—but the leader is the senior partner, giving the direction to the call.

Two conversations in the room at the same time spoil each other. If someone in the home commences to talk separately to one of the partners, he should try to get back into the main conversation as soon as possible.

d. Get into the House

A satisfactory call can rarely be had while talking through a door. The visitors should introduce themselves at once, mention the church and tell why they have come—"We are from Bethany Church and we have come around for a call." If, through surprise or the habit of talking to solicitors at the door, the visitors are not invited in, they may say, "We would like to come in, if you are not too busy."

It may appear that it is a poor time to call. The visitors cannot take at face value their hosts' insistence that they want to postpone dinner or waste concert tickets or have an addition to the company they are entertaining. When other visitors are in the home in a very intimate and informal way, there may still be a good evangelistic call. There have been cases in which both those whom the callers came to see and their guests have been won. Friends who have dropped in uninvited may insist that they were just about to leave, which may be a good thing all around. But usually, when there is any appearance of inconvenience, it is better for the callers to set a time to return. Then when they come back they will find an unusually cordial welcome.

e. Get a Favorable Situation

The callers should try to be seated where they can most easily talk with the people they came to see. The confusion of getting seated may result in some very awkward positions unless the visitors are careful.

A television set can be a serious handicap. The classical method for dealing with it is for the callers to drop their voices lower and lower until they are talking in such subdued tones that someone shuts the thing off in order to hear what they are saying. This may be reversed by saying, "I did not quite catch what you said, do you mind if the radio is turned down?" Television is more difficult. If it is near the end of a program a caller may say, "Don't you want to see the rest of this program? We can talk when it is over." That (a) raises the question and (b) sets a time for turning off the set. If children or others not interested in the call are watching the television, the visitor may insist, "I am afraid we are going to bother them. Can't we go into the next room to talk?" Proposals that the visitors should carelessly toss a coat over the television set, or leave their car engine running with the spark plugs ungrounded, have not found general acceptance.

All of those in the home who are prospective members should be included in the conversation if possible. It may be necessary to say, "Is Mr. Jones in? We would like to talk to him too," or of a grown child, "We came to see Ruth also, if she is here."

f. Make a Friendly Start

The callers should show a cordial interest in those they are visiting. Sincere praise of something in the house or of some accomplishment or of the children can be expressed. A mutual friend or interest can be mentioned.

g. Get Soon to the Real Purpose of the Call

While a little friendly small talk establishes a pleasant atmosphere, not much time should be spent on nonessentials. The callers are there on great business, and they should get to it without delay.

It can be introduced by a reference to the reason for the church's interest: "Your children are in our Sunday school and we know that the church cannot do all it wants to do for your children without a close connection with you too"; or "You have been attending the services and we want to talk to you about the church"; or "Since you have moved to our town we want you to think of our church as your home."

h. Ask Questions

Questions discover the attitudes and church background. Until these are known the visitors are working in the dark.

Questions get people to talking—and thinking. Psychologists say that people are persuaded less by what is said to them than by what they say.

The questions should be asked so as to give the benefit of the doubt—not "Did you ever attend a church?" but "What church have you attended?"; not "Are you a Christian?" but "Don't we all need more help in being Christians?" It should be assumed that the other person: (1) wants to be a Christian, (2) has a religious background, (3) believes in God and Christ. If these assumptions are not correct, it will soon be known.

Questions which are likely to be answered affirmatively should be asked. These questions should go farther and farther until people are ready to answer "Yes" to the great ones. For example: "How long have you lived here?" "What church were you interested in before?" "Have you affiliated with any near-by church?" "I know you are trying to give a Christian training to your children —wouldn't it be a help if you professed your own Christian faith and came into the church?" "I guess some of us who are older need help with our religion as much as the children do, don't we?" "Is there anything as important as trying to follow Christ and helping our children to know Him?" "Wouldn't it be a good thing for you and for your home if you were all in the church together?" "Have you ever thought of doing this?" "Wouldn't you be happier if you got it settled now?"

Obviously, the questions do not come as rapidly as that. They are spaced by conversation. But such a line of questions can lead on to the goal.

Care must be taken not to ask questions which sound prying or rude. The manner should not be that of a cross-examination, but of a desire to share the thinking of a person whom you like and whose opinions you respect.

i. Talk about the Spiritual Motives, Not about the Church Activities

Most modern Americans already have too many things to do; they will be very little interested in the offer of another schedule of meetings to attend or another set of social obligations—however enthusiastically these may be described. They will be interested in finer living, in an answer to their deepest questions, in the help of a more than human wisdom and power. The call must awaken the desire to live closer to Jesus Christ. Church membership will then seem desirable as a way of knowing Him better and of obeying Him. The Church has little appeal for those who do not love Christ—it is almost irresistible for those who do. An intention to be loyal to Christ must come before a decision to join the Church.

The direction to make the call "Christ-centered" raises a difficulty which, for many callers, seems as high as a mountain. How can one sit in a stranger's home and get into a conversation on spiritual matters? How can one even pronounce the name of Christ in a social visit without having it seem queer and forced?

The difficulty is not the lack of something to say—or an unwillingness to hear it. Most visitors have things they would very much like to say about what Christ has done for them and for their homes; most people who are visited would like to talk about those things. The difficulty is in getting started.

Callers can learn how to bring a conversation to religious matters only by experiment. With a hesitating word at the first home, and a little more at the next, they learn.

Many instructors would be shocked to discover how many of the visitors they send out never mention spiritual things at all. More than the bare advice to do so is required. Ready-made formulas cannot be handed over. But suggestions and descriptions of how others do it are essential in helping the visitors to work out their own methods. Here are some of the ways that have been used:

A hardware salesman began his calls by making fun of himself, "There are plenty of people who would faint if they caught me doing this. Why, for twenty years my wife and I never went near a church! Then we got started, and last summer they even had me lead the prayer meeting. There was my chance to get some things off my chest, and here is what I told them. . . ." In a half-humorous way, recalling his prayer-meeting effort, he made a beautiful statement of what the Christian faith was meaning to him and of how much he regretted his years outside the Church.

A young foundryman on the first evening had declared that he would go along to drive the car, but could never talk religion to anyone. By the third evening of the calling he was saying, "I guess you find in your work, like I do in mine, it's mighty hard to be a

Christian—don't you? If it weren't for the Church I don't know where I'd be tonight." He would then speak of what he had learned at the church, and of the difference it was making.

A woman likes to talk to parents about how children need to learn of Christ and His teachings. Then she suddenly applies it to the parents, "I'm making the Church sound like a kindergarten! The fact is we grownups need it even more than the children do. I guess as long as we live we will need all the help we can get in knowing Christ and in living like Christians."

Another experienced visitor takes his start from world conditions, getting agreement that the world's only hope is in religion and in the teachings of Christ. He then speaks of how the same thing is true of his business, and of his home. Then he gets to everyone's personal need of God and of prayer and of the Church.

A statement of one's own experience is often a good introduction. While a prolonged autobiography is not effective, a brief and grateful statement can be very convincing. Some callers may need warning against the delights of self-dramatization. Those who are too shy to talk about themselves can tell about the experience of some friend.

Though the calls must not be "church-centered," there is no reason for not commencing by talking about the church and its activities, as a way of leading the conversation into deeper things. A glowing description of the church services can make it easy to speak of how they keep one conscious of God and give a faith by which to live. A delighted account of some of the church activities can lead to a statement of how they help one to know and follow Christ. There is danger that the talk will not get beyond the superficial attractions—the minister's eloquence, the well-organized program, the social enjoyments. The temptation to talk about the church as a splendid club—and nothing more—must be resisted. But a reference to what the church does may usefully bring the talk to the Church's faith and purposes.

One of the best and easiest ways to bring a call to essential matters is to say, "I suppose you would like to know what they ask of those who join the Church, wouldn't you? Well, first of all they ask . . ." Then, either conversationally or referring to a card or application form, the caller reviews the questions which are put to the candidates for membership. After each of them he asks, "You could say that, couldn't you?" If there is no difficulty, he goes on to the next statement. But as soon as one of the questions raises an uncertainty, the person says so, and immediately the conversation is on the great religious issues, as naturally as talking about the weather. "They will ask you whether you believe in God—you do, don't you?" "Then they ask whether you accept Jesus Christ as your Divine Lord and Saviour—couldn't you say that?" Here the reply may be, "I think Jesus was a great teacher, but I have never made up my mind about His being any more than that. What does it mean to say that He is a Lord and Saviour?" When the first questions about God and Christ have been faced, there is a basis for answering the later ones about one's attitude to the Church.

Mature callers may not need any special ways of bringing a conversation to spiritual things. A young man told a conference of his misgivings when he was assigned to make calls with a man of whom he was very much in awe—an educator of national renown. The younger man, new in the church, expected to have a very stiff and formal evening with the distinguished scholar. But he was deeply moved when his partner commenced the first call by saying, with simple earnestness, "I want to tell you what Jesus Christ means to me." All callers can hope to acquire that sort of easy directness. But until they do, they will need to be helped to learn ways of bringing Christ into their conversations.

j. Give a Reason for the Decision

Though it is important to ask questions and to get those they visit to talking, the callers must also have something to say. They must give reasons for the decisions they hope will be made. They try to determine, from the situation and from what is said, which reasons are most likely to be influential. For example, the need to follow Christ in serving humanity is likely to appeal to young people; a recently married couple can be told how their love of God will support their love for each other. Some of the reasons which callers use most often will be given in the next chapter. Other motives were mentioned in Chapter VI on "The Evangelistic Appeal."

Should Bible quotations be used? Most people who have not accepted Christ have not accepted the Bible, and they will not regard quotations from it as proof. Even so, an apt verse or an unquoted reference to something in the Bible can be impressive. When visitors find that they are talking to people for whom the Bible is God's Word, direct quotations from it can be very persuasive. Extended reciting of memorized verses or reading from a pocket Testament can seem showy and tiresome. It is usually better for the visitors to be able to give the Bible's thought in their own words. Visitors need to know the great Bible truths, but they do not have to be able to quote them verbatim, though an ability to do so is often very useful.

Old-time phrases are a barrier between Church people and others. Worn-out expressions may be a substitute for reality. Callers should use their own terms, not a churchly vocabulary. They can practice by telling themselves in fresh language what they mean. For example, it will probably be more natural to say "think differently" than "repent," "goodness" instead of "grace," "interesting" instead of "challenging." People who live with their religion every day can learn to refer to it with simple naturalness. A sanctimonious manner is fatal. Reverence does not demand a forced solemnity.

k. Relax and Enjoy the Call

Tension is a barrier. The grave importance of what they are doing makes some callers overintense. Embarrassment at an unfamiliar sort of contact with people may make the callers stiff and ill at ease. The more uncomfortable the visitors are the more uncomfortable it makes the people they are visiting. They should expect to have a good time in each home—and they will. An unfriendly reception is almost unheard of. Even those who cannot be won appreciate the visit. New callers, who would almost have prayed as they rang the first doorbell, "Please, don't let anybody be at home," usually come back amazed at the welcome they have received and overjoyed at the delightful contacts they have had. Visitors should enter into a call as though anticipating one of the happiest experiences of their lives. That attitude will help any shy or reserved people whom they visit to lose their inhibitions and enjoy the conversation.

l. Avoid These Five Mistakes

1. Do not risk a refusal too soon. If people are asked early in the call for a decision they are likely to say "No," since that was their attitude before the callers came. And once having refused, there is often a stubbornness which makes them hate to reverse themselves. The early refusal will thus remain as a barrier. The callers should first give the reasons, or wait until there is some indication that the answer will be favorable, before they ask people whether they will profess their faith and join the Church.

2. Do not argue. We do not get people to come with us by pulling against them, but by walking by their sides. The old rule still holds—"If you win your argument you may lose your man." A flat contradiction only drives people to think up more reasons for their opinion. For example, when someone says, "The churches are full of hypocrites," the loyal member is easily stung into a sharp defense of the people he loves. He may be tempted to give Dwight L. Moody's famous answer, "Come on in, there's always room for one more." But he will do better if he says, "I know the church is not as good as it ought to be. That is why we need people like you who see what a church should be and can help us make it that." Agree with people as far as it is honestly possible, and then start on with them from that common position. When agreement is impossible, recognize it, but do not get stuck on that point. Move to a line of thought on which you can make progress—"Even though you find some of the Bible hard to believe, isn't it true that in the teachings of Christ we have what the world most needs?"

3. Do not overtalk. Two eager callers, who are full of things they want to say, may easily drown those they visit in a sea of words. When one partner talks and then the other has his chance and then the first one starts again, those at whom they talk are the audience, not participants. People are not merely talked into a decision—they must partly talk themselves into it. That is why the visitors should say things which will lead to a constructive response. They give their reasons; when the conversation turns to useless topics they bring it back. But they give other people their full share of the chance to talk. When people have not much to say to the visitors, it is usually a sign that little can be accomplished, though occasionally those who are naturally uncommunicative will still be sympathetic and responsive.

4. *Do not waste time on nonessentials.* It is easy to get so involved in minor matters that all progress toward the main purpose of the call is blocked. People may introduce fine points of belief—predestination or angels or the unpardonable sin. To these the caller may wisely answer, "Christians spend a lifetime inside the Church learning about those things. But to join the Church all that is required is faith in Jesus Christ as Saviour. That is all we have to think about now."

It may be questions of conduct which threaten to lead to a useless detour—"I like to smoke and I have always thought that Church members are not supposed to do it." Here again the conversation should be led back to the essential issue—"People have to settle such questions in the light of their loyalty to Christ. The Church requires only your sincere willingness to do whatever you think He wants you to do."

5. *Do not change the subject.* Like the woman of Samaria, who tried to turn the conversation with Jesus from herself to the abstract question of where the temple ought to be, people today try to evade the real issue by introducing something irrelevant. It often seems like the last struggle of whatever sin has kept them from Christ or from the Church. The visitors, if they are not to seem brusque, often have to show a brief interest in the new subject; but they should leave it to get back as soon as possible to a conversation that can lead toward their goal.

Sometimes it is the visitors' carelessness which causes the diversion. A young couple were almost ready to make their decisions when one of them spoke of having missed church in order to redecorate the house. The visitor spoke admiringly of how beautifully it had been done, and immediately he was taken on a tour of the whole house, from the attic to the basement. Such long interruptions usually mean that much of the progress which has been made is lost—and there is less interest in a warmed-over conversation. Much patience is needed by those who are given teammates whose idea of helping is to keep getting the conversation off the track.

m. Get Decisions

Evangelistic visiting has a definite purpose—the securing of decisions for Christ and for Church membership. There is another sort of calling which is also important in church life—the sort which is intended merely to get acquainted with people and to create a friendly feeling for the church. These two sorts must not be confused. Unless a church makes a definite distinction between evangelistic visiting and good-will visiting, they will both be weakened.

It is usually a sign that they have failed when visitors report to their pastor, "These people are almost ready. If you go to see them, I know that they will decide." The securing of that decision is the function of the lay visitors. Experience shows that in most cases they have a better chance to gain the decision than does the pastor. They are assigned to finish the task, if possible, and they have not done their duty if they are content to leave its completion to anyone else.

Moreover, the benefits of the finest visit are likely soon to disappear unless they are fixed by some definite result. The good which has been accomplished will be lost if it leads only to a vague hope of seeing each other again. When people can remember that call as the time at which something definite took place, its results are preserved. (See Chapter I:3 and Chapter IV:B:1.)

If people wonder whether it is reasonable to expect a life-changing decision to take place during one brief visit, they should remember: (a) The decision is asked only of those who presumably already have some knowledge of what it is to be a Christian and a member of the Church. (b) God has prepared for the call and is working during it. (c) The minister will call on those who make decisions, to show them more completely all that is ahead.

The decision must have some sort of expression. It must be marked by an exercise of the will. There must be evidence that something important has happened. The promise to Christ must be definite. Just as friends shake hands on an agreement and lovers give rings, so there must be some act which will make it clearly understood and remembered that a religious decision has been made.

The expression which most evangelistic visiting uses is the subscription to a written statement of faith and purpose. That could be done in a way which would seem very commonplace. To climax a conversation about the Christian faith by thrusting out a card and saying, "How about signing this?" could be highly inappropriate. But it can be done in a way which is beautiful and symbolic. The word "sign" may well be avoided. "Record your decision" is a better expression.

People can be shown that a written decision is needed so that the church can have definite notice of those who wish to be received.

MY DECISION

I accept Jesus Christ as my Lord and Saviour and intend with His help to live a Christian life.

I desire to unite with the..Church by

............Profession of my faith
............Reaffirmation of the faith I professed in another church
............Transfer of my membership. For certificate of transfer

write to...............................at.................................

Signature..

Address...

Just as soon as it seems likely that the person is ready, not hurrying it but not delaying a moment longer than is necessary, the visitor takes out a decision card. He may read its statements and then ask, "Is that not what you would like to say?" Or he may hand the card to the other person, after marking the statements which apply, and ask, "Will you read that?" He has a pen or pencil ready. If there is hesitation, he can say, "If that is what you believe, won't you put your name to it?"

Sometimes there is still hesitation. In that case, the card should not be taken back immediately, but left in the person's hand. It serves as a focus for the thinking. It is a visual aid and a symbol of what the visit is trying to accomplish. Gentle persuading can continue, giving more reasons and answering difficulties, as long as this is welcome. When something is so serious, people are often slow in doing what they know they should do. Tactful urging may go on for some time.

But persuasion must never go beyond the point at which it begins to seem embarrassing. Trying to force a decision by insistence or overtalking will not succeed, and it will justly cause resentment. There is no place for high pressure in evangelism. When a refusal has been clearly given and further talking about it is making little progress, the call should soon be ended. The decision card may be left, with the request to think about it and pray about it, and an indication of what is to be done if the person later comes to a decision. Then, with a friendly invitation to the church or to some special church event, trying to leave as happy an impression for the church as possible, the visitors go. They later write on the assignment card their advice about future action.

It may develop that there is some other church the people ought to join. The visitors may receive the decision for that church with great rejoicing; they are working for the Kingdom, not for a local organization. Or they may pass on the information to the other church, which will then be able to win the people.

Sometimes it is clear early in a call that not much good is being done. People may obviously be uninterested, or they may give only monosyllabic answers to questions. It is unwise in these cases for visitors to keep beating their heads against a wall. It benefits no one, and they are needed where their time can be better used. They should leave soon, hoping that at least they helped the people to have a good feeling about the church and its members.

No rule about the length of a call can be given, save that it should never be unnecessarily prolonged. Thirty minutes is a good average length. Decisions may often be won in twenty minutes or less. Most calls should not last more than three-quarters of an hour; but occasionally it will require much longer than that to deal with problems about which people are eager to talk.

The visitors should be able to explain the various ways of joining the Church: (1) Profession of faith for those who have never belonged to a Church—with baptism for those who have not been baptized. (2) Reaffirmation of faith for those who have once belonged to a Church but are unable to get a letter of transfer. Visitors need to know from which religious bodies their denomination allows this sort of reception. (3) Letter of transfer for those in good standing in Churches which issue such letters. The visitors should offer to have their minister write for the letter, and should get the information he needs. This is more orderly and definite than expecting people who may be forgetful to have the matter taken care of in time. If they feel that this is too impersonal a way to break a connection which means much to them, it can be suggested that both they and the pastor write about the matter. If it is not certain that a letter can be secured, the understanding can be that, if a letter does not come, the reception will be on reaffirmation of faith. (4) Restoration for those who wish, upon promise of renewed loyalty, to be reinstated in a church which has dropped them from active membership.

n. Family Decisions

The New Testament often treats conversion as a family matter. It would have seemed strange for Peter to deal only with Cornelius, without paying attention to the rest of his household. To think only of winning people as separate individuals would be a departure from Christian tradition. It would not be realistic or sound. A home is a religious unit. And it is often easier to win a whole family than to win a single individual. Their feeling for each other makes them take the step together more readily than any of them would take it alone.

Visitors should try to have in the room during a call all of those in a family who might be brought into the Church. They seek to learn the church background of each one. As the talk progresses they see which person seems most ready to make a decision. They are sometimes surprised to find that husbands make up their minds more quickly than do their wives. When the time comes to ask for a decision, the visitors turn first to the one who seems most ready. When that is settled, they turn to the next most ready. Each decision makes the others more likely. If it is a minor child who is to be asked, the visitors first ask the parents' permission, which is usually gladly given. Then, being careful not to take unfair or embarrassing advantage of the child's presence, his or her decision can be referred to as a reason for the parents to decide. They can be shown that the child needs the support of their being together in the Church and the Christian life. The advantages of having the home unified religiously, and the great thing it would be to have all coming into the Church at the same time, can be pointed out.

o. Tell What Happens Next

After a decision has been made, the callers should explain what is to follow. They tell about the pastor's call and about the occasion on which new members are to be received. If there are preparatory classes or other requirements, these should be explained.

The callers can give those who have just made decisions for the Christian faith some brief advice about church attendance and participation. They may express the hope of an increasing friendship with them in the church. Older visitors can advise younger people about personal devotions and Bible reading and grace at the table.

It is unwise to continue a call very long after decisions have been made. That is so great an event that everything afterward seems like anticlimax.

When they are ready to go, the visitors need not grope for some way to wind up the call. They simply rise. After that, everything slopes to a conclusion. Let them beware of prolonged holding onto the doorknob.

p. Close the Call with Prayer, If Possible

Visitors are likely to find that to end some calls simply by shaking hands and saying "Good-by" would seem inappropriate and incomplete. When they have been talking about God and about the deepest issues in human life, when there has been the moving experience of a dedication of life to Christ, the Divine Presence seems very close. At such times, to pray seems more natural than not to.

Many new callers think that they could not pray in someone else's house. That inability does not disqualify them; they can still be very useful callers. But they should try to come to the time when they can make such a prayer.

The rule in all evangelism is this—never drag in something awkwardly pious because the occasion is supposed to call for it, but learn to think of God as so real and so present that it becomes natural to talk about Him and to talk to Him.

The prayer should be brief and simple. As they rise to go, one of the visitors may say, "We are certainly happy about what has happened here tonight; let's thank God for it," or "Let's ask God's blessing on this home." By prearrangement one visitor can say, "We are surely glad we came here tonight; John, won't you offer a little prayer before we go?"

Even when no decision has been made, it may still be important to have prayer. Many people have said that the prayer was the most helpful and moving part of the call. It is often surprising to find how grateful for it people are.

A SAMPLE CALL

A standardized call is impossible, fortunately. But there are so many new callers who ask, "Just what do you say?" that such an outline as this may be of help to them.

1. Introduce yourselves. Say that you are from the church and have come for a visit.

2. Refer to the connection between the people you are visiting and the church.

3. Take a very few minutes for compliments, friendly interest, topics of common concern.

4. Tell something about the church, showing your gratitude and enthusiasm for it.

5. Ask about church experience and attitudes.

6. Give some reason for the decision which you seek: the need for Christ and Christian practices, the good of the family or of the world, your own experience—whatever seems most suitable.

7. Tell about the questions which are put to those who join the Church. After each of these, ask whether it would raise any difficulties.

8. If the way seems open, ask whether this important decision should not be made now.

9. Present a decision card. Quote the statements which apply. Explain how a decision is to be recorded.

10. If there is hesitation, tell why this is the time to make the decision.

11. When the decision is made, express your pleasure and tell of the happiness it will bring.

12. If it seems tactful, give brief advice about family worship, prayer, church attendance.

13. Explain what happens next—the pastor's call, the process of joining.

14. If possible, offer a prayer, thanking God and asking for His blessing.

15. Leave, after expressing your hope of an increasing friendship, and of meeting at the church the coming Sunday.

4. After the Visiting

The full report on each call should be put in writing at once. Memory is so fickle that a day's delay might bring all sorts of embarrassing confusion. Information which belongs in any of the prospect files should be recorded, with recommendations for future action. Decisions must be reported to the pastor so that he will make his counseling calls and take whatever action is needed to prepare for the reception.

The most important part of evangelism comes after people join the church. The next steps for them are described in the chapter on "The Care of New Members."

5. Continual Evangelistic Visiting

A church needs to provide for Lay Evangelistic Visiting in two ways: first, through brief, intensive efforts; second, through visitors who are always ready to serve.

The intensive periods have indispensable advantages: (a) They offer the best occasion for enrolling new visitors. (b) They afford the best opportunity for training the visitors. (c) They bring new members in larger groups, which makes a good assimilation program easier. (d) More prayer and concern can be rallied behind the work for a limited period. (e) They dramatize to the whole church the work of evangelism.

But those who should be seen ought not to have to wait until the next seasonal calling program. The old idea that evangelism should be restricted to a few weeks before Easter, or to midsummer revivals, is one from which the modern Church, fortunately, is getting away. Evangelism is a constant concern. There should be provision for evangelistic calls between the special periods. There are several ways of making this provision.

a. The Zone System

When a church divides its parish into zones, as described in Chapter XVIII on "Organizing for Evangelism," the leaders of each zone arrange for evangelistic calls throughout the year. When they are told of evangelistic prospects within their areas, they go to see them or arrange for someone else to do so. The leaders are alert to discover for themselves the prospects in their zones, and to see that calls are made on them.

b. Evangelistic Visitors' Clubs

Many churches have special groups which are devoted to evangelistic calling. They are likely to take Biblical names—"The Seventy" (Numbers 11:16; Luke 10:1), "The St. Andrew's Fellowship" (John 1:40-42), "The Fisherman's Club (Matthew 4:19).

Some of these clubs meet on Sundays after the services. Others have monthly evening meetings for assignments, reports, instruction, discussion of their problems and prayer for each other and for those they hope to win.

A church may have more than one such club—perhaps a group of businessmen who meet downtown at lunch for assignments and inspiration, and a Deaconess Guild. One of the official boards may consider itself to be also a calling organization, devoting a part of each meeting to reports and assignments. Youth groups, couples' clubs or a women's "pastors' aid committee" may make evangelistic calling a permanent project.

The members of calling clubs are sometimes pledged not only to evangelistic visiting, but also to such personal disciplines as daily prayer and Bible reading. They often have some token of membership—a pin or a pocket cross or a membership card, with a statement of purpose and reminders of spiritual habits.

c. Direct Assignments

There may be those who have agreed to make calls whenever they are needed. Assignments are given or mailed to them, with a calling partner designated. The partners arrange to get together and make the call within the specified time.

A Pennsylvania church has an evangelistic honor roll—a dignified plaque on which is recorded the names of all who have brought another into Church membership. A star is added for each additional person who is brought. A Chicago church presents a small pin or lapel emblem to every member who has won another. This pin also designates the wearer as one who is pledged to make the winning of others a chief concern.

d. Spontaneous Evangelistic Conversations

The formalizing of evangelism is always a disaster. It happens when religion has gone dead. It associates evangelism with a special sort of people—the clergy; and with a special place—the church; and with a special vocabulary—the stale verbiage of a former generation. Whenever religion is alive, evangelism becomes an informal, normal, happy part of daily life.

Those who have gotten started in personal evangelism through being given training and assignments in visitation programs often make the winning of others a continual private enterprise. They take seriously the saying, "The supreme business of every Christian is the bringing of others to Christ." A basic rule for all evangelism is this: WHATEVER IS TO BE DONE ALL THE TIME HAS TO BE LEARNED AT SPECIAL TIMES. All of the skills learned in evangelistic visiting are important in this privately undertaken evangelism.

The most striking stories of "personal evangelism" often are of contacts between strangers—in trains or restaurants. People who know they will not see each other again have the fewest restraints. This should not mislead us into making this the typical example. Valuable though it is, it is the least important sort of evangelistic conversation. There is no way to carry it on to a lasting result. We can hope that God will see that what is started will be finished, but His normal way is to have us keep people in our prayers and care until we see them brought into the Christian fellowship. Fersonal evangelism needs to be anchored in a local church. Like the familiar picture of the man on the rock reaching out to save those who are tossed in the sea, the personal worker needs to have one hand holding fast to the Church as he stretches out the other hand to those who are spiritually adrift.

Every Christian needs his personal prospect list, for the intention must be specific. But we must also be alert for the sudden opportunity, the chance conversation which may start the great thing to happening. Every occupation has its special possibilities. One can think of those offered to homemakers, lawyers, teachers, nurses, doctors, members of labor unions, welfare workers, students. Every social club or neighborhood contact offers possibilities.

After the death of a Chicago physician it was said that among the possessions he left there was none so precious to his friends as the little black notebook which contained the list of names of people he was praying for and seeking to win to Christ. It was a varied list, members of his own family circle, doctors, nurses, patients, druggists, businessmen, students, clerks, taxicab drivers, boys and girls of the neighborhood. They were all there—a grand company, all of whom he believed had been committed unto him and for whom he had a definite responsibility before God. Great was his joy when he was able to note beside the name that that one had given his or her heart to Christ.

There is no finer career a Christian could have. A layman in Des Moines, since his retirement from business, has been bringing two-hundred people a year into his church. He averages four hours a day at this work, calling and following his calls with letters. His pastor gives him fifty names at a time. He has people who help him by praying for his work. A St. Louis layman, in a section of the city that is considered difficult for church work, has been winning seventy-five people a year by devoting every Monday evening to it.

A church can produce that sort of members by giving them a great desire to see others won, and giving them a start through a lay evangelistic calling program. It can urge upon its members the necessity of praying for those whom they would like to see brought to Christ. "If you speak to God about your friends you will soon find that you are speaking to your friends about God."

A women's society in Arkansas asks all its members to repeat daily the prayer,

Lord, lay some soul upon my heart,
And love that soul through me;
And let me nobly do my part
To win that soul for Thee.

Young people can be reminded that the time they spend having dates does not have to be tossed carelessly away. Those who are most attractive have a change of pace which includes both high gaiety and deep seriousness. Youth friendships may be brief or they may be lasting, but with Christians they can all mean the permanent enrichment of a life.

Friendship is still the basic evangelistic method. It can almost be said that no person was ever brought to Christ save through another person.

Those who wish to talk to their friends about religion have to learn how to bring it into their conversations. One of the best ways is to talk about the church. That can be done as easily and normally as we talk about a club or a hobby. Enthusiasm for what is going on at a church is a sort of confession of faith in what the church stands for. To ask another person where he goes to church, or to invite him to a church, can lead straight to a conversation on worship and belief. A Christian should have more to talk about than an institution. But a reference to church affairs is a useful introduction to deeper matters.

Everyone is talking about race relationships, war, the atom bomb, industrial strife and all the social predicaments. It is not hard to turn the talk from such questions to how Christians look at them, and so to the reasons for belief, and so to Christ.

One can comment on a religious book that has been read or a sermon that has been heard—just as a matter of general interest. A book or a leaflet can be given to a friend, with the request for an opinion of it. Indiscriminate tract distribution among our friends might not be the thing, but a good piece of literature can be the basis for a rewarding discussion.

The best argument for Christianity is a Christian. While it is not true that "a good life is all the witness that is needed" (gospel truth is never conveyed by radiation) it is true that if people like us they will take seriously what we say. Many a testimony has been canceled by an ungenerous personality. Housman's definition, "a saint is someone who makes goodness attractive," suggests the first necessity for our spontaneous evangelism.

IX

What to Say

Evangelistic workers, like doctors, find the same cases constantly recurring. By thinking in advance of what to say, they can be prepared for most of the situations they will meet.

Memorized conversation items could scarcely be edifying. But there is great value in studying what other people have said. What is given here has been used by many. It is a part of the accumulating wisdom of the Church. It is intended: (a) to help all who talk to other people about the Christian faith and Church membership; (b) to provide material for instructors who train evangelistic visitors; (c) to give suggestions for evangelistic preaching and writing. (Chapters III and VI also deal with what to say.)

1. Reasons for a Decision

a. Now Is the Time.

The most common response to an invitation to make a profession of faith and come into the Church is "I know that is the thing to do, but not right now." Sometimes, of course, this is simply a good-natured attempt to avoid giving a flat refusal. But often it is sincerely meant. It means that procrastination, that deadly enemy of the good, is winning again. Whether or not the student was right when he wrote on his examination, "The best-known doctrine of the Presbyterian Church is procrastination," it is certainly the favorite doctrine of the unchurched.

Sin is subtle; it persuades people, who would never say "No" to Christ, to say "Not yet" to Him—and to say it forever. All the evils which keep people away from discipleship put up a running fight behind the defense "Not now—later." Visitors tell them what their consciences have already been saying and get the same answer, "Not yet."

The excuses which people have been giving themselves, and now give the visitors, are often plausible—"We thought maybe next Easter would be a good time." "With something so serious, we do not want to rush into it." "My husband and I want to talk it over a little more; we will let you know." "My father belonged to another denomination, and I want to explain it to him before I take this step."

In much of this the Church is meeting in stark, hand-to-hand combat the very evil that keeps people from it. It must not be taken lightly or dismissed with the cheerful thought that these things take time but it will not be long. That hopeful aspect is often deceptive. Every postponement may make a decision less likely.

The weapons of this warfare are not carnal. Every suggestion of hammering at people or slick sales procedures must be avoided. But gentle persuasion can go on after the first refusal if there is no sign of embarrassment or resentment. It takes time for the sin of delay to finish its last desperate struggles. That is why visitors let people hold the decision cards for a while, though they at first decline to use them. That is why preachers sometimes prolong an invitation or repeat an invitation hymn—the struggle to decide takes time.

There must be things to say after the first invitation. "Will you ever be better able to decide than you are right now?" "What are you waiting for that you do not already know?" "Haven't you post-poned this before? Isn't this the time finally to face it?" "Not to decide is to decide not to." "I have known people to hesitate, but I never yet knew anyone to regret having said 'Yes.'" "You will be a great deal happier once you get this settled. Won't you have a good feeling after you have done this?"

People can be shown that they will be vexed by the problem until it is settled. No question is escaped until it is settled right. The habit of indecision grows harder to break with each repetition.

Visitors can express their faith that it is God Himself Who sent them for this very time. He is the One Who is offering this opportu-nity. The thought, "Do you believe God wants you to wait? Will

He be pleased if you make your decision?" can be introduced. (This all has a place also in appeals from the pulpit.)

Sometimes people are like the vicar on his first visit to Paris, who bitterly regretted that he had not had the sense to go there before he was converted. They are convinced that the Christian life is a duty, but they are not yet convinced that it is preferable. They look on it as a regrettable necessity which they would like to postpone as long as possible. They must be made to feel that it is a joyful existence which makes every day out of it seem sad by comparison.

Those who say that it will eventually be the thing to do can be asked, "If it is right for you to give your life to Christ, isn't every minute that you wait wasting that much of your life?" "If Church membership is a good thing, are you not losing something valuable by delay?" Make it plain that to say "Now is the time" to something good is God's victory.

b. Logic

Logic by itself cannot bring belief, but it can be used to show what should follow from beliefs which have already been accepted. Indecision often comes from hazy thinking. The issue may never have been clearly faced. Thinking may not have been complete or orderly enough to lead to practical conclusions. People can be helped to recognize what, to be consistent, they ought to do.

The line of reasoning can start with God. If there be a God, then He is the central fact of all existence. Without a right relationship to Him everything goes wrong. To "get right with God" is logically the first necessity, if there be a God at all. This can be shown to those who have a theoretical belief in God, but have not been doing much about it. Many lines of thought branch out from here—our response to the love of God, God's seeking for every person, God's plan for every life, the maladjustment of life apart from God, etc.

The fact of Jesus Christ can start a chain of logic which leads straight to the need to acknowledge faith in Him and to enter the fellowship of His believers. "What shall I do then with Jesus which is called Christ?" is a question which many who claim to believe in Him have evaded. They can be made to face it and to give some definite answer. A lay visitors's club might accurately call itself, "The Hounds of Heaven."

It can be shown that a person who believes in the Church cannot consistently remain aloof from it. "If God established the Church for humankind, then is it not for you?" "If the Church is good for other people, are you different?" "If children need the Church's influence, are we not, in God's sight, children all our lives?" "If your community or your country needs the Church, then is it not your duty to support it?"

People who accept the Bible can be shown from the Bible that they should openly confess Christ (Matthew 10:33, Mark 8:38, Romans 10:9), that they need religious fellowship (Matthew 18:20, Acts 2:42, Hebrews 10:25), that the Church is God's will for men (Matthew 16:18, Acts 2:47, Ephesians 5:25).

There are other first steps which many people have taken without ever seeing where they must logically lead. It is the business of evangelism to guide thought to the right conclusion. This guiding has to be done with the sort of gentle respect for the other person's mind that can win agreement.

c. Regard for Jesus Christ

The appeal of the person of Christ is Christianity's finest argument. Many outside the Church have a profound reverence for Him. They will be inclined to do something if they can be shown that "Christ wants you to do this." "If you love Him you will do it." "He will mean more to you after you have done it."

d. A Christian Home

Most parents will do what they plainly see is for the good of their children. They must be shown why the children need to feel that their home is definitely Christian—with the parents openly recognized as followers of Christ, with religion regarded as necessary. They can be shown what it does for a family to go together to a place of worship, and what it does for a home to be connected with a church home. Those who send their children to a church for moral and religious training can be told that the church has a poor chance of succeeding unless the parents are its partners. The power of example can be stressed. The parents' practice is more important than their preaching. The very age at which boys and girls most need the church is the age at which they are likely to drop out unless their parents are with them in it. At this age it is not enough to tell them what to do; they have to be shown. There is truth in the old saying that "A boy loves his mother but he imitates his father."

Religious companionship is a powerful tie between married couples. Their love for each other is supported and hallowed when they connect it with their love of God. They need regular and definite reminders that God is a partner in their marriage. When they are out of sorts with each other, the very act of going to church together can bring them back together as nothing else can. "Families that pray together stay together."

In a denominationally divided family, the aim should be to bring all into one church, if possible. Such differences can mar the harmony of a home. Or the desire to avoid disharmony often leads to minimizing the Church and drifting away from it. Though parents may keep alive two denominational loyalties, they have only a half chance of getting the children interested in either Church. They lose the beautiful family tie which a shared church interest gives. They miss the values of a family pew and a church home. Children vitally need the feeling that the church is a family interest. Religion is always a family matter. The Bible, from the patriarchs through the Epistles, describes godly homes as being united in their religious observances. A young couple, seeking to share all the finest things in life, should be able to share something as important as religion.

All this can be pointed out in a divided home. It should be made plain that the church is not just trying to win a member, but would be willing to lose one if that would help the family have a strong, united church interest.

Sometimes a couple's denominational convictions are so strong that neither is able to go with the other. Occasionally, in such cases, they can get together in a third denomination which is free from what they object to in each others' Churches. More often the best that can be done is to persuade both to become active and loyal members in their own Churches. Church enthusiasm, though turned in different directions, can still be a tie between a married couple, and an example for the children.

e. Christian Fellowship

Those who are enthusiastic enough about anything—stamp collecting, Shakespeare, birds—form clubs. Those who share the greatest enthusiasm that life can know—the love of Jesus Christ—cannot stay separated. We will never get what we should from our religion apart from others who are our natural comrades in faith. They increase our enjoyment of it and decrease our difficulties. We need the spiritual warmth which kindles from heart to heart. Almost everyone, even those who do not know it, crave close, loyal friends. Christians can promise, because of their own experience, that the best friends are those who are found in church.

f. Spiritual Help

All of us miss much of life. Our spirits become smothered. Tired bodies dull our sensitiveness. The routine of earning a living and housekeeping and all the material necessities which constantly press on us tend to make us less human and more mechanical. We need everything which can keep our souls alive and make our spirits strong. We need regular reminders of God and goodness and love and beauty. We need to be called from the passing to the eternal. All this is what the Church has for us. It keeps steadily before us the things we might otherwise forget. It makes us notice what is invisible. The rites which express a faith in Jesus Christ keep Him in the front of our minds. Regular prayer and Bible study and comradeship in religious interests keep our hearts stirred and save us from emotional stagnation. This is the way to a healthy mind and to an inner strength which can take whatever life may bring and go on happy and triumphant.

g. What the Church Offers

The rule that the call should be "Christ-centered and not church-centered" does not mean that definite church attractions cannot be offered as inducements, if they are offered as a satisfaction for religious needs. The beauty of the Sabbath services and the good the minister does and the benefits of devotional meetings can be described in glowing terms. The excellence of the church school and what is offered for young people and the adult organizations can be described in a way that will make people feel the desire to have such advantages. Visitors should be able to describe the organizations and activities of the church and their times of meeting.

h. Duty

We are all debtors to Christ for what He has done for us, and it is our duty to do all we can for Him.

We are debtors because of our Christian homes and what our parents taught us, and it is our duty to pass this on undiminished to the next generation.

It is our duty to our country and to our fellow men to support every influence for good.

Gratitude brings some people to God. Gratitude—for wife or husband or children, for the good things of life—makes them feel they must express their thanks, and so they come to church.

i. Service

Men crave a satisfying use for their lives. They need to start each day looking forward to something worth doing. They need to feel that when they die they will have accomplished something. This craving can be satisfied by giving one's life to Christ and to His service. He is a glorious leader and the sense of fighting for His cause in the world makes life a thrilling and immensely satisfying adventure. This motive for definitely pledging one's life to Christ and entering His discipleship has a strong attraction for youth. It has an appeal to which discontented and frustrated older people will respond.

People with sensitive hearts are appalled by all the misery in the world; those with consciences are indignant at the evil and injustice. They can be powerfully drawn to the Church if they are shown that it is struggling to establish peace, uphold democracy, help the poor, relieve the suffering, correct social wrongs, purify government, spread the gospel. They must see that whether the Church does this poorly or well depends on how many members it has who are dedicated to its tasks. Those who long for a better world can be shown that the Church is the one best hope of man, and that there is nowhere we can put our support where it will accomplish more for human welfare. They must not be led to expect always the sort of sudden satisfactions which superficial remedies provide. Grubbing out the roots of evil is often less glamorous than attacking the fruit. Teaching a Sunday-school class may not be as exciting an expression of patriotism as marching in a parade, but the Church knows that it is even more important. The person who joins the Church and helps keep it strong and true to its mission is doing a great thing for mankind today, and for future generations.

A reference to world conditions may help people see why they should support the Church. In every land the Church is in the forefront of the struggle of democracy to survive against ruthless tyranny. With the threat of its most awful war looming over the world, the Church is trying to implant in men's minds the ways of peace. The problems in America can only be survived if Americans learn to live by the principles which Jesus taught, and which the Sunday schools and pulpits in every community are trying to instill. To join the Church is to join in the fight to make decent living possible on earth. "The world needs the Church and the Church needs you" is an appeal which can be made very forceful.

j. Influence

All of us are in contact with people who will be influenced by what we do. There are some whose example powerfully affects many lives. If we openly profess our faith, other people will be influenced to find the good that Christ can have for them; if we keep our faith a secret, our example will lead others to ignore religion. Most of us are not likely to mount a soapbox to shout our faith to our business or social acquaintances. But when we join the Church, we are letting them know where we stand.

We are surrounded by bewildered people who are groping for a faith, and many of them are turning to false gods. They desperately need to know what we have found. If Christ and the Church have done anything at all for us, our honesty and our concern for others compel us to let it be known. When it is said of anyone, "He is a Church member," his vote has been counted—he has witnessed to his belief in Christ.

k. Personal Interest

It can powerfully help a person in making a decision to know that there are others who are greatly interested in it. "All of your friends at the church are hoping so much that you will do this." "It would mean a great deal to me to have you with us in the church." "It is because we think so much of you that we are so anxious to have you give your life to Christ." The desire to please friends should not be the motive. But when a person is spiritually ready, the influence of friendship may properly be used.

l. Salvation

The language of the pulpit is not always suited to the parlor. In face-to-face contacts we have to use terms that are normal for a conversation. Those who have confessed obvious evil may think of themselves as sinners needing salvation, but most people do not. They may have known sin under so many aliases that its original name has been forgotten. To talk to them about their sins will only convince them that the Church is obsessed with offensive make-believe. But it means something to them to be told that faith in Christ and religious living will take away fear and give peace of mind and make them able to get along with people and introduce them to a finer and more satisfying way of life.

Repentance can be thought of as getting a fresh start; reconciliation is coming to a right relationship with God; sanctification is living at our best. We never understand such terms ourselves until we can translate them into everyday speech. The translation is what we need to use in much of our evangelism. There is danger in this of being superficial. But it is better to give a part of the truth and be understood than to state the doctrine properly and mean nothing.

It may spare offense if we talk to people about sin in the first or third person, not in the second. "I have found out . . ." "People need . . ." rather than, "You are . . ." or "You need . . ."

We can talk to people about getting rid of bad habits, about changing one's way of living, about losing the sense of inadequacy, about release from the past and its nagging regrets. We can talk about the happiness and the freedom and the victory of the Christian life.

2. Getting Membership Transferred

Ninety per cent of those who hesitate to transfer their church membership will give one of the following reasons:

a. *"I do not know how long I will be here."* One may reply that this uncertainty is the reason for finding a church home. Provision must be made for the possibility of staying. If it turns out the other way, the certificate of membership can at once be forwarded to the new community. Explain that church membership can be moved more readily than one's clothes or bank account, and should be just as much a part of daily living. Adults should transfer to a local church just as their children transfer to a local school.

Ask, "How long have you lived here?" The laughing admission that it has already been a long while may bring the recognition of the foolishness of waiting longer. Ask also, "If you move, will you be going back to where your church membership now is?" If not, it is clear that it is at least better to have the membership where it may be temporary than where it can never again have any significance at all. Ask, "What do you count as your home and business address? It should also be your religious address."

People often mistakenly associate with a transfer of membership the same gravity and awe they felt when they first joined the Church. It should be explained that the great thing was done once for all, when they came into the Church of Jesus Christ. Transfers of membership within that Church are merely a matter of record keeping. It is not transferring membership soon which is casual and irreverent, but the failure to do so. The Church of Christ is injured when its members remain for a while inactive or let the record of their church participation conflict with the fact.

In these nomadic days the church is a ready-made home whereever one may move. To go within its door is to find the same well-loved and congenial friends that have been known in the old home town. The Christian simply walks in, says, "I am one of your members you haven't met; it is a nice church we have here," sends for his letter and settles down as one of the family.

The visitors should know, and sometimes say, that delay in getting transferred is dangerous. Habits of church neglect are soon formed. After the transition period, with practices and friendships in the new community becoming settled, the place for the church keeps getting smaller.

b. "I love the old church too much to leave it." Sometimes this takes the form, "I would hate to leave my parents' church." Those who say this need to understand that a church membership on paper means nothing. If they cannot get to the old church they cannot really be members there, regardless of what the roll book says. Church membership is not an heirloom that can be left to gather dust. It is a part of life or it is nothing.

Love for the old church is not demonstrated by having no part in any church. That is the sign of its failure. We show our affection for it by our eagerness never to lose the sort of church participation which we had with it. We remain a part of its fellowship when we are in active Christian fellowship somewhere; we break away from it if we let ourselves go outside the active fellowship of Church members. It is no favor to a church to clutter up its records with out-of-date names; it may cost it the per capita assessment which many denominations ask of their local churches.

Many people say that they do not move their membership because the old church needs their annual contribution. If that really is a worthy claim on their benevolent giving, there is no reason why they cannot continue to send it after their membership has been transferred. It is the gift, not the meaningless name, the old church needs. The share of the expenses for light and heat and pastoral services belong to the church whose benefits are being used, regardless of where the names are enrolled.

People can be reminded that the sentimental reason for not transferring membership cannot be normal or right because it would mean the ruin of the old home church and almost every other, dependent as they are on transfers for the larger part of their strength.

Most parents would actually be delighted to have their children who have moved become active again in a church. In any case, one's first responsibility is to his present home and to his own children and to his own Christian life.

We honor our Christian parents and our old church and our Lord when we keep our Church connection normal and alive. Our loyalty and love belong, not to a former local congregation, but to the great Church of Jesus Christ.

c. *"I have not decided yet which church to join."* In response to this, one may ask how long the deciding has already taken. The question of what is being waited for to get the matter settled can be raised. There can be some discussion of which church would be most suitable. A visitor may offer to forward the decision to any other church, and explain that his interest is not in promoting his own congregation but in helping the person to find a church home. The danger of becoming a chronic church window shopper and sermon taster can be pointed out. If active church membership is a good thing, then every day it is postponed is a loss. People in prolonged transition are in the grotesque position of being Church members without being members of a church.

d. *"I am enjoying the freedom from responsibilities."* That is not a reason people often give, but it may actually be the most common reason of all. There is something very beguiling about having no duties, no pledge cards, no restraints on flitting from service to service, sampling the anthems and the preaching and playing shy with those who try to be friendly. It seems to offer all of the advantages and none of the disadvantages of church membership. But it is delusive. Many of the most important benefits of the Church are missed entirely. And the final fate of all lotus-eaters will not be escaped.

This reason must be answered on suspicion, as it rarely is expressed. It is often well to volunteer a reminder that the church is not merely a place for public performances but a home, where people who know each other meet to learn and pray and work together. One definite church is needed to be the religious center of one's life. It is the anchor for a family. The familiar pew, the pastor-friend, the well-loved scene of many glorious experiences have a spiritual value which is indispensable.

Those who call themselves Christians and believe in the Church have an obligation to support it, regardless of where their membership is listed. This duty is not escaped by a failure to transfer. After they transfer it will still be their consciences, and no organizational requirement, which tells them how much time and money they should give.

Church duties are duties. If we believe in the Church and get good from it, we cannot honestly take a course which would, if generally followed, break up all churches. And church duties are blessings. We benefit most from what we do for a church. When we get without giving we go stagnant. It is only in Christ's service that we know Him as we should.

3. The Roman Catholic—Protestant Marriage

In dealing with a couple one of whom is a Protestant and the other a Roman Catholic, it is well to find out whether they were married by a priest. If they were, and if the Roman Catholic is devoted to that Church, then it can be pointed out that for them both to have a strong church interest will be a bond between them, even though their attachment is to different communions.

But if a priest did not marry them, then the nominal Roman Catholic is actually outside of his or her Church and cut off from its sacraments. That is a distressing state. Those who are caught in it need, and perhaps are hungry for, a Church. They have a powerful claim on our Christian concern.

One need not hesitate to discuss religion with such people for fear of proselyting, for they are not members of any Church at all. A Protestant Church is their only hope. Those who wonder whether an invitation to them can do any good should know that many congregations are successful with a large proportion of those they approach. And it may be a surprise to discover how welcome a tactful raising of the question often is.

It may seem queer that many such couples have never talked much about the matter. An evangelistic visit frequently brings out more of the thinking of the husband and wife on the subject of their religious difference than they have learned in years from each other. That is one of the advantages of having tactful and sympathetic callers raise the question. There will be cases in which an immediate sign of distaste for the subject will make it clear that there is no use in pressing it. But such cases are by no means the rule.

Early in the conversation it is well to point out what the two Churches have in common. They worship the same Christ, repeat the same Lord's Prayer and Apostles' Creed and use almost the same Bible. Both hold confession to be essential—though the Protestant makes his confession directly to God, while the Roman Catholic confesses through the priest. Many Protestant Churches do not require Roman Catholics to be rebaptized, and their Church accepts Protestant baptism. The beliefs which we require of those who join the Church are largely those which Catholics also hold. (It may be helpful to summarize these, in brief, untechnical terms.) Many Catholics, whose knowledge of the Protestant Church is based on prejudice and hearsay, will be astonished to learn how much there is in common.

The great importance for a married couple and for their children to have a home that is unified religiously should be emphasized. How much a person misses by not having a Church and an active connection with the Christian fellowship can be mentioned. The former Roman Catholic can be advised to avoid the pressures which may be brought to bear if the matter is discussed with relatives, and reminded that the first obligation after one is married is to the present home, not to the former one.

Disparagement of the Roman Catholic Church should be avoided. Differences need not be discussed unless they are an obstacle. If necessary, it can be explained that Protestants revere Mary as the holiest and most honored of women, though they do not pray to her. We interpret the "rock" on which Christ promised to build His Church to be not Peter but his confession of the deity of Jesus (Matthew 16:18). The sort of reasons that are listed in the first section of this chapter can be very telling. The emphasis can be on how much the Protestant Church has to give. In a good many churches the most grateful and enthusiastic members are those who have come from just this situation.

4. Answering Excuses

The best response to an excuse someone gives for not joining the Church is often to restate the excuse very deliberately, as though understanding it and sympathizing with it—and then go on to something else. Or frequently the answer can be very brief. The excuse is often given just because something has to be said, while the real reason is something else. Or when an objection is sincere it may seem important only because there is no real interest in the

Church. If a strong motive for church membership can be given, the objection will be forgotten. Therefore little time should be spent on the objections and much attention given to the motives. Prolonged argument is almost always futile.

It may help to encourage people to give some petty objection in full. Getting it off their chests may help them get it off their minds. And as they tell about it they may begin to see how trifling it looks.

Sometimes, however, the excuse will be a serious barrier. Then it must be dealt with. Because the ones given here are heard repeatedly, it is well to think about them in advance. One must not be so ready with the answer that it will sound glib and therefore contemptuous. But the Christian worker must never waver in the conviction that there can never be an adequate reason for a person to reject Christ or His Church.

a. *"I am waiting until my husband (wife) is ready."* "Experience proves this to be poor strategy. You are much more likely to bring him (her) to the church after you are a member than when you also are unattached. Once you are firmly anchored in a church you have more pulling power than when you are adrift. With both of you out of the church, the question of membership remains purely theoretical. As you meet other couples in the church and church people become family friends, their influence will be added to yours. Besides all this, you have your own obligation to yourself and to God to consider. The fact that one parent is not in the Church makes it even more important to the children for the other parent to establish the Church connection."

b. *"I can be a Christian without joining a church."* "That may be possible, but could you not be a better Christian in the Church? No one is so good that he does not need all the help he can get to be better. With all that the world does to turn us from our loyalty to Christ and our consciousness of His presence, we need something outside ourselves to keep us reminded of Him. We need the Church's teaching and its regular calls to worship and the inspiration of others who share our problems and our faith. Did not your ideas of what it is to be good and to be a Christian come originally from the Church? Then will you not be able to be more true to them if you are living closer to the source? One may be a Christian outside the Church, but the Bible makes it plain that he cannot be a fully obedient or normal Christian. Jesus commanded His followers to profess their faith openly and to come into the fellowship of believers. He put the Church on earth to give blessings which all of us need, and which we cannot get in any other way."

c. *"Some of us outside are a good deal better than some of the Church members."* "Even one of the twelve Jesus chose to be nearest Him betrayed Him. There will always be disloyal members in the Church, just as there have always been traitors in every army. You are so shocked by hypocrites in the Church because you know there is reason to expect a Church member to be good. The Church is the only organization in the world whose first requirement for membership is that the candidate be admittedly unworthy to join. Imperfect people should be in the Church, and they are. It tries to bring in the worst people in the community, and some of them come—promising to try with God's help to be better, but only gradually succeeding. Remember that they criticized Christ by saying, 'This man receiveth sinners and eateth with them' (Luke 15:2).

"The Church is not a museum where saints are exhibited, it is a school where sinners are trying to learn goodness. Is not that where you belong? You are right in feeling that if the Church has what it claims to have there should be some evidence of it in the lives of its members. I believe that there is. Imperfect as we are, most of us in the Church are infinitely better than we would ever have been without it.

"It is because you see what a Church member ought to be that the Church needs you. Whenever you see a church or its members behaving unworthily, that is not a reason for Christians to go away from it but to run to it to help make it what Christ intended it to be. He has given it to His followers as a trust, to be defended and purified.

"We do not join the Church because we want to be like the other members, human and fallible as they are, but because we want to be like Christ. He is the Head of the Church; He has promised His help through it."

d. *"I have too many doubts,"* or *"I do not know enough."* "The Church does not ask people to wait outside until they have made up their minds on every question of belief. They spend the rest of their lives growing in faith and knowledge after they are in the Church. Only a few basic questions are asked of those who join, for example—(a very brief and not technically worded summary). If you are uncertain about these, perhaps we can talk about them; or our minister would welcome a chance to come and discuss them with you. Your doubts can be healthy—they show that you are thinking. The Church does not want blind faith. It respects your mind. It wants its members to examine its doctrines and to think about them until they are convinced. The Holy Spirit will guide you; you will get light from the Bible and from prayer. The Church will be your great helper as, within it, you struggle for a surer faith.

"You do not have to understand all about science before you start to use it. You do not have to have all your questions about Christianity settled before you can practice it. Knowledge often follows practice. There is much about the Christian faith we can never understand or appreciate until we have begun trying to be followers of Jesus Christ."

Sometimes this excuse is a valid barrier to membership. The spiritually indifferent, those who say with frivolous smugness, "I am just not very religious," those who are skeptical about essential Christian beliefs do not belong in the fellowship of faith. A church must beware lest its love of people and its evangelistic eagerness tempt it to lower its standards until membership has no meaning. To say to those who are not spiritually ready, "Well come on, you probably have as much faith as most of us did when we joined," may sound generous, but it is the worst sort of unkindness. It may block people from ever knowing what the Christian faith and the Church really are. And it is a sad damage to the Church to turn it over to members who will secularize and cripple and discredit it.

The Church must reassure and welcome with open arms those who are so abashed by the sublimity they have glimpsed that they humbly feel unworthy—those whose prayer is, "Lord, I believe; help thou mine unbelief." But it cannot welcome those who are unconcerned or unconvinced about Christ or who have no real intention of following Him. When these are met, the first thing to do is to tell them as much about Christian belief and the reasons for faith as the occasion permits. One conversation, like one sermon, has been known to bring a genuine conversion. It is more likely to be only a part of the process which leads toward faith. When people remain vague or unresponsive a brief call is better than trying to plant the seed and push it up into a harvest in one evening. The church should try to keep every possible contact, with the hope that through friendship, through its organizations, through Sabbath services and through classes God will finally make the person ready to come into His Church.

e. "*I am not good enough to call myself a Christian; I do not live as a Church member should.*" "If you thought you were good enough, the Church would not take you. Its first requirement for membership is the acknowledgment of sin. The one who sincerely says, 'I am not good enough,' is not far from the Kingdom. Jesus said, 'I am not come to call the righteous, but sinners to repentance' (Matthew 9:13).

"If you really want to live as a Christian should and fear you will not be able to, you can trust Christ for help. You will be amazed at the power He gives to change habits and resist temptation. If you broke your resolutions in the past, it may have been because you were counting on your own power. Now with Christ helping you, strengthened by prayer and by the influence of the Church, it can be different. Through faith we can do things we never would have dreamed were possible. Can you trust Christ to keep you from slipping today and tomorrow? Make your promises for one day at a time, and leave the future to Him.

"But if you are not sure you want to give up the things which you think would be wrong for a Christian then, of course, you are not ready to join the Church. We cannot purposely give Christ half of our lives. It is a good thing that you are too honest to want to compromise. Remember that He never asks us to give up anything that is worth having. He takes away false pleasures in order to give us true happiness. The ethics He requires may cost us money, but 'what shall a man give in exchange for his soul?' The day when a person says, 'I want to give up everything which is contrary to Christ's will for my life,' is the day when he first discovers what a glorious thing living can be. There is nothing gloomy about the Christian life. Christ gives us the real pleasures at their very best—friendship and love and homes and beauty and recreation. The happiest-looking people in town, by and large, are the church people.

"If you are thinking of those debatable things which some people question but which you are convinced are all right for you, you do not need to worry. The Church does not require you to give up anything which Christ permits. If your conscience is clear before Him, that is enough. It is only things which harm you or hurt someone else which have to be given up. If you need more light on these questions, you can be getting it as a member of the Church."

f. "I cannot attend the church services." "Many people who are prevented by duty or infirmity from coming regularly to the Sabbath services are loyal and grateful members of the Church. Many of the advantages of Church membership are open to them. There are meetings which they can attend. They enjoy being a part of the fellowship. There are ways in which they can serve the Church. They have a church home and the satisfaction of a definite religious tie. In being known as Church members, they are taking their stand for Christ.

"But if you would be kept away from the services because you do not want to come, or because you prefer to do other things on Sundays, then you should not join the Church. People ought not to come into the Church halfheartedly, but only when they expect to be faithful and loyal members. Christians are intended to assemble regularly to worship God and to receive guidance and strength. This is plainly shown by the example of Christ (Luke 4:16), by the promise of His special presence with those who gather for worship (Matthew 18:20), by the practice of Christians from the beginning (Acts 13:42), and by the Bible's express instructions (Hebrews 10:25). The Church and Christian practices have never been maintained without regular Sabbath worship.

"Anything we do requires giving up something else. Something will have to be left out, of course, if you start attending church. I suspect that church people actually have as good lawns and better health and as much information as those who spend their Sundays gardening or golfing or reading the Sunday papers. But even if they did not, all they get from those hours of worship would certainly be worth much more than what they give up. Anyone who is too busy to go to church is busier than God intended him to be. God gives us 168 hours every week; we surely should spare one of them for worship in His Church.

"If you feel that you need Sunday for rest, remember that you can rise late and have an unhurried morning and still be at the services in good time. All the rest of Sunday will be more calm and refreshing when you go to church. You will find that the peace and relaxation and uplift and changed state of mind you get at the church are the finest sort of rest. Our Creator can give us the re-creation that is the best sort of recreation. There is nothing that will build up worn-out nerves and energies as does the worship of God. 'They that wait upon the Lord shall renew their strength' (Isaiah 40:31). Church services are filled with people who work so hard that without the Church they could not keep going. The busier people are, the more they need the Church."

g. *"I had too much religion forced on me when I was young."* (This is one of the most common and least weighty of all excuses. Some people have told it to themselves so long they have come to believe it, though it is an obvious substitute for the real reason. The attempt to rationalize by blaming one's parents is not too respectable and deserves little answering. But if people persist in this excuse, something may have to be said.) "I am not quite sure I understand. Do you mean that you got stocked up with enough religion for a lifetime? Or did you come to disapprove of the Church? Or did your parents turn you against it? Or did some sort of fanaticism take away your chance of enjoying wholesome Christianity? (When people try to explain this excuse, they may recognize how empty it is.)

"The sort of church you turned against is not the sort of church we are talking about. You should visit our youth departments and see how beautifully everything has been planned to suit the age and needs of the boys and girls, and to make the church attractive to them.

"We cannot get enough nourishment in our youth to last us the rest of our lives—either physically or spiritually. What the Church has for people is something they need all of the time to keep them living at their best. We cannot as adults wear the clothes we wore as children and our youthful religious conceptions will not be what we need when we are grown. Life comes at us every day with new difficulties and new temptations and new opportunities, and just as steadily we need the help with these the Church provides.

"Whatever mistakes may have been made in your religious training, at least you got the idea of what it is to be a Christian. You are still traveling on some of the momentum it gave you. But if you break the family's religious tradition, your children will have it only by hearsay, and your grandchildren will have nothing left of it at all."

h. "I am hard pressed for money just now and could not afford to make a contribution to the Church." "The Church is different from most societies and clubs—it has no entrance fee and no set dues. It follows its Lord, Who said that the poor woman who gave two tiny coins had done more than the rich who made great gifts. It gives to those who have little money the same privileges of full and regular membership that it gives to the rich. It lets its members decide for themselves how much they will give. No one should stay outside the Church for financial reasons.

"A Christian who believes in the Church and does not support it is neglecting his duty, whether or not his name is carried on the membership roll. The Church teaches us the true value of money and shows us where to make the best use of it. The desire to avoid hearing appeals for money is a desire to avoid financial advice which Christians need. The Church is a wise investment counselor. But it always leaves it to every member to decide before God how his money shall be used."

i. "I don't like the minister." "The minister is not the church. We join a church because of what we think of Christ, not because of the attraction of the minister. We like our pastor and we believe you will too when you know him better. All of us are getting a great deal of good from our church. Here are some of the things we admire about our pastor (tell of incidents or qualities which have endeared him to you). Ministers come and go, each with special things he does well and others he does not do so well, but the Church of Christ goes on. If you really cannot join our church because of the minister, let us help you get into some other church."

j. "I had a bad experience and I am never going to join a

church again." "We know how deeply something like that can hurt. But were you not so hurt because you were so disappointed? You were expecting great things from a church—and you still should. Those are the very things we have come to talk about—and we believe you will find them in our church. Do not let one bad experience rob you for all your life of what God wants you to have in His Church. Your experience was not typical.

"Every church is a gymnasium where God is training people to live as Christians, and He does not always make it easy. We have to learn to forgive other people, as they forgive us. Does not your feeling about the Church mean that you have not been able to forgive—as Christ said we must? You will never be free of the pain of that bad experience, or of the injury it has done you, until you are able to forgive and to get back into a church again. Will you not come with us? We need your help to make our church what a church should be—and we promise to do our best to give you everything you have been wanting from a church."

k. "There are too many denominations. I want to be a Christian; I am not interested in being a ——ist." "A musician does not improve his contribution to an orchestra by having no special instrument. Most modern denominations do not think of each other as rivals—they are all contributing their part to the one great Church of Christ. You can take your place in the Church through any of its branches. Eighty per cent of American Protestants are in six great denominational groups, and most of them could be at home in any of these groups. Strong councils of Christian churches unite us—internationally, nationally and locally. When you join one church you are coming into the fellowship of all. Until you join one, you are separated from all. We are not talking for a denomination. It would make us very happy to help bring you into any church."

l. "Your church seemed cold and unfriendly." "Then it has failed in its purpose and I apologize for it. Our church, I have thought, has a reputation for being warmhearted and cordial, and I am very sorry the people you saw there were not like that. There are a good many visitors in our services and it may be that the people near you were strangers who were waiting for someone to speak to them. Won't you meet me there next Sunday so that I can introduce you to some people I know you will like? It is really because our church is interested in you that we have come tonight; people have spoken of how much they wish to get to know you and to have you in the church. We need to have you there to help make us the sort of friendly church that we so much want to be."

X

Evangelistic Preaching

His pulpit still offers the minister his supreme evangelistic opportunity. No form of communication the Church has ever found can compare with preaching. In almost every urban neighborhood and country crossroads in America there is a place where people assemble to hear what a spokesman for Christianity has to say. Every seven days the pulpits have uninterrupted access for at least twenty-five minutes to the minds of more than ten million people.

This generation has discovered, or rediscovered, some other wonderfully effective evangelistic methods. But it would be the sheerest folly to think that these have replaced evangelistic preaching. The minister, like the physician, does not give up all the other cures whenever a new one is developed. Each evangelistic method does something which none of the rest can ever do.

The health curve of the Christian Church throughout the centuries can pretty well be plotted by the warmth of the evangelistic fervor in the pulpits. In the periods of decline, sermons were intended only for the edifying of the saints. But when a fresh spiritual life has come surging like a springtime through the Church, into the preaching has always come the pleading with men to give their hearts to Christ.

Indeed, Dr. C. H. Dodd of Cambridge questions whether sermons which lack the evangelistic note are entitled to be called preaching at all. In *The Apostolic Preaching and Its Development* he says that in the New Testament to "preach" always means to evangelize. *Kerygma,* "preaching," always refers to speaking to the unsaved.

159

Much of our preaching in the church at the present day would not have been recognized by the early Christians as *kerygma*. It is teaching or exhortation (*paraklesis*), or it is what they called *homilia*, that is, the more or less informal discussion of various aspects of Christian life and thought, addressed to a congregation already established in the faith.

1. The Advantages

One clear advantage in preaching, as an evangelistic method, is the time it gives for persuasion. Most people who have not already taken a public stand for Christ require a good deal of convincing before they are ready to do so. A sermon, or a series of sermons, has a long enough hold on their attention to make this possible.

A second advantage is the extended chance which preaching gives to explain to people what it means before asking them to accept Christ. The best evangelistic preachers have also been good teachers, so that their converts have come into the Church with some knowledge of what they were turning from and what they were turning to. A good series of "special meetings" covers many of the same subjects as does a communicants' class; those whom it wins are already partly instructed.

The glorious sense of communion can be a mighty power for good in public evangelism. It is true that mass psychology has been improperly used. But the warmth which comes from a company of joyfully singing, ardently worshiping people can melt the ice which has insulated a heart against the Spirit's influence. There are errors which can be held only in solitude; there are insights which come from others. Take a person who has dismissed single Christians as freaks, put him in a room where almost everyone believes, wrap him around with the glowing atmosphere of faith and the happiness of devoted hearts—and belief may begin to seem natural and right and greatly to be desired.

The impulse which comes through fellowship is surely appropriate for bringing a person to a religion whose key word is "love." Mass motives are sound when they come from a new sense of men's unity in Christ. If the herd instinct helps bring the wandering sheep into the fold, it is God Who put that instinct there.

There are good reasons why a conscientious pastor approaches mass evangelism with an uneasy wariness. It has been discredited by flamboyance, spiritual trickery, high pressure, greed and shallow emotionalism. Too many evangelists have had a bigoted outlook and a distorted gospel. But none of these abuses has any sort of necessary connection with the method. The finest things always have the worst perversions.

A method which, from the day of Pentecost, has been of incalculable effect in spreading Christianity throughout the earth is not likely to have become outmoded in our generation. Indeed, there has been more mass evangelism in our time than ever before in human history—though it has been used by the Church's enemies, not by the church.

2. Relation to Revival

The preaching service is at the heart of the Church's life. If a revival is to flame throughout America, it is most likely to be kindled from the pulpits.

Strictly speaking, a revival is not evangelism. Only a Christian life which has already been started can be revived. But in practice, revival and evangelism are often combined. The same appeal which brings the unchurched to dedication can bring church members to rededication. A service which is radiant with the sense of the Divine presence can introduce the unsaved to Christ while it is keeping Him as a daily reality in the lives of the saved.

Every church is built up of concentric circles. At its center are those who seem to understand Christianity and to be deeply committed to it. On the fringes are those who have never had much idea what the Church is and whose impulses come almost entirely from non-Christian sources—though these fringe members may be the most vocal in some church affairs. The whole hope of a church is to be pulling its membership in toward its heart. An evangelistic service can do that.

3. At the Sabbath Services

a. Three-Minute Evangelism. Many ministers make a brief invitation a part of the order of worship. This may be done every Sunday or at special times. It is more than the mere announcement that new members will be welcome. It is one-paragraph evangelistic preaching. It needs something to dramatize it—a Bible story or verse, a vivid illustration, a poem. Special Sundays or the sacraments offer opportunities for striking appeals.

Though there may often be no response, this three-minute evangelism is still worth while. Its effect on those who are undecided is cumulative; and it keeps a congregation reminded of a church's evangelistic purpose.

b. One-Hour Evangelism. Every part of a normal Sunday service may be designed to make a strong appeal for Christian faith and Church membership. Some way to express decisions may be offered.

It is important that church members know in advance when such a service is to come. They can then make a special effort to bring their friends who are not members. The minister can prepare for the service with the knowledge that nonmembers are likely to be present.

Some churches have a regular schedule for such services, so that the members can always be trying to bring others on those days. "Evangelism Sunday" may be the first Sunday of every month, or the Sunday before the sacraments are celebrated.

c. Six-Week Evangelism. Though there are advantages in having a series of evangelistic services on weekday evenings, there are some peculiar advantages in using consecutive Sundays for them. There is a ready-made attendance in the normal congregations. The minister has a week between services in which to prepare his messages and change his methods. There is less of an adventure into the unknown for preachers who lack experience. There are six days between Sundays to promote attendance, and consecutive weeks during which interest can grow. Evangelistic visitation between the services can powerfully increase their effect. Newcomers get started in a normal church activity. The congregations can be brought to accept evangelism and invitations as proper in a Sabbath service.

Such services are usually held on Sunday mornings; but some churches have used them as a means of recommencing evening services which have been dropped.

As with any series of evangelistic meetings, a great deal of preparation and advertising and prayer is needed for these consecutive evangelistic Sundays. The church should start its planning for them many weeks in advance.

4. Special Meetings

a. The Reasons

(1) At a regular church service, evangelism can be only an addition to other purposes which must be served. (2) Many who are not members will come to a special meeting more readily than to a regular church service. (3) Features which are proper and of great value in an evangelistic meeting would be inappropriate in a Sabbath service. (4) The tonic exhilaration of something fresh and different, an intensity of feeling set free from the pall of sameness, can be valuable in evangelism. (5) A week or two of meetings can be promoted with a concentration of effort and of interest which cannot be maintained for a longer time. (6) Sermons from night to night can be linked with a cumulative effect which would be lost if six days came between them. (7) People from other churches, and those who are employed on Sundays, can come to evening meetings. (8) A pastor who could not leave his church on Sundays can be brought in to help with special meetings.

b. The Name

"Preaching Mission," "Mission," "Revival," "Special Meetings," "Protracted Meetings," "School of Life," "Enquirers' Meetings," "Adventure in Living," "Quest for Truth"—the name should have the sound of what is interesting and important and inspiring. The right name for one community may be wrong for another. A name with which people have unpleasant associations can be a handicap.

c. The Dates

The earlier in the church year the meetings are held the more chance there is to assimilate new members and use the inspiration. Winter is often the least crowded season. Summer is the expected time in many communities. There is an old saying that summer revivals get people over the sins of the spring, and get them ready for the sins of the fall.

A series which opens on Sunday and closes on Friday is common. Or it may close on the second Sunday, with no Saturday meeting. A two- or three-week series is better.

d. Community Mass Meetings

Services by one church have the obvious advantage of connecting the converts immediately with a congregation and of reviving the church members in terms of their special needs and at the scene of their church life. But there are also important advantages in union meetings. (1) They set the whole community to thinking and talking about religion. (2) The excitement of a large effort gets it supported by widespread enthusiasm and interest. (3) Free publicity is easier to get and paid advertising is easier to finance. (4) There is an inspiring demonstration of Protestant solidarity. (5) At a time when the Churches are hard beset by unbelief and evil, Christians need to stand together in their witness to Christ and in their opposition to unrighteousness. (6) In union evangelistic meetings the world can recognize Christianity as an imposing force for good. (7) The social message of the gospel can be directed against evils which infect the whole community, or to the solution of social problems which are a community responsibility.

5. The Preacher

a. The Pastor

There are great advantages in having evangelistic services conducted by a pastor in his own church. Converts will have their great experience with the one who will be their pastor, not with a stranger whom they may never see again. Many who join a church during special meetings with a special preacher never become interested in the ordinary church services with the regular preacher. The local pastor can best speak to the needs of people whom he knows, for revival or evangelism. He will know how to fit his methods to the mentality of the community.

All of that must be weighed against the advantages which a preacher who is not the pastor has. He is not restricted to new ideas and material, but can draw upon the best that he has ever had. The conduct of evangelistic services uses a craftsmanship which many pastors have had small opportunity to develop, and talents with which some men are extraordinarily endowed. A series of meetings with a specialist in this work may equip a pastor to hold his own meetings in the future. Church people are more likely to come to hear someone whom they cannot hear every Sunday. A pastor can advertise another man's preaching in terms in which he cannot advertise his own. A person from a distance can be given the aura of celebrity.

b. A Variety of Preachers

A pulpit exchange, by which the ministers of the co-operating churches will go from one to another through a series of meetings, is sometimes used. Or co-operating pastors may take turns in preaching at union services. This has the advantage of letting each preacher concentrate on one special sermon; it permits church people to hear ministers of other churches. But it gives a variety program when a linked series is what is needed. It inevitably has the effect of an oratorical contest. A preaching mission of this sort may be excellent for inspiring and instructing the church members. It is not the best method for evangelistic services.

c. The Minister of Another Church

A church which wishes to invite in an evangelist will do well to look for the pastor of a church. Though there are some excellent full-time evangelists, there are not enough of them to take care of more than a small part of the need. Such work is seasonal and many men with special gifts for it have pastorates so that they will not be idle for a large part of the year. A parish minister is able to interpret church membership to members and to non-members with a sympathetic insight which a preacher with no settled church connection sometimes lacks. During a week of meetings the leader often meets with various church groups to give them inspiration and suggestions for their work—which a pastor can do best.

Churches often err in assuming that a great preacher will be a great evangelist. Celebrities are least likely to adapt themselves to a request. They assume, with reason, that people will be pleased with their sermons, whether or not they meet the need for which they were invited. Many of them recognize that their greatness is not in evangelistic preaching and they are too wise to venture into an untried field merely because that is what they have been asked to do. Ours is a generation of Sunday morning preachers. The report on "evangelistic" meetings which churches most often make is "They did us a great deal of good, but it was not at all what we wanted."

We must also face the fact that guest preachers, like pastors, fear to give an evangelistic appeal because they do not like to make themselves ridiculous by pleading for decisions for Christ when everyone present has made that decision long ago. Many a speaker who has prepared to address an "evangelistic" service finds that his audience holds only the most faithful of the saints.

Before inviting a pastor to lead its evangelistic meetings a church must inquire particularly about his special ability in this. It must learn whether he uses his own pulpit for evangelism. It should correspond with those for whom he has conducted services.

d. The Specialist

Paul said that there are some who have a special calling as evangelists (Ephesians 4:11). It is an office which has always been of great importance in the Church. It is much needed today. While almost any preacher can learn how to be effective in evangelism, there are some who have a rare genius for it. Specialists develop skills which God can greatly use. The scarcity of such leaders is one of the most serious weaknesses of our time. The appearance of a new generation of them will be one of the surest signs of a revival in the Church.

There are two contrasting types of specialized evangelists. Some are brought to that work by their strength, and others by their weaknesses. The latter have considerable skill in looking like the former—up to a certain point. The least worthy ones are the most intent on providing good references and forestalling any questions which might be raised about the very weaknesses with which they are afflicted. Therefore, any church, before issuing an invitation, must make its own investigation.

It must learn where the evangelist has held services and find its own people there to whom to direct inquiries. Those whose names the evangelist supplies for reference may be those who share his peculiarities. Such questions as these must be asked: (1) Is he an able preacher? (2) Is he personally likable—free of boastfulness, egotism, crudities, narrow censoriousness? (3) Does he exalt the Church—making its membership and work seem important? Does he work to anchor converts in the normal program of the Church? Does he strive for sensation by sweeping denunciations of churches? Does he deliver pronouncements on what the pastor ought to do? (4) Does he stress some peculiar theological opinion, implying that those who do not share his view cannot be Christians, and stirring fruitless arguments? (5) Is he so critical of young people that he will alienate them? (6) Is he a person of intelligence, whose mental processes will appeal to thoughtful people? (7) Does he preach the Bible and the eternal Christian truths, or is he a lecturer with a religious coloration? (8) Do his humility, spiritual depth, kindliness and courtesy give evidence of his knowledge of Christ? (9) What financial arrangements does he make?

Many churches find that a stated honorarium is better than a share of the offerings. With no pressure at all, an offering for an evangelist whom people have come to like may be so large as to cause criticism. Or it may be so small that he is badly treated. The willingness of a church or a council of churches to exploit an evangelist in order to get a large offering for itself cannot be justified. When a financial motive comes in, the evangelistic value is diminished.

6. Bringing Hearers

The greatest discovery about evangelistic preaching is that it requires the members to be partners of the minister. The finest sermons will move nothing but the air unless someone has been brought to hear them, and that is what the laity are best equipped to do. The decline in soul-winning preaching comes less from the lack of evangelistic passion in the pulpit than from the lack of evangelistic prospects in the pews. Many preachers who were eager to introduce men to Christ have lost heart when they lost hope of having hearers who were not already long-time members of the Church. A planned partnership between the minister who brings the message and the members who bring the hearers is the first essential for evangelistic preaching.

Preachers of the unusual groups devote their intelligence to getting an audience and trust the Holy Spirit to provide a sermon. Ministers of the usual sort devote their intelligence to getting a sermon and trust the Holy Spirit to provide an audience. The right way is surely to devote all possible thought and prayer to both.

The minister's chance to bring those who might be won is very limited. He has not the contacts with the unchurched. He cannot give a glowing account of his own preaching. There is a notoriously loose connection between the quality of the sermons and the size of the attendance.

When one of this country's ablest preachers came to his church, the pulpit had for some time been vacant. Attendance had declined and it stayed small. After several months, some of the men in the church began to regret that so few people were getting the benefit of the splendid sermons. Without the knowledge of the pastor, they pledged themselves to tell several people each day about the great services at the church. By this one means, within six months the attendance was more than doubled.

Church members who are walking advertisements are worth acres of newspaper space. Church people talk of their clubs and sports; they have as much opportunity, and better reason, to talk with enthusiasm of their church. Just to tell how fine it is and how much it is doing for them has value. But a personal invitation is far better. To say, "Let me stop by for you," or at least, "Let me meet you at the church," is the only adequate way to bring those who need to hear the gospel proclaimed.

That sort of inviting can be an easy start in personal evangelism for those who are timid about it. It is not enough—the Christian has more than a church service to which to witness. But to begin by telling about the church can be a way of learning to talk about religion. And it often goes directly into a conversation about why the church is important and what it believes.

The minister is called to be an evangelist, and his pulpit offers him an incomparable opportunity. If he is going to use it, he will have to start by training the members to bring people to be evangelized. This has become an enthusiastic tradition in many churches.

Here again is the faithful rule—WHATEVER IS TO BE DONE ALL THE TIME HAS TO BE LEARNED AT SPECIAL TIMES. Church people are taught to be trying always to bring their friends to church by being given special times and ways to do it. This general duty becomes specific with an "evangelism Sunday," or a series of evangelistic Sundays, or a week of meetings.

These are some of the ways of bringing hearers:

a. Impersonal Ways

(These impersonal ways, by themselves, bring very few. But they are of great value in preparing for personal invitations, and in making both church people and those outside feel that the services are important.)

Use *every church meeting* for weeks in advance to tell about the services. Written announcements should be sent to the organizations.

In the *Sunday bulletins,* or any other church publication, put attractive publicity and invitations.

Print *leaflets* or *cards,* and issue them in quantity to all church members. These can be handed to friends, put in letters, slipped under doors or into maiiboxes and given to all visitors to the church.

Put *posters* in the church, in stores, in other public places.

Write *letters* to all church members, to those on the prospect list, to all with whom the church and its organizations have any contact.

Put a *sign* on the church building or in its yard.

Get *news stories* into the papers. A dull announcement is not news. Color can be found in the biography of the preacher or singers, a massed choir, pictures, dramatic features in the program. An interestingly worded sermon title has advertising value.

Pay for *newspaper advertising*—preferably not in the religious section of the paper. One large advertisement is better than several small ones. When churches have their own services on the same days, they may unite in one large advertisement with their separate announcements in small type at the border.

Get *radio* announcements. If the speaker can have a daily radio time it will add to the benefits of his presence in the community and increase the evening attendances.

b. Personal Ways

Use *cards* on which church members pledge: (1) to attend, (2) to bring nonmembers, (3) to pray for the services. These pledges can be made in church meetings or the cards may be mailed to members. They may be passed out at the first two or three of the evangelistic services.

Have an *every-member visitation* at church homes to urge attendance and the bringing of friends. The visitors may take cards on which co-operation can be pledged.

Have a different *church organization* sponsor each service, making it responsible for filling the church with its own numbers and those whom they bring. Give recognition to the sponsoring group during the service.

Have a *Family Service,* at which family groups sit together. At less formal services, families with the largest number present or the most generations can be discovered and honored.

Have a *visitation of those on the prospect list,* inviting them to the services, or offering to call for them or to meet them at the church.

Have a *telephone campaign,* inviting nonmembers and urging members to attend and to tell and bring others.

7. The Connection with Visitation Evangelism

a. Before

(1) Those whom evangelistic visitors cannot win may next be asked to promise to attend the services, where the messages may do what the visitors could not do. The callers should be cautioned not to give the invitation to the meetings until they have done their best to win the great decision. (2) Those who make decisions during the visits can find the meetings a deeply moving introduction to the Church and a training for the Christian life.

b. During

All the great evangelists have counted for much of their success on "personal workers" who talked to people at their homes or places of business during or after the mission. Visitation Evangelism, on the evenings between special evangelistic Sundays or on the afternoons during a week of meetings, can bring people to the services or can win those who have not responded to the invitations from the pulpit.

c. After

Evangelistic preaching can bring people close to a decision which will still not be made until someone in private talks to them about it. Special services may make church people able and willing to do evangelistic visiting.

8. The Message

Ministers who are timid about their evangelistic ability can be reassured by Paul's statement about his, "I was with you in weakness, and in fear, and in much trembling. And my speech and my preaching was not with enticing words of man's wisdom, but in demonstration of the Spirit and of power" (I Corinthians 2:3-4). A study of the sermons of some of the Church's most effective evangelists gives plenty of evidence that it still pleases God "by the foolishness of preaching to save" (I Corinthians 1:21). Some enhanced their very ordinary sermons by striking pulpit personalities. But others who were greatly successful have been described as merely matter-of-fact in manner. The one necessary distinction seems to have been the deeply earnest reiteration of the simplest Christian truths—"God is," "God loves you," "Jesus Christ can set you free," "Jesus wants your life."

The Bible is still the basic handbook for evangelistic preaching; prayer is the primary method in sermon preparation; a loving study of people is the best source of ideas. Aside from these, the surest help comes from studying the sermons of those who, at the present time, are most successfully applying the gospel to human needs. Some inspiration may come from the preaching of the great evangelists of the past; but an imitation of the revivalists of the last century is as out of place in a modern pulpit as would be the style of Daniel Webster at a luncheon club.

It is essential that the preacher be able to translate the Latinisms of the creeds into the basic English of everyday experience. He must put the timeless Christian truths into such timely terms and applications that a modern listener will say, "This is for me!" Deeply loved expressions which are full of meaning for Church people may seem offensively hollow to those who have not learned their content. Technical terms in any field are the shorthand which must be written out in full for the uninitiated. Even for the preacher, a sonorous old phrase may be a substitute for thinking out exactly what he means. He must remember that the vocabulary of his seminary days goes out of date. The surest sign of spiritual stagnation is the dependence upon metaphors which sprang from the fresh experience of a past generation.

This does not mean that the poetry of faith has to be put into prose, or the eternal mystery made commonplace. Even the practical man-in-the-street loves a resounding word. But every specialized religious expression must be explained and applied until it has a living meaning for the hearers.

There will be no great religion without great emotions. Jesus did not argue philosophy with people—He won their love. The heart is the antenna, the brain does the tuning. Anyone who thinks that this generation is not emotional has never been to a football game. Emotions which are not rightly used will be perverted. It was the sophisticated youth of the European universities whose emotions were exploited by fanatic leaders. The youth of America will be saved from the emotional appeal of false religions only by the emotional appeal which is the Church's birthright.

There is a sentimentality of the cheapest sort in much of the bitter scorn of emotion in religion. The *amor intelligentiae* may be one of the coldest of sentiments, but it is an *amor* all the same.

In *Mass Evangelism Today* Dr. Edwin T. Dahlberg has vividly described the use and the abuse of emotion in evangelism:

> The furnace man must melt the metal into a white hot, fluid condition, and the pattern maker and moulder must prepare the forms into which the liquid metal can be poured. If a church becomes exclusively evangelistic without any great social ministry or

teaching method we have the menace of red hot emotional revivalism poured out over the community without any definite forms of character or citizenship in which to take shape. If on the contrary we have religious education or pastoral calling without evangelism, we have the hopeless situation in which many teachers and pastors now find themselves, whereby they are trying to fit chilled, unemotional and unresponsive lives into the patterns of the kingdom of God. No blacksmith could shape his tools by hammering away at cold iron. Just because evangelism has sometimes put the emphasis a little too heavily on the bellows, we must not be afraid of those mighty spiritual enthusiasms which fan a flame, and make possible the shaping of a new human order in the world. . . . We need to be roused from the deadly spell of religious quietism that has settled down with such paralyzing influence upon the church. Religion is the one realm in life where people are literally starved for emotion and action. . . . What is needed is something electric, joyous, and vocal—such reckless expressions of the Spirit as have always characterized mass revival.

9. Decisions

a. The Reasons for a Decision

An emotion is saved from degenerating into emotionalism only by giving it some way of proper expression. The fear that giving an invitation in a public meeting may lead people to do something for which they are not ready must be balanced against the fear that not giving an invitation may keep people from doing something for which they are ready. That last may well do the greater psychic and spiritual damage. To stir people religiously without giving them anything they can do about it leaves them far worse off than they were before.

It is the sin of evasion which keeps most people from God. They reject Christ, not by denial, but by postponement. An evangelistic sermon which issues only in advice to give the matter·thought simply strengthens this habit of evasion.

There must be a note of urgency in all evangelistic preaching. The minister is like a lawyer pleading for a verdict, and that verdict has to be definite.

The effect of the finest sermon will soon drift away unless it is tied to something. There must be some act of the will which fastens it. When a new direction has been given to a life, there must be some landmark which will keep it from being lost.

After all, the danger is not that too much will happen at the service but that too little will happen afterward. An evangelistic meeting which does not lead to training and nurture in the Christian life can do great harm, but the harm will be done whether or not an invitation has been given. The danger that public decisions will bring into the church those who should not be there will not threaten a church which carefully prepares its candidates for membership. The decision must not be an end in itself; but it is an essential and all-important turning point.

The decision does not have to be the last step before joining the church. The decision to accept Christ may lead to entrance into a communicants' class, or into whatever program the church has to prepare people for membership. There are many sorts of decisions which may be sought in a public service.

b. How an Invitation Is Given

The invitation to make a decision must be given: *Naturally,* with no forced imitation of another's manner. The minister must learn by steps, going only as far each time as he can go without feeling awkward. *Firmly,* with no fumbling or timidity. *Confidently,* as though expecting a response. *Clearly,* telling exactly what the decision means and how it is to be expressed. *Gently,* not with high pressure or dominating methods. In a *friendly* way—not oratorically. *Earnestly,* as a solemn and holy matter—not as an unimportant item in the service.

As in all evangelism, the preacher is counting on effects which are far greater than the human causes. He gives the invitation knowing that neither it nor the sermon could be expected to move people unless the Holy Spirit is impelling them. He therefore must do a great deal of praying in advance, and have the sense of praying as he speaks.

The invitation is usually given from the pulpit, though some ministers come down to the main floor level so that they will be closer to the people. An invitation may be woven into the sermon, but it has more effect if it is set apart for its own emphasis. It is better to address it to "Those here who have not . . ." rather than to "Any here who may not have . . ." implying that they are peculiar. The invitation may repeat an appeal from the sermon or the text. It may quote one of the great Bible invitations or promises.

The minister may reinforce the decision with such thoughts as these: The invitation is from God. Christ wants the decision to be made. The decision is a very simple thing, but it will make an amazing difference. The congregation is a loving family, which is eager now to see others come into its fellowship. Continued postponement is a sad mistake. There will be a glorious happiness once it is settled. The surrender of our lives to Christ has to be definite. He needs us to take an open stand for Him. It will be the most important and the best act of a lifetime. Some of the reasons for decisions given in Chapters III, VI and IX may be used.

Repeating the invitation may be necessary. Unsympathetic onlookers often criticize this—and if the invitation hymn is sung "just once more" too often, they have reason. But experience shows that if the invitation is given again it wins some who do not respond at first. People have to think it through, and often struggle it through, before they are ready. Sin and the habit of postponement are hard to get around. If the hearers are told early in the sermon or before it that they will be asked to make decisions, they will be better prepared to do so when the time comes.

c. Ways of Expressing a Decision

The method must be suited to the mood of the occasion. Some of those suggested here might be appropriate for a youth conference but not for a Sabbath worship service.

It is often helpful to lead people gently by two or three progressive decisions, going from the easier to the more difficult. For example, the minister may ask those who wish to live nearer Jesus to raise their hands, then ask those who raised their hands to meet him in a conference room after the service, then talk to those who meet him there about professing their faith and coming into the Church. They are perfectly free at any stage to turn back. The purpose is not to snare them but to help them come by separate steps to a higher level than they could reach by one leap.

People may be invited to:

1. *See the pastor* at some stated time—after the service or the next day. He may tell when he will be in his study for that purpose. Church people may be urged to bring their friends at that time.

2. *Think it out and pray it out in private*—then tell someone of the decision which has been reached.

3. *Write out a statement of faith and purposes* before the day is over.

4. *Remain for an "after meeting."* The instruction will be related to the sort of decision that has been made—how to follow Christ, how to join the Church, how to have family worship, how to pray.

5. *Come to an inquiry room* after the benediction. People may be asked to come as a step toward joining the Church or simply to get guidance in what the Christian life requires and to have their questions answered. Church members may be designated to show people to the room and to relieve any stiffness before the pastor arrives.

6. *Sign cards.* The cards may have such statements as, "I accept Jesus Christ as my Lord and Saviour and intend with His help to live a Christian life," "In obedience to Christ I desire to unite with His Church," "I would like to know more about being a Christian," "I rededicate myself to the purposes of the Church of which I am a member," "I promise to try to live nearer Jesus Christ and to serve Him better," "I would like to transfer my membership to this church," "Name, Address, Church Membership."

The cards may be in the hymnal racks, or passed out by the ushers, or printed at the bottom of the bulletin, or given to those who stand or who raise their hands to express a decision. Pencils should be within reach of everyone.

The minister may ask people to look at their cards as he reads the statements to them, pausing after each one for a simple, earnest plea for the making of that affirmation.

Everyone present may be asked to sign a card, marking on it at least a record of attendance. That will make it easier for some to mark other statements.

Time to study and sign the cards may be given while the choir sings an invitation hymn. People may be asked to take the cards and then to bow in prayer over them, making the signing of the card a record of the promise they have made to their Lord while they prayed.

7. *Raise their hands or stand*. People are usually asked to do this after a time of prayer and while all heads are bowed. Unless this is joined to some such later act as meeting the minister or signing a card, it may have no lasting significance.

8. *Come to the front*—usually during a hymn or choir music which reinforces the invitation. The fact that this takes courage and is a public witness has spiritual value.

It is easier for a person to come forward if others are doing so. Some ministers ask the members of the official board to come to the front of the church, when the invitation is given, to greet those who respond; thus those who make decisions do not have to come down the aisle by themselves. If it is known that some people are ready to join the Church, they may be asked in advance to come forward when an invitation is given, with the thought that this may encourage others to do so. In an appeal to youth, the church-school teachers or youth leaders may be asked to come to the front.

The minister usually descends from the pulpit so that he may greet those who come, and may be closer and more personal as he renews the invitation.

9. *Make a verbal statement*. Those who are ready may be asked to rise and repeat after the leader some such statement as, "I am trusting Jesus Christ as my Lord and Saviour." Or they may be asked to make their own statement—perhaps not more than ten or fifteen words. This is often done in young people's meetings or out-of-doors services.

d. Aids to Decision.

Early in 1950 Bishop Cockin conducted six meetings for large student audiences at the Sheldonian Theatre in Oxford, England. Each evening there was a forty-minute talk on Christianity as a reasonable, challenging and life-giving faith. Then there was a five-minute break for reflection, with quiet organ music. Then in a ten-minute summary Bishop Cockin drove home his arguments and made his appeal. Some ministers have three minutes of silence after the sermon, then an invitation to an after-meeting,

then a brief prayer and benediction. Canon Bryan Green sometimes closes the after-meeting by suggesting to those who stayed
for it that they scatter throughout the now largely empty church
and kneel for private prayer. They may pray for a minute or an
hour. He or his helpers are ready to come to any who wish them;
otherwise they do not intrude.

After the sermon a lay member may be asked to give a testimony
and appeal. Those who have joined the church during the past
year and are happy in having done so may be asked to come to
the front. One of them may be asked to tell what the church has
meant to him, and to invite others to share what he has found. Or
it may be the fifty-year church members who come forward for
that purpose.

Symbolism may be effective. A lighted cross in a partly darkened
room may strengthen an invitation. A candle-lighting ceremonial
may illustrate the light we have from Christ, or His commandment to let our faith be a light in the world.

e. What Follows Decisions

Every decision must be a step toward some definite result. Sometimes people may be trusted to follow out the new purpose by
themselves—as with a pledge of private prayer. But more often
it is necessary for a church to keep a connection with those who
have made decisions and to guide them. If it is a decision for
Church membership, the person must at once be connected with
the process which leads to joining the Church.

10. Arrangements

Special evangelistic services need something to make them fresh
and vivid. They must give the exciting sense of immediate religious
reality. There must be the feel of the moving of spiritual power.
It is fatal if they are just one more round of sameness. One should
not hesitate to experiment. Dullness is a greater danger than is
novelty.

Music is of the utmost importance. It can make or break the
services. Church music is not an end in itself—it is a device for
producing certain spiritual results; it is an instrument for opening

hearts to religious influences; it is a vehicle for taking religious truths into minds; it is a form of religious expression.

A church service is not a class in which a musical education is to be forced on a captive audience. Its music should be of whatever sort is best able to reach people at their present level of appreciation. Choir masters like to insist that it is only ignorance which prevents congregations from preferring the "best" music— which is a dubious irrelevancy.

A hymn is a good hymn when it does what religious singing is supposed to do. No other musical or literary canons have any bearing—including the tastes of the minister or the organist, neither of whom is normal musically. The fitness to secure the particular effect desired with the particular sort of people who will be present is the one proper basis for selection. Evangelism is sadly handicapped by the music in many of our churches— something to be endured, not enjoyed.

An evangelistic service is not the place to learn new hymns, except for a theme hymn which may be used repeatedly. Hymns which older people know and love may be disliked by teenagers. Such liberties with sense as fervent utterances "when the death-dew lies cold on my brow" or when taking off "from Mount Pisgah's lofty height" are likely to give younger people the uneasy feeling that evangelism is fatuous.

It would be wrong for the Church to insist that Africans learn English in order to hear the gospel. It is just as wrong for it to insist that Americans learn a certain musical idiom in order to understand a church service. Obviously, a conservatory graduate and a day laborer use a different musical language. The Church has too much made the impossible requirement that laborers and bankers and farmers learn the musician's vocabulary if they are to express themselves or be taught through music. An artificial dignity and self-conscious "good taste" will simply cut the Church off from the people.

To describe a tune as "catchy" would seem to condemn it for church use. But there is value in the sort of tuneful hooks which make a great Bible truth catch in people's minds. Those who hum on the way home from church, "I'll go where you want me to go, dear Lord," are taking something important from the service. When the housewife accompanies her sweeping, or the carpenter his sawing, with the easy rhythm of, "On Christ, the solid rock, I stand, all other ground is sinking sand," they are working in the shadow of the Mount from which that first was said.

Music which is within the range of those whose musical tastes and religious vocabularies are not highly developed does not have to be the sort which has discredited evangelism. Some of the popular hymns have bad theology and absurd imagery and tunes which stay in one's head like a toothache. But there are others which are among the most powerful expressions of its faith Christianity has ever had. They need not all be cast out together. Like sweets with children, too much sweet and easy music can become a bad habit and a source of weakness. But a church should be musically equipped for a variety of needs. Unfortunately, the editors of denominational hymnals try to protect the churches from their ministers' bad taste by not letting them have within reach any hymn which would not be appropriate for the most dignified occasion. It may therefore be necessary to purchase extra books for evangelistic meetings—and for prayer meetings and Sunday evening hymn singing.

Some of the gospel choruses are sacrilegious; but the common unintelligible anthem, whose only message is that Christianity is a boresome and meaningless matter, is also a sacrilege of the worst sort. People have been turned against the Church by cheap hymns; but a great many more are being kept away by the pain of mumbling at half voice through hymns which no one really wants to sing.

An evangelistic meeting should use only hymns and special music which will seem beautiful the first time they are heard. They should put great religious truths so plainly that everyone will understand. Their wording should be within the range of apprehension of those who are unsophisticated in church usages. And there should be not one verse more than people enjoy singing.

The larger the choirs, the more homes and friends there are with ties to the service and the more power there is in the singing.

A good song leader is excellent, but a good song leader is rare. There are not a few like the one who said, "After we go to town

on this next verse, let's have a real peppy prayer from the pastor!"
But a leader who keeps his personality out of the way of the
mood of the singing can add real power and beauty to it.

The churches, moving more slowly than some of the freer groups,
are discovering the value of mass meetings which use such instruments as the harp and the violin, which employ unusual lighting
effects and have the close timing of a good radio program. A series
of brief messages with strong human interest can be more impressive than a long speech. There can be laughter and spontaneity.
Celebrities, who have Christian convictions and whose lives are
uncompromised, can attract crowds to popular meetings, and
their testimony, however brief, may have great influence.

Roman Catholic preaching missions have used two priests in
separate pulpits. A message does not always have to come from a
single voice. The interchange will hold interest and make a dramatic impact. If one proposes questions and difficulties which the
other answers, it can lead the audience through exactly the process
by which minds must come to conviction.

A guest evangelistic preacher can give valuable help to a
church in addition to the preaching. He may have a morning Bible-
study hour with the women. He may give instruction in lay evangelistic visiting. After consultation with the pastor about church
needs, he may help an official board with its problems. He may
have a prayer meeting with the young people. Some leaders follow
every service with an instruction period on prayer, tithing, voca-
tions, etc.

The method used by Rev. Mark L. Koehler in his church at
Yakima, Washington, illustrates a well-rounded revival and evangelistic program. The whole church is prepared, well in advance,
to bring nonmembers to six special Sunday morning services. These
services center on six great Christian themes, each with a strong
evangelistic emphasis and an invitation to come into the Church
or to join an Inquirers' Group. The sermon each Sunday evening
deals with the personal and social applications of the doctrine
presented in the morning. After a Thursday evening supper, there
is a study of the Bible basis of the Sunday theme, and a discussion
of it. Each organization which meets during the week is asked to
give a part of its meeting to a study of the week's theme. The

church paper takes a written treatment of that theme into the homes each week. Groups in homes for the women, and one for business-men downtown, meet during the six weeks to pray for better Christian living in the Church, and for the bringing of others into it.

When outsiders are coming for special meetings, it is important for the church to make a good impression. The building should be at its most attractive. The ushers should be coached in how to make strangers like church people.

11. Prayer

There is unlimited evidence that prayer is the most important factor in evangelistic services. It has most to do with the power of the messages and the size of the attendance and the effect in people's lives. A failure to make provision for prayer in planning the services is poor spiritual craftsmanship.

Prayer can be had by making arrangement for it in: (a) every church meeting, (b) special prayer meetings, (c) prayer gatherings on the days of the meetings, (d) cottage prayer meetings in the members' homes, (e) asking the shut-ins to support the services by their prayers, (f) asking all church people to keep the services in their private prayers—perhaps using cards on which they pledge to do so.

XI

Evangelism through the Church
Organizations

Our modern culture tends to confine religion to religious institutions, and then thrust those institutions so far from the main stream of affairs that people have to go out of their way to notice them at all. Most unchurched Americans do not hate the Church —they do not care that much about it. The Church simply has no place in their scheme of living. The gulf must be bridged from the Church's side. The Church must someway catch the attention of its secular-minded neighbors and seem worth noticing.

Its organizations are an ideal bridge between the Church and the world outside it. Many who would never think of being in the church for any other reason will come for the Men's Club banquet or the teen-age canteen. They will let their children attend the church school. In the Red Cross sewing or the Scout Troop Committee those who are thoroughly secular-minded may be working side by side with some of the most devoted members of the church. The contact thus made can be cultivated until people begin to understand the Church's deeper values and wish to share them. This will usually not happen unless it is planned.

Bait is legitimate for the fishers of men—but the Church's fishing is too often all bait and no line. Nonmembers come for the book reviews and bowling clubs and teas and drift away again because no one ever tries to connect them with the church. We must confess with shame that countless numbers come to our churches for all sorts of reasons without being given the slightest glimpse of what the Church is really for. Most churches greatly need some plan, both for making contacts and for making the most of them.

A church is an assembly line whose finished products are delivered in heaven. Its raw materials come from several sources. One of these is the maternity hospitals; but a church which counts on its births as a major source of supply is doomed. The rate is too low; some are sure to be lost; and the lack of concern for winning the rest of the world to Christ would make a fatal atmosphere in which to bring up Christians. Some of its human supply comes to a church by accident—people bring themselves to the services or send their children to the church school. But these accidental additions are too few and too casual to be an important source.

It is this lack of a source of supply which ruins many a church's hopes of being steadily evangelistic. Prospect lists are soon exhausted. After the third round of evangelistic calling, or the third year of special services, there are no more names of people to invite.

If a church is to remain a church—introducing human beings to Christ and building them up in Him—it must train all of its members and all of its organizations to reach out into the world to draw people toward it. This requires a definite way of working.

Churches have greatly needed a long-range method of evangelism. Most of those outside the Church are not able today to make an intelligent decision for Jesus Christ. If some overpowering appeal could induce them to join the Church at once, it would be a mistake to receive those who would know so little of what they were doing. If great numbers are to be reached the Church must have some more deliberate methods than the sudden approaches which too much pre-empt the idea of evangelism. It must have ways of preparing people spiritually and mentally for the great commitment which may not come until many months after the first contact has been made.

The old jest that "no souls are saved after the first twenty minutes" has this unhappy truth—after the first twenty minutes we often do not have anything else to try. When people do not respond to an appeal from the pulpit or a visit in their homes, we do not know what to do next. We sadly put the prospect card back into the file with a vague idea of trying again. But if nothing happens in between, at the next attempt the person will be even less likely to respond. Evangelism through the organizations gives churches what they have so plainly needed—a six- or twelve- or eighteen-month evangelistic method.

A church is obliged to give every one of its members a share in evangelism. It must enable them to do what Christ has commanded them to do. They can never be spiritually whole without it. But there are some who cannot be brought immediately to do those things which are too often all a church proposes in its urging to evangelism. As has been noted, there are a few who are temperamentally unqualified to do evangelistic visitation. There are more who are so shy or so unused to a direct religious approach that they must be started in evangelistic work at an easier level. Evangelism through the organizations is something in which every member of the church can have a part. In it, they can be learning how to do evangelism of a deeper sort.

Many new members slip from the Church and go back to old habits and associations because they never get into the church fellowship. This danger is far smaller for those who get into the fellowship before they get into the Church.

Church organizations die of dullness. Without clearly worthwhile aims, they lose the respect of busy people. When an organization begins to think of itself as a door into the Church, it has an exciting purpose. In a program to win others it finds the stimulus of dramatic service and the satisfaction of a definite accomplishment. Moreover, many a frivolous and therefore feeble church group has found itself in its trying to show Christianity to others. For an organization as for an individual, the evangelist is his own first convert.

A New Jersey pastor had been trying in every possible way to get his young people to put more serious content into their programs, with no success. But when they came back from their week of calling they revised all their plans for future meetings "because we need to know more about religion." A Pennsylvania church reported, "The Young People's Fellowship wrought wonders in their visitation—stepping up interest and attendance and participation in a most remarkable way. Partly as a result of this, four of the boys decided to enter the ministry."

1. Getting the Organizations Interested in Evangelism

Sermons, literature, an annual leaders' conference or a permanent evangelism council representing all the organizations can keep them all concerned with evangelism. In some churches the pastor and members of the official board meet early every fall with the officers' cabinet of each organization. They discuss the great motives for evangelism by the organization and what can be done. Each new set of officers needs to be educated early for evangelism.

A group in a local church can be stimulated by a conference which its officers attend or by a speaker who is brought to the church. Programs at regular meetings can make all the members eager about evangelism.

There is danger that organizations will see in this nothing but a drive for members. If the final religious goals are not continually stressed, they will never be reached, and the needed force will be lacking. The desire to boost the organization or to turn in a good score will not supply enough incentive.

2. A Program of "Evangelism through Fellowship"

Exhortations to evangelism save no souls. Church organizations, like individuals, will readily agree that evangelism is their Christian duty. But nothing will be done about it until they discover just what to do and how to do it. That is the reason for the "Evangelism through Fellowship" programs which are becoming increasingly popular. Their purpose is to show the organizations how to bring people from outside the church into their fellowship in order that through their fellowship those people may be brought to Christian faith and Church membership. There are three stages:

a. The Organizations Become Competent

There is no use putting on a campaign for new members who will find the meetings so dull that they will immediately quit coming. There is no evangelistic purpose in bringing people to see movies on salmon fishing or to hear a discussion of how to finance the silver tea. It is false strategy which tries to keep meetings from being "too religious" for fear of boring the worldly minded. Secular attractions can always outbid the Church in everything save its one specialty. Church organizations which grow fastest manage to touch the most important matters in a fresh and vital way.

At a self-study meeting an organization asks itself such questions as: "Is what we do interesting and valuable enough to make those who come once wish to keep coming?" "Will we seem friendly and attractive to newcomers?" "Will they find with us anything which will make them want to become Christians and Church members—or are we just a cut-rate social club?" It adds realism if statistics have been prepared showing the organization's record in: (1) adding new members, (2) holding its members, (3) bringing its members into Church membership.

With the weaknesses located, remedies can be planned. These may be: a new sort of programs, greater attention to social occasions or to worship, instruction in how to be friendly, the use of decision meetings or of interviews with members about joining the Church, a better system for getting new Church members into the organization.

b. There Is an Enrollment Effort

1. A Prospect List of those who may be won is prepared by much the same methods as those described in Chapter VII. Every organization needs its own well-kept file of prospective members. Those who are tempted to scorn such card thumbing as mechanized religion need to be reminded that we do not prove our spirituality by carelessness, nor do we save our time by doing things the hard way. The cards are the tie with people. A Neighborhood Religious Census and a program of Evangelism through Fellowship fit each other perfectly; each is likely to need the other in order to be successful.

2. Callers are sent out. They are enlisted and trained and assigned much as are evangelistic visitors (see Chapters VIII and IX). They use many of the same methods in calling. They require less spiritual and mental competence than do those who seek decisions for Christ and Church membership. They can be trained in an hour—though at least that much training is essential. One who calls for an organization may be getting ready to try the more exacting sort of evangelistic visiting.

The calling period should not be longer than three weeks—two is better. It is aimed at a definite date—that of the Welcoming Meeting.

Callers may go singly, though there is great advantage if they work in pairs. Children often go with older people for calls on children.

3. *The callers seek decisions:* (a) to join the organization, (b) to come to the Welcoming Meeting—either or both. A decision card, with a reminder stub to be left, makes the decision definite and important.

At the Welcoming Meeting there is (a) a specially good program, (b) a glowing description of what the organization does and offers, (c) an enrollment of the new members, (d) a time for fellowship. Those who have promised to come are reminded a few days before the meeting and someone offers to bring them. Success is shown less by the number of new members at the Welcoming Meeting than by the number at the three or four meetings after it. Therefore it is important that these next meetings have unusually attractive programs. There should be attention to bringing the new members and checking on any who miss. An old member may be assigned to get each new member to the meetings and to help him or her to become acquainted.

c. The New Members Are Drawn toward Faith and Church Membership

The group must keep demonstrating Christianity to its new members—in programs which have the thrill of real religion, in service projects which show Christianity in action, in the fine fellowship at the church and in the members' homes. Meetings may mention the importance of Church membership and of a definite stand for Jesus Christ.

As soon as they have had a chance to become ready, members of church groups should be offered a definite opportunity to profess their faith and join the Church. Unless this is systematically arranged, some will be missed. The church's evangelistic visitors may be sent to them. Some organizations have their own visitation evangelism programs. Teachers and leaders may have private interviews about decisions. Groups may arrange to get their members to evangelistic preaching services. Many church-school departments have decision days. Other organizations can have them. A conference or a rally may offer an ideal opportunity for winning commitments to Christ and the Church.

Failure in this may make an organization a substitute for the Church. If members of a class or church group are allowed to assume that they have done all that is necessary, they soon become confirmed adherents of the outer courts.

Any church organization or older church-school class can have its own program of Evangelism through Fellowship. But it is a magnificent experience for a church to have all its groups unite in such a program. There is the excitement of a big enterprise and the increase of church unity which comes from working together on the planning and the prospect lists and the enlistment and training of callers. On the same evening each group may study its evangelistic competence and then join the others to compare findings and plans for improvement. When there are several groups which have reason to call in the same home, one team of callers can speak for all of them.

Christian fellowship should be a tremendous evangelistic power. A program of Evangelism through Fellowship simply makes it possible to use this power intelligently and on purpose.

3. The Church School

Education without evangelism makes Pharisees; evangelism without education makes fanatics. There has been generation-long controversy between those who insist that a person must be taught to be a Christian and those who insist that a Christian is made by a decisive act of the Holy Spirit. The acrimony has been increased by a sense of guilt and inadequacy on both sides. Many educators know that they are temperamentally not equipped to help anyone have a searching experience of commitment; and many warm evangelists are confused and ignorant in the field of education. There has to be a combining of goals and methods. Ardently evangelistic pastors need to give a great deal of well-informed attention to their Churches' educational techniques. And denominational training schools and agencies for Christian Education have to show how the learning process can help bring pupils to a dedication to Jesus Christ as the Lord of life. The command "Make disciples . . . teaching them" cannot be broken up.

This merging of methods is overdue. There are hundreds of thousands of people who can name the day on which they became Christians, and still have very little idea what a Christian is. And secular America is to a large extent populated by those who had their time in Sunday school without ever being given any first-person application of the things they learned.

Bishop Praetorius reports that of every 100 pupils in American Protestant church schools, 75 drop away from the Church. Fifteen of these will later be rewon, so the final loss is 60 per cent. Those lost 60 represent the Church's most shocking failure in evangelism, because so clear an opportunity was thrown away; they also represent the Church's most wide-open possibility of improvement in evangelism.

Seventy-five per cent of those the Protestant Church receives on profession of faith come through the church school. Most of these are children from church homes—the school was not the chief reason for their coming. But it has a large responsibility for the quality of every generation of Church members.

Church agencies which deal with children and young people have the best chance for evangelism. Ninety per cent of those who join the Church do so by the time they are twenty-one years old, and 95 per cent by the time they are twenty-four. The greatest number come between the ages of eleven and thirteen. While attempts to win older people are abundantly worth while, it becomes more difficult as age increases. Dr. Edward Judson says that going from the world into the Christian life in youth is like crossing a river near its source. It is just a short step then, but the farther one travels along the bank the more difficult it gets until only a few make it later on.

The sharp drop in church school enrollment is therefore alarming. The school age population has increased, but of the five largest Protestant denominations, only the Southern Baptist has a growing church school. The others—the United Methodist, United Presbyterian, Episcopal, and Lutheran Church in America—from 1960 to 1970 lost approximately 3,136,000 pupils—a fourth of their 1960 enrollment.

Church-school evangelism suffers from the dilemma of the teacher who said, "My intentions are good, but I find I am not so much trying to set little feet on the golden stairs as to keep them off the varnished chairs." It is hard to prevent week-by-week problems from crowding out the evangelistic purpose. Teachers need continually to be reinspired to that purpose. And they need to be shown the different ways by which pupils of different ages can be brought to know Christ as a personal Friend and Saviour.

a. Evangelism through Fellowship Program

All that is said in this chapter about a program of Evangelism through Fellowship applies to the church school.

b. The Cradle Roll

Babies are wonderful evangelists; therefore, every effort to enlarge the Cradle Roll should be made. Baby-supply stores and photographers watch the birth announcements and send callers who offer to help meet the parents' needs. The Church should be no less alert. Enterprising Cradle Roll management, which works hard at enlarging the roll and at giving the church's help to the parents, can be a mighty evangelistic source.

c. A Church-School P.T.A.

A Parent-Teacher Association is a thousand times more needed for a church school than for a public school. Everyone recognizes why parents need to know one another and to know the teachers in secular schooling; all those reasons are vastly multiplied when the schooling has to do with religious faith and living.

Occasions are needed in which parents come to the church to meet their children's teachers and the pastor. They need to be told exactly what the church is trying to do for their children, and what is expected of them. They should know about what goes on in the school and what should be done at home to supplement it. They must understand the importance of bringing the children into

Church membership and be prepared to co-operate in it. It is irrational for a church school, which has direct contact with its pupils for only one hour a week, to try to operate independently of their homes.

The Roman Catholic Church makes very intelligent use of its parochial schools to win the parents of non-Catholic children. In some parishes such parents are required to take a course in religion and morality and to attend Catholic services if they wish to keep their children in the school. They are not obliged to go beyond that, but in some cities this is a chief source of converts to the Roman Catholic faith.

A church school must reach all the parents it possibly can in order to bring their children to Christ. It must reach all the children it possibly can in order to bring their parents to Christ. Both merit a church's best planning and effort. Its school offers a church an opportunity to win countless children and parents who could be reached in no other way.

Teachers' visits in the homes are important. Teachers are working in the dark until they have some knowledge of their pupils' family background and problems. That contact increases their intimacy with the pupils. Such visits give a chance to explain to the parents what the church school does and what they need to do. The visits are much more likely to be made if the school sets the time for them and gives some specific reason—perhaps the delivery of a piece of study material which needs to be explained to the parents or a conference on the lessons for the period just ahead.

d. Vacation or Weekday Church Schools

These schools can be powerful arms of the church in reaching the secular community. Too often the contacts they form are broken off when the school ends, with nothing left save a fading memory. In most cases a great deal more may easily be done to bring the pupils and their parents into the church's regular program.

e. Neighborhood Story Groups

Many churches are training women to gather the unchurched children of their neighborhoods in their homes for a weekly Bible-story hour. When the group is well established it may be transferred bodily to the Sunday school. This is a growing movement.

f. Teachers' Training for Evangelism

As a part of a project in Evangelism through Fellowship, and from time to time in any case, there is needed a meeting of all the officers and teachers to consider how pupils may be led to know Jesus Christ and to give their lives to Him. At this meeting the teachers are inspired, they study the evangelistic use of the teaching materials, they plan contacts with parents, they discuss how to be sure that every pupil who is old enough is offered a definite opportunity for making a decision.

g. Decisions

If talking to the pupils about Church membership is left to the initiative of each teacher, it is almost certain that some pupils will be missed entirely. There must be a systematic and thorough way of being sure that every pupil is brought face to face with the question of an open commitment to Christ. General announcements about joining the Church or entering a communicants' class are not enough.

"Decision Day" has become a valuable tradition in many churches. It is held for the entire Intermediate Department—sometimes also for the Seniors. Here is a typical arrangement for it: A month in advance the teachers are given written advice on how to talk the matter over in the class and with the pupils privately. Letters to the parents explain the day and ask them to counsel their children about their relationship to Christ and the Church, or to talk with the pastor about it. The classes concerned assemble in a room which is carefully planned to give the sense of reverence. After a brief worship service, the pastor talks for ten minutes about the claims of Christ and the Church. A hymn—perhaps "Jesus Calls Us"—is then sung. Pupils who intend to come into the Church may be asked to sign cards or to rise or to come forward. The teachers are sitting with their classes, ready to encourage any timid members. The teachers may come forward to stand with the pupils they have helped to win.

It is essential that the pupils and their parents be told in advance about the day. This may properly be a time of deep emotion. But the emotions aroused should be those that will grow stronger with the years, not those that will be remembered with embarrassment and resentment. The impulses which come from doing something with one's fellows are appropriate when coming into the Christian fellowship. But the arrangement must not be such that pupils will feel trapped into doing something they have no real desire to do.

h. Communicants' Classes

Most churches now recognize that special classes for the boys and girls who are coming into Church membership are indispensable.

There seems to be a tendency toward increasing the duration of these classes. Some churches now have them for an entire year, many continue them for a quarter, though the six- to eight-week period is still the most common.

Some churches bring into the communicants' class all the pupils of one of the grades in the Intermediate Department. This has the disadvantage of automatic membership instead of the sense of high purpose in entering the class. But it has the great advantage of winning some who at the outset had no thought of dedicating themselves to Christ through the Church.

Entrance into the class may be the result of a great personal decision. The attempts of earnest young people to bring their friends into the class can be a splendid form of youth evangelism.

If the classes are required of all who join the Church, this must be explained in writing to the parents. Otherwise some will be justly aggrieved if their children are barred at the time when their friends come into the Church.

The communicants' class must never be treated as just a matter of routine. The announcements and the conduct of it must reflect something of the romance and beauty and adventure of the Christian faith.

4. Young People

Most of the theory of evangelism and the methods discussed in this book apply to young people. Youth organizations can be extraordinarily successful in Evangelism through Fellowship. There are also some special methods for them.

a. Youth Week-end Program

Several denominations have recommended a program which is concentrated into three days. At a Friday evening supper the young people receive instructions and assignments. After two hours of calling they come back to the church to report and discuss their experiences. On Saturday morning there is a devotional period and more instruction and calling. Saturday afternoon there is instruction and calling. Saturday evening, after a dinner at the church, workers tell what they have learned, and their pastor helps bring the discussion to practical conclusions. On Sunday the church school and the youth organizations make special provision for welcoming and enrolling the young people who have been brought through the calling. The skills learned in this intensive period then become a permanent part of the youth work of the church.

b. Cells

Small groups, which meet regularly but informally for religious discussion or study or prayer, have had striking evangelistic results in some colleges. They generate a desire to help bring other students to a definite faith. They may include those who at the outset are only curious and seeking. The multiplication of such groups in dormitories and fraternity houses has been a remarkable recent development on some campuses.

c. Dates

A Church leader recently said that the influence which guided him toward Christianity at a time when his decisions were in the balance came from a girl he has not seen since the summer camp at which they were together. Christian young people can use for Christ the time they spend with each other. Such a purpose, too humorlessly pursued, might seem grim. But there is something about the mood of the boy-and-girl friendships which at times opens up the deepest subjects. At such times it is possible for a follower of Christ to give someone else an insight for which he or she will be grateful as long as life lasts. Church young people need to be reminded of this possibility.

d. Conferences

When anyone bewails the decline of some of the older evangelistic methods, the Church can point to the rise of youth conferences as a new method which can be far better than any which have been lost. Such a conference, when well conducted, is unsurpassed as a way of bringing young people to a lasting experience with Jesus Christ.

This purpose may be inhibited by the theory that such conferences should concentrate on the development of young people who are already in the church. But the two purposes can be combined. Abundant experience shows that the presence of unchurched young people does not have to lower the religious tone of a conference. Indeed, the eagerness of the church young people to win these others may keep the conference on a higher level of religious intensity. The same appeal which will win a beginner to dedication can bring a Christian to a much needed rededication. Study courses which increase the knowledge of a Church member can be opening up the possibilities of the Christian life to one who has not yet accepted it.

Conferences have learned how to use emotion in a wholesome way. The council ring, the dedication service, the Lord's Supper can be powerfully used to bring young people to give their lives to Christ.

e. Retreats

Many churches each year take their young people away for a week end to some spot from which they can get a new perspective on themselves and on the youth work of their church. Young people from outside the church are often included. The fine fellowship, the sense of God in the beauty of the out-of-doors, the times of worship and the great purposes discussed may be wonderfully effective in opening young hearts to Jesus Christ.

f. Older Young People

The forgotten age in many churches is the late teens and early twenties. The high-school-age classes and fellowship clubs have been left behind; there is no interest in adult groups. The strongest tendency to drift away comes at the very age when a series of crises make the Church specially necessary. Those at this stage are making the trying transitions from school to job, from dependence to independence, from immaturity to citizenship. They are in the midst of the stresses of courtship and marriage.

This age is admittedly difficult to hold in the usual church program. It is a period when reverse evangelism is especially severe. But the hopeless way in which many churches simply let their older young people go cannot be justified—there are other churches which are eminently successful with them.

A program for this age cannot follow the well-worn paths of least resistance. It requires unusual initiative. Some of the denominations supply excellent guidance. A local church will be wise to study the suggestions of more than one denomination.

g. Young Couples

There are vistas in romantic love which give glimpses into infinity. Having a baby is a miracle by which even the most frivolous are awed. This may be why young married people are among the easiest for the Church to win. Young people who have drifted from the Church are often ready to come back to it again just after they have married. Those who have never felt any need for the Church may turn to it eagerly when their children are small.

The young married couples' club is the greatest evangelistic agency in many churches. The youthful high spirits of the members, combined with a new earnest view on life, often makes them the most ardently energetic in winning others. They are at the age when those whose friendships have been largely with the unmarried are anxious to form friendships with other couples like themselves. A church which does not have a special club for young married couples has not opened the door through which the greatest number might be coming into its fellowship.

5. Choirs

In the past few years pastors have been discovering the wonderful evangelistic possibilities in their choirs. Adults who at first would come for no other reason come to the choir because they love to sing; through that they are brought into the church. Boys and girls in youth choirs grow in their appreciation of Christian truth and worship; their parents, who come to services because their children are participating, keep coming. Adding new choirs, and new members to the choirs, is one of the most effective evangelistic methods the modern church has developed.

XII

Inquirers' Groups

The Inquirers' Group is a powerful evangelistic method which is being increasingly used. Many pastors are discovering that they can present the claims of Christianity in a peculiarly forceful way in a small group where people hear and discuss. It is a twentieth-century adaptation of the Catechumenate on which the early Church relied for converts. It is more directly personal than pulpit evangelism and can make a more thorough appeal for faith than does visitation evangelism. It is peculiarly suited to modern minds. It will win some whom nothing else can reach.

Many who are spiritually hungry and confused stay aloof from the Church. They will not be won by preaching; visitors will find them prejudiced against the Church and skeptical. But intellectual curiosity and restlessness may make them glad to attend a group where beliefs are discussed in an informal, undogmatic way.

A suburban pastor urges his church members to bring their nonmember friends to a five-week "School for Skeptics." One of the most rapidly growing churches in the country directs much of its evangelistic effort to bringing people who have no intention of joining the church into its adult communicants' classes; for many the result is a conversion experience. A New Jersey pastor has several times each year a series of five fireside evenings at the manse to which his young people or his couples' club bring their friends who are not church members. One of the most successful presentations of Christianity to Jewish people in New York is done by a pastor who invites his Jewish neighbors and friends, and their friends, to his apartment for extended religious discussions, with various leaders. In a famous Eastern university for the past few years there have been groups of unconvinced but searching students who meet regularly in several of the dormitories to discuss what Christianity can have for them.

Like many modern evangelistic methods, this one saves much more time than it consumes. A minister can do far more in six evenings with twelve people together than in twice that many evenings spent in calling at their homes.

"School of Life," "Seekers' Forum," "Faith Clinic," "Inquirers' Group"—a wide variety of names has been used. The informal ones usually take no name at all.

1. Starting

Some of the best groups are started by lay members. This helps give the feeling of the unusual—which is essential. There is great advantage when a group invites a pastor to be with them rather than the pastor inviting the group. But the idea may have come from him. He may publicly recommend the plan or discuss it in private with some of his members.

Church people may ask their pastor to come to a series of meetings in their homes, to which they can bring their unconvinced friends. A workman may arrange for his pastor to meet with him and some of his fellow workers while they eat their lunches. One of the church organizations may start such a group. A public forum on beliefs may be held at the church.

Such a gathering must never seem like just another church meeting. Doubters must be able to discuss their doubts without feeling out of place. For that reason, the nonmembers should outnumber the members. It is well to announce that a church member may come only when bringing a nonmember.

Lay evangelistic visiting, or an appeal from the pulpit, having failed to win a decision, may next offer an invitation to a class on what Christianity is. This will often be eagerly accepted. An Inquirers' Group may start after a series of evangelistic preaching services which have asked for decisions to attend such a group. A group may be started after a neighborhood religious census, with personal invitations being taken to all who seem available.

The minister, in his private conversations and in his sermons, may ask people to come to the group.

Nonchurch parents of church-school pupils may be told that

their attendance at an Inquirers' Group is an important part of the church's training of their children.

Such groups are of great help in the problem of mixed marriages. The non-Protestant often welcomes the chance to learn more about Protestantism. Whether or not this leads to Church membership, it can at least make a more sympathetic understanding.

Reminders by mail or telephone will keep those who have started from missing meetings.

2. Content

Inquirers' Groups consider Christian beliefs, behavior, the Christian view of social problems, the Church, the reasons for Church membership, the ways to spiritual health.

A good sequence to follow in the meetings is this: (a) an explanation of some basic Christian belief, (b) the reasons for believing it, (c) the differences it makes in daily living, (d) discussion of whether the belief can be accepted as true, (e) an attempt to reach some agreement about it.

Discussion is valuable, but only after something to discuss has been clearly presented. Members of large groups may be asked to present their questions in writing.

Some way to combine religious practice with the theoretical discussions is important. Those who come may be asked to try church attendance between classes, Bible reading, the use of some prayer method or a devotional help. These experiences can then be discussed when the group meets. Prayer at the meetings may seem out of place at the start, but grow more appropriate as the intimacy and spiritual interest develop.

Some manual, or a selection of pamphlets on the subjects to be discussed, may be used. Many pastors mimeograph study material or reminders of what has been presented to the group. Outside reading may be proposed.

3. The Leader and His Methods

The pastor is the natural leader for such a group, though some lay leaders have been highly successful. On a campus a popular professor is often invited to lead.

Much that is said about the teacher of a class for new members and his methods (in Chapter XIV:B:5) applies here. It is important that the class be kept lively. The leader's manner should be friendly and conversational, with his enthusiasm for the subject making it shine. Too churchly expressions should be avoided, unless they have the lift of poetry. Humor and illustrations are good. Moving pictures, slides, charts and a blackboard are very useful with larger groups.

Words cannot be wasted. Great subjects must be covered briefly. The leader must exercise stern self-discipline to keep from stealing the time from the discussion. Therefore careful preparation is essential. The first attempt with such a group may be the least satisfying. The content and methods will improve with experience.

Some leaders review each time all that has gone before. In large groups written or oral examinations add excitement and the sense of importance.

Private conversations with those who are attending give a chance to talk about questions or needs which would not be mentioned in the group. Such conversations can be arranged by appointment.

Some groups have an understanding that each member expects to have a private interview with the leader.

The question of joining the Church should be raised with the whole group. It becomes definite in private interviews or in the use of decision cards or by asking openly who intend to join. There may be one or two extra meetings for those who decide to come into the Church.

4. Arrangements

The name, address, and church experience of each one who attends should be recorded. This may not be done at the first meeting, for fear of frightening some away.

Schedules vary greatly—from four to thirty meetings—from twice a week to once a month. Most meet on week nights, though some come on Sunday mornings or evenings. The seasons before and after Christmas and before and after Easter are the most popular, though good Inquirers' Groups have been held during the summer.

Two or more churches may unite in holding an Inquirers' Group—with the ministers sharing the teaching, or with one the teacher and another the administrator.

XIII

Evangelism by Pastoral Services

1. Marriage

A pastor's interview with a couple he is going to marry deals with the deepest issues of life. It is therefore an incomparable evangelistic opportunity. He explains that marriage is not a human arrangement—it is a divine institution, established by God for human blessing. The ring is passed among the bride and the groom and the representative of the Church because God is a party to the contract, and the promises are also being made to him. (See also pages 30-31 and 139-41.)

In many cases a pastor cannot or should not bring a couple into his own church. In his dealing with them before the service and in his solicitude afterward, he is trying to bring them to some church somewhere.

2. Baptism

Most churches which practice infant baptism require that at least one parent be a "professing Christian." This one-time profession may have had so little value that evangelism is necessary if the baptism is to have any meaning at all. The occasion may offer the best of all chances to bring the nonprofessing parent to faith.

Many parents take it for granted that a baby should be baptized, without much idea why. It may have little more religious significance for them than the christening (i.e., Christianizing) of a battleship or a supermarket. The minister must begin at the rudiments to explain what sort of faith and practice are required of the parents if the child is truly, as the sacrament means, to be brought into the presence of Christ from the very beginning of its consciousness. Whatever be the scriptural arguments for or against infant baptism, certainly the practice of many pastors in treating it as

though it were magic—neither instructing parents in their obliga·
tions nor looking for evidence that they are prepared to fufill those
obligations—has no sort of justification.

The preparation of the parents is straight evangelism, and it is
one of the most favorable occasions for it. Pastoral calls or interviews at the church may be the method. Some churches set quar-
terly dates for infant baptisms, with meetings in advance at which
the parents are prepared in a group. Written materials may supplement the verbal instruction. Godparents, on the assumption that
they are stand-by parents who may have to perform a parent's
duties, can be asked to take the preparation.

Denominations which do not baptize babies, but do have a
service at which they are consecrated and their parents ordained
to their holy office, may make the preparation of the parents for
that service an evangelistic process.

When a minister tells parents, "We will not baptize your baby
until you are a professing Christian," there is danger that he may
seem to be trying to use the baby to force the parents into membership. He must explain gently and carefully why evidence of Christian faith is necessary, why the Church is needed in the Christian
rearing of a child, why a sacrament of the Church can have no value
to those for whom the Church has no value. He may seem less
arbitrary if this explanation can be given in a printed form, together with a quotation from the rules of his denomination.

Adult baptism may give evangelistic contact with those who are
present when it is administered, or who can be brought with the
candidate for the preparatory talks—parents, husbands, wives and
friends.

3. Funerals

The evangelistic use and abuse of funerals is endlessly perplex-
ing. There is no conventional way to have a burial without a religious service. This gives a minister access to many whom he can
reach at no other time. If he uses his visits with the family to give
very pointed evangelistic urging, they may feel that they have
been trapped. If he uses the service to stress the importance of
preparing for death by accepting Christ, he may find that a captive
audience is not a very receptive one.

In his attempts to comfort a stricken family, or to impress a callous one, the minister must remember his Lord's consideration for the bruised reed and the smoking flax. He tries to waken as much faith, and to bring as much help through prayer, as he possibly can, without going too far beyond where he will be followed. At the service he can speak a good word for Christ and refer, perhaps in a prayer, to God's intention for life, without seeming to exploit sorrow for promotional purposes.

Those who have found a minister's kindness and sympathy to be their great help in time of trouble will be gratefully drawn to him and to his faith. The direct evangelism which this makes possible may best be commenced after the distraction of the funeral and the first grief have passed.

4. Pastoral Counseling

All pastors are sought out for counsel by some who are not in the church—parents of church young people, distressed neighbors. Pastors who let it be known that they are available to give help, and who announce stated times and ways for people to come to them, may have many who seek them for advice on personal or family problems or emotional upsets.

A pastor will fail these people if all he has to offer is pat admonitions to pray and read the Bible and come to church. In many cases that will be like advising a drowning man to swim. But it is equally sure that a pastor will not have given his best help until he brings people to rely on a higher power than their own and to seek wholeness and wisdom from communication with God, as Jesus Christ revealed Him. He will need to bring people to the health which comes through fellowship and to the support of sound spiritual habits and to the guidance of the Scriptures.

A sudden evangelism may not be the first answer to people's troubles, but all Christian counseling must point people to Christian faith and living. If it stops short of evangelism, it is unfinished.

"Just how do you get at it?" "What do you say?" are questions which bother many pastors. Love and prayer and experience are dependable teachers. Much can be learned from such books on counseling as those by Dr. John Sutherland Bonnell. Chapter 6 of *The Practice of Evangelism,* by Bryan Green, has splendid help.

XIV

The Care of New Members

A. The Principles

1. The Urgent Need

The most encouraging feature of modern evangelism is the increased attention it is giving to better ways of receiving, training and holding those who join the Church. This is long overdue. The most important part of evangelism comes after decisions have been made. The greatest weakness of the evangelism of the past was that it stopped too soon.

The saddest figures in all the statistics of American churches are those which tell that, of every two persons received on profession of faith, one has been dropped as a failure. Think of that, next time new members are being welcomed into a church. Mentally cast half of them out the door again because, in the typical church, that is what is going to happen.

As disastrous may be the unrecorded number of those who remain on church rolls, considered by themselves and others to be typical Church members, but almost totally unaffected by the Church and its faith. The whole impact of the Church on the world is weakened because it has so many in its membership who have never really understood what the Church is. On an average Sunday, two-thirds of the members will not be at the churches to which they have vowed loyalty. As Dr. Frederick H. Olert has said, "Of every 100 enrolled members, 5 cannot be found, 20 never pray, 25 never read the Bible, 30 never attend a church, 40 never give to any cause, 50 never go to Sunday School, 60 never go to church at night, 70 never give to missions, 75 never do any church work, 80 never go to prayer meeting, 90 do not have family worship, 95 never win another soul for Christ."

We are so familiar with this record of failure that we are in danger of accepting it as something to be expected—like the wasteful prodigality of nature. But there is no law of nature to excuse it. It is the direct result of our careless and unrealistic practices. This is shown by the fact that congregations which give exceptional attention to the care of new members often keep more than 90 per cent of them loyal and enthusiastic.

On that melancholy evening when the church officers meet to purge the roll (and what a dreadful expression that is!) they are likely to be in a critical mood—"These people never kept their vows; they were unfaithful." In all honesty it is more likely to be the church which broke its vows and was unfaithful. As a lawyer said when he returned from evangelistic calling, "It suddenly came to me that we had made these people a proposition, and they took us up on it. Now we are on a spot, and I don't know whether we can make good or not." The casual way in which many a church leaves it up to its new members to shift for themselves shows small regard for the solemn obligation it assumed in its expressed pledges of "affection, nurture and care."

Not one person in fifty joins the Church without expecting to make a success of it. Almost all come looking for something, led by the vision of a better sort of life. Everyone who is lost is a spiritual disaster. Each broken hope is a shameful indictment of a church. A church which has "cleansed" itself by dropping a long list of names never comes out looking very clean.

If we treated newborn babies as carelessly as we treat newborn Christians, the infant mortality rates would equal the appalling mortality of Church members. The obstetrician must be followed by the pediatrician. As William J. McCullough sagely says, "I never saw a bassinet without sides."

The "losses from the back door" are a major problem in every denomination. The best place to prevent losses from the back door is at the front door. There is much anxious talk about how to reclaim those who left the Church of Christ when they left the little home-town building, and how to revive those who were stillborn years ago. Overshadowing all our necessary struggles with these problems is the fact that we have waited too long. A tenth of the work would have had ten times as much chance of success if it had been done earlier. Halfway evangelism leaves people farther than ever from the Kingdom. Those with whom a church has failed have been so damaged that they are the hardest to win. A guard rail at the top of a cliff is better than ambulance service at its foot.

2. The Doctrinal Basis

Our unrealistic practice has partly come from a misunderstanding of what happens when a person joins the Church. We have assumed, because of a newly professed faith in Christ, that a soul has been born into the Kingdom and the miracle of regeneration has occurred. In that we are presuming to know what only God can know. Most Americans have a sentimental liking for the name of Jesus Christ, even when they have very little idea Who He is. An apparent convert may have accepted, not the living Christ, but an imaginary character who is called by His name. Most people who have heard Christmas carols over the radio think that they know what Christianity is, and they may answer in all sincerity that they accept it. The words of the questions which are asked can mean so much or so little that the church may not realize how many of its members are received on confusion of faith.

By our visitors or from our pulpits we ask people, "Would you like to be a follower of Christ?" and if they reply that indeed they would, we are likely to say, in effect, "Then come to the church next Wednesday night and you will be one." When to our question, "Do you wish to be saved?" the answer is "Yes," we sometimes seem to conclude, "Good! Now you are."

There is no Bible support for the idea that when people have made an apparently sincere acceptance of Christ, they are soundly launched in the Christian life. The Great Commission puts "baptizing" before "teaching them to observe all things"—the part we are too likely to neglect (Matthew 28:19-20). The three thousand who were baptized on the Day of Pentecost next were given intensive "teaching." The statement that "the Lord added to their number day by day those who were being saved" clearly implies that more time and nurture were required within the Church (Acts 2:42 and 47, R.S.V.). That also is seen in the arrested development of the Samaritans whose progress toward being full Christians stopped just after they had been baptized—a not unfamiliar happening today (Acts 8:14-17). While we are finding texts, it is not wresting Scripture to apply what the wise man of the Proverbs said, "The slothful man roasteth not that which he took in hunting" (Proverbs 12:27).

When we encourage new members to feel that the decisive thing is finished when they join the Church, it is no wonder that they think they are doing all that is necessary when, like beaming old graduates, they return for the annual alumni reunion at Easter.

3. The Historical Development

The New Testament Church required little preparation before candidates were baptized and received into the fellowship. All the members were first-generation Christians and beginners; the whole Church was a communicants' class. In the centuries immediately following, however, beginners were required to wait for a two- or three-year period of probation before they were admitted to the company of established Christians. During this time they were given intensive instruction and examined for evidences of the genuineness of their faith. That is the practice of some Protestant Churches in mission lands. In Korea candidates are supposed to bring another person to faith in Christ before they can be received into the Church.

In America many Churches receive anyone who will express a desire and accept a very brief statement of faith. There are reasons for this. In a culture which is at least nominally Christian it is difficult to assume that those outside the Church are not in any sense Christians. We may believe that those who sincerely wish to follow Christ will become what Christians ought to be more readily if they are taken into the Church than if they are left waiting outside the door. The miracle of regeneration may be more likely to occur within the fellowship than in the cold uncertainty of a period of probation. Some believe that any hindrance to the impulse to join the Church is an interference with the working of the Holy Spirit. Though many liturgical Churches prescribe confirmation classes for both children and adults, and Pentecostal Churches require the experience of a crisis as evidence that the

Holy Ghost has been received, the tendency has been to snatch people into the Churches at the first evidence that they are willing.

Moving up the date for reception does not in any way lessen the need of a period for guidance and instruction. The Church's responsibility to members who are received immediately is exactly what it would be if they were still on probation.

Recently more and more Churches have been increasing their requirements for membership. This is a recognizable movement. One denomination stated as an aim of its three-year, nationwide evangelistic crusade: "To make church joining twice as frequent and twice as difficult as ever before." Among these new requirements for membership are a course of preparatory classes, attendance at services over a stated period, a financial pledge, the reading of literature, the writing out of a statement of personal faith or experience, a detailed private conference with church officers.

Many declare that the adding of such conditions, instead of diminishing receptions, increases them. The First Presbyterian Church of Hollywood often led its denomination in the annual number of receptions. When this church made the completion of a series of classes a requirement, the number of those seeking admission immediately began to grow. Dr. Louis H. Evans, the pastor, said, "People value what is not too easy; the more seriously a church takes its membership, the more important it seems to those outside."

There is danger of trying to make admission to the Church so easy and painless that people will scarcely know that anything has happened. The fear that people will not join the Church if any effort is required may not be wholesome. Such effort may have a value in eliminating those who are not really in earnest. A church which will enroll as a believer anyone who has been heard to say, "Thank God it quit raining," is sometimes supposed to have an advantage over its more exacting neighbors; that supposition is probably not well founded. People prize what costs them something. The characteristic zeal of members of the immersionist Churches may owe more than is generally recognized to the requirement of a physical ordeal at the beginning of their membership.

4. The Practical Necessities

New members require much which they will not get in the regular program of a church for all its members. Pastors who believe that their sermons will serve as communicants' instruction are not very realistic. New members have a great deal of catching up to do which must be done in a direct, intensive way. They do not have the feel or the knowledge or the attitudes which healthy church participation requires. Unless they are given some sort of special treatment, they are likely to assume that their immature state is normal for Church members, and so they never will grow out of it.

"Form them while they still are pliable," must be the rule. After people have been in the Church for a year, they are likely to assume that their opinions on religious matters are as good as anyone's. From then on, an attempt to change them very much may seem to them to be presumptuous. It is during the period of joining that people are most humbly ready to be told what Church members ought to be.

New Church members may not understand that Christians are a different sort of beings, with a completely distinctive way of thinking and living and dying. "If any man be in Christ, he is a new creature: old things are passed away; behold, all things are become new" (II Corinthians 5:17). Christ may be accepted as a good influence, instead of as the all-commanding center of existence. People are likely in all honesty to think of joining the Church merely as forming a helpful connection, instead of as entering into a new and all-inclusive way of life. An ardent sentiment for the Church may be cherished by those whose opinions and decisions are governed entirely by the motives of the world.

Dr. E. Stanley Jones says that goldfish taken from a bowl and put into a pond will at first only swim in small circles no larger than their bowl was. Those who have formed outside the Church their business ethics, their attitudes toward other races, their ways of having a good time and their ideas on the use of money are likely to retain them without change unless they are shown the peculiarly Christian view of such matters. New habits are notoriously hard for adults to commence. Help will be needed if there is to be a change in long-established customs of speech and behavior, of home life and Sabbath use.

No great thing, from building a bridge to playing a violin, is ever done without techniques. That finest of masterpieces, a Christian life, can be achieved only by using the techniques which have been prescribed in the Bible or developed through centuries of experiment. Christians should not be expected to discover those methods for themselves. They are a birthright which the Church is supposed to transmit. New Church members are defrauded of their heritage when they are merely told in general what to do, without being told specifically how to do it.

Regular participation in the Sabbath services is of vital importance for bringing new members into Christian fellowship and understanding. But long-established habits of nonattendance will not be broken by a few blithe words of advice. When people are told to read their Bibles without being told how, they are likely to end bogged down in the statistical tables of the book of Numbers. Exhortations to pray without practical advice on how to do it may bring people only to the point of suspecting that prayer is vastly overrated. The family altar can be had in a wide variety of modern styles; but unless these are described, people may despair of fitting so Victorian a furnishing into present-day homes. Many church members have remained handicapped in public worship because they have never understood just what the parts of the service are getting at or what is expected of the worshiper.

Every Church which is bringing real Christianity into the lives of people is giving its converts meticulous instruction in techniques. The Wesleyans became great, and became Methodists, because of their insistence upon methods. Every Church in which faith is going dead begins to take an aloof view of rules.

Rules are as important for Protestants as for others. Protestants are more likely to get their rules observed by promises than by threats. They allow some personal latitude in deciding what the rules will be. Their discipline is self-discipline, under the guidance of the Church. But Protestant churches know that if they do not give those who come to them specific and down-to-earth rules for spiritual health, they become flabby and dispirited.

Peter gave a good outline of what must be covered in the training and assimilation of new members (II Peter 1:5-7, R.S.V.). As a check list for the growth of new Christians he specified: (1) Faith (the feeling for Christ—dedication of life to Him). (2) Virtue (right behavior). (3) Knowledge (of the facts about Christianity and the Church). (4) Self-control (freedom from lapses, i.e., firm habits). (5) Steadfastness (strength of character). (6) Godliness (spiritual practices). (7) Brotherly affection (being at home in the church family). (8) Love (the distinctively Christian attitude toward one's fellow men). It is training in those things which an adequate program for new members will include.

Transplants are often more fragile than seedlings. Those who are received by letter of transfer require special care. The new congregation will not seem like the familiar friends back home. The different ways of doing things may seem wrong. Homesickness may turn into resentment of the new church. The precarious process of adjusting to life in a new place may let church habits be crowded out. It is therefore important that those who come by transfer be brought into as much of the new-member program as possible. They will need the preparatory conference with the minister who is to take the place of their former pastor. While it might not seem realistic to require loyal, long-time members from another church to attend classes on belief and churchmanship, they are often anxious to do so. If it is shown to be desirable, a good many of them will come without being required. They will need the introduction to the organizations and activities of their new church. All the ways of making them feel a part of the church family are particularly important—calls, social events, sponsors.

5. Two Prerequisites

We need to remember always that any methods we may use to establish new Church members in the Christian life depend for their success upon previous conditions.

First—the new member must have had *a definite sense of turning to Christ* in a warm and personal way. As Dr. Samuel M. Shoemaker has well said, "Many churches are carefully shepherding and trying to train a lot of people who have never begun a decisive spiritual experience. How can one nurture a plant before it has taken root? How can one bring up a child that is not born?"

This spiritual experience may have been brought through a church service or a young people's conference. It may have come from a conversation with earnest visitors. It may have first been recognized in some moment of flashing insight or have developed so gradually that it is connected with no definite event. It may, indeed, come during the process of training new members. But unless it comes, that process will be useless. Let us never think that by classes and sponsors and all the other techniques we can make Christians of those who have never had the feel of faith.

Second—there must be *a genuinely spiritual quality in the church.* The most elaborate system for "processing" new members would fail unless the church itself, in its fellowship and program, is revealing to them what Christianity is.

That does not mean that a church should say, "First we must have a revival and then we will start being evangelistic." God will never give a revival to a church that is postponing its concern for those outside it. But in every step of its evangelism it must keep an anxious eye upon itself and be finding, in its very desire to win others, a motive for striving constantly to deepen and purify itself.

We can be shocked into self-examination by a grim phrase Samuel Chadwick used. Blaming himself for allowing some of his young converts, who had soon lapsed, to get into a church which was cold and apathetic, he said that "It was like putting a baby in the arms of a corpse."

This explains why we have to be very dubious about a church which declares that its policy is to win fewer people and to win them soundly. It gives a new member a poor start to bring him into a church which is purposely soft-pedaling evangelism. The most healthy possible atmosphere for a new Christian is found in a warmly evangelistic church which is so enthusiastic about its faith that it is eager to share it. There is a tonic for new members in the sense of lay activity and spiritual awareness and exciting accomplishment which a strong evangelistic program brings.

The facts fit that theory. Throughout the country it will be found that the churches which are doing most for the members they receive are the ones which are working hardest at winning more. There is danger of admitting members faster than they are being assimilated. That danger, however, is not removed by receiving fewer—a self-defeating strategy—but by working harder at assimilation. A well-organized church could double its membership every year, and do it soundly. A church which begins to talk about limiting its receptions to some sort of quota is simply trying to escape the labor required by a good new-member program.

Good methods for the care of new members work backward and affect the whole membership. Those who, by calls or talks or sponsoring, are trying to show what Christianity and the Church are all about, are impressing themselves. If each group of those admitted is ardent and devoted, a new spiritual springtime will begin to spread throughout the congregation. A church membership can best be transformed at the point of entry.

6. How to Organize for It

Abuse of congregational freedom is responsible for much of the shockingly inadequate care of new members. Most denominations specify a bare minimum of what must be done for those who join them, on the theory that the local churches should be allowed to provide in their own way for the great deal more that is needed. But often the result is that the local churches do nothing beyond the prescribed minimum.

The official board of every church must annually devote at least one full meeting, with no other business, to its methods of caring for those who join the church. This must be done regularly because without regular upkeep all church machinery rapidly falls into disrepair, and because improvements in the methods will always be needed. This cannot be left to the pastor—it is lay business. Of the methods to be listed in this chapter, it will be seen that, while some depend almost entirely on the minister, the larger number are the responsibility of the lay members of the church. It requires a large amount of manpower for a church properly to assimilate its new members. The officers should never have a chance to forget that this second half of evangelism makes large demands of them and of the other members.

A committee may need to do preliminary work before the official group has its meeting on this—determining how well the church has been succeeding with those it has received, learning whether past plans have been carried out, investigating what other churches are doing, examining new literature on the subject, drafting recommendations to be proposed.

Here again we come to that primary axiom—SHORT CUTS IN EVANGELISM NEVER WORK! There may be time-wasting ways which should be dropped, but no quick and easy ways will ever be discovered. Christian lives are never mass produced. A great number of personal encounters are required. A church which cannot get a good many of its members to give time for the various phases of its new-member program will surely fail in its evangelism.

This second half of evangelism is less exciting than the first. Getting decisions is thrilling. It is like a game that can be scored. The results come rapidly. But bringing those decisions to fulfillment in an established Christian life is not very dramatic. It takes months instead of minutes. That is why churches are so prone to stop their evangelism in mid-course. It is this unglamorous second half which reveals the real heart of a church. The romance is there —but not for the superficial. There is no way for a church to get around God's exacting tests. Only those who prove their devotion by their patient, painstaking efforts can succeed.

There is wry humor in the fact that, when any method for church work is proposed, large churches are likely to dismiss it as useful only in a simpler setting, and small churches say sadly that they are not big enough to try it. The requirements for the care of new members are the same in the country or the city, in artless or sophisticated churches. The methods to be considered in this chapter are being used in churches of every size and sort. They are not too intimate for large churches, whose tendency to be impersonal makes the provision for friendly contacts specially needed. They are not beyond the capacity of the minister with no employed assistance, who most of all has to have efficient ways of organizing his work.

One more caution about the methods—churches are notoriously prone to congratulate themselves on beautiful plans, quite apart from their performance. The most impressive machinery is useless unless someone turns the crank. When the officers have laid out a sound new-member plan, let them give particular care to the you-go-do-it part. At their meetings they should, as a regular order of business, check on how well it is operating.

A new member plan never works well the first year! With no smooth routines and with annoying loose ends, it is burdensome and irregular. But if the church persists, in the second year it becomes far easier than the old disorganized way of worrying about what ought to be done, and by the third year it can be an exciting success.

Some churches make the Membership Committee or the Evangelism Committee responsible for the various parts of the new-member program; others have a special New Member Committee, under a lay chairman who will find in this an immensely satisfying service. In any arrangement, guidance and reminders from the pastor will be necessary.

B. The Methods

1. The Pastor's Preparatory Conference

A preliminary interview with the pastor is essential.

a. Even those who are completely committed to Church membership will need to know more about it than could be told them at the time of their decision, however that decision may have been made. This may discover a few who are not really ready to join the Church. It is much more likely to bring a great increase of enthusiasm and dedication.

b. The new purpose may have made it seem urgently important to discuss certain questions of belief or conduct. For example, a man who had gratefully promised to join the Church began to worry over what the Church would say about his divorce of many years before. A prospective Presbyterian was unhappy about predestination.

c. Spiritual guidance for new members is important in this call —advice about prayer and Bible reading and church attendance and religion in the home and witnessing.

d. The mechanics of coming into membership need to be arranged and dates set.

e. The pastor needs to become a friend of those who will be members of his flock. He needs a knowledge of their backgrounds and interests and personalities. They need to think of him as someone whom they like and trust.

Some ministers schedule these interviews at their studies. It is usually better to have them in the homes of the prospective members.

This interview gives a good opportunity to introduce literature which new members are supposed to read. Some ministers center a part of the conversation on a printed application for membership or on a mimeographed list of questions.

There is danger that this conference will be largely a social call —discovering mutual friends and interests. While that has some friendly value, there is too much to be done to waste the opportunity in casual chatter.

Knowing that the whole church career is influenced by the view at the outset, the minister tries to show the deep importance of the step that is being taken and the majesty and glory of Church membership. He tells about the local church and its opportunities. He mentions the responsibilities of membership. He gives a preview of the questions which will be asked at the time of reception. He tries to get the prospective member to ask questions and to talk.

Some churches have a lay committee which interviews separately each candidate for membership. While this can be of great value, it does not take the place of a conference with the pastor.

If there is a probation period, there may be a series of conferences to guide the candidate's progress.

2. Written Forms

A typical *Application for Membership* (sometimes called an *Invitation to Membership*) contains: (a) Spaces for biographical data—name, home and business addresses and telephone numbers, date of birth (some add delicately "if under 25"), church history and activities, whether or not baptized, other members of the family and their church connections, where to send for a letter of transfer. (b) An explanation of the ways of joining the Church, with the one which applies to be checked. (c) The statements of faith which new members accept. (d) The vows they take. (e) A listing of the church organizations and forms of service, with those in which there is special interest or experience to be checked.

The following are less common: (f) Spaces for a financial pledge. (g) An outline of the new member program (classes, etc.)

and a promise to participate in it. (h) Information about the church—a picture, a brief history, a description of its activities, a cordial invitation to it. (i) Inspirational statements, Bible verses, poetry.

There are great advantages in application forms:

a. They give prospective members a chance to think in advance about the faith they will be asked to profess. They are expected to make the most searching statements the human mind can conceive. If the questions are asked on the spur of the moment, with no opportunity to meditate about them, the candidates may properly feel that this is just a traditional formality, not to be taken very seriously. They may rightly be resentful if they think they have been tricked into saying things they do not really mean.

b. When the vows are presented in writing, they can be given serious consideration. By those vows people bind their whole lives; they pledge thousands of hours of their time; they make promises which affect every hour and every minute—every attitude and act. It is unfair and absurd to ask that to be done suddenly. When members are suspended for unfaithfulness, if they had a chance to talk back many of them could say with complete justice, "We didn't take the vows seriously because you didn't take them seriously. They were sprung on us at the last minute when we had no chance to say anything but 'Yes.' It was plain that they were not supposed to mean very much." The wording of admission forms is often not in the language of every day and needs to be explained. Many who have readily promised "to make diligent use of the means of grace" would be astonished to learn that they had promised to go to church.

c. Written forms collect in an orderly way the personal information which it is otherwise endlessly troublesome to get.

d. Impressive and attractive written forms emphasize the importance of joining the Church.

e. A written form makes it easy to bring a conversation to the great issues of the Christian faith and of the Church. The pastor in his preliminary conference with a prospective member can refer to the written statements of faith and the vows and, without any groping or presuming, be straight on the subjects he came to talk about. Evangelistic visitors sometimes use an Application for

Membership. A long form may be a distraction and obscure the decisive issue, which is why a simple decision card is more often used. But that danger can be avoided. Some experienced evangelistic visitors declare that the easiest and most natural way to get onto religious subjects is to read aloud the statements of faith and the vows on an Application for Membership, and to ask after each one, "You could say that, couldn't you? Does that raise any questions?"

The form most often used has four six-by-nine-inch pages, usually with a picture or a Bible verse or an inspirational passage on the front cover. The next most frequent size has four pages about eight and a half by eleven inches. Many use four-by-six-inch cards, printed on both sides. Cards cannot be very complete and must be cramped, but they can be more conveniently carried in pockets or used in the pews.

Some very attractive examples have been mimeographed, but the final cost even for excellent printing is not large, since only one copy is used for each new member. Good thought and careful design are more important than expense. Some of the best have been produced by very small churches. It is better for a church to design its own than to try to order some standardized form. It must fit the program and ideas of the local church and have that church's personal touch.

A *Certificate of Membership* is a record and memento of one of the great events in life. The Application must finally be returned to the church, but the Certificate can be kept. It contains the statements of faith and the vows, so that these need not be forgotten. It has the official record of the date and mode of reception, over the signature of the pastor and any lay officer who signs official documents. Often there are Bible verses or other inspirational lines. There may be a set of brief rules for spiritual living or for how to get the most from church life.

Membership certificates are often considerably ornamented, perhaps with a picture of the church or of a religious painting. They may be printed on one of the impressively engraved blank forms which stationers supply. Some churches give a certificate small enough to be carried in a wallet, folded double. The best ones may be supplied by the denominations. Unlike the application, a membership certificate does not have to be specially adapted to a local situation, and there is some advantage if it is a tie, not only to one congregation but to the whole Church.

A *description of the reception and assimilation procedures* is often given to new or prospective members. It tells to whom the various methods of admission apply; it explains about baptism; it describes just what is done in receiving members and why it is done; it tells about classes and literature and any other features of the new member program. This written information is valuable in helping candidates to understand what is to be done and in gaining their co-operation.

3. The Reception by the Officers

(This section is for denominations in which members are received into the Church at a meeting of an official board. Some of its suggestions may be adapted to other forms of reception.)

The greatest event in a Christian's life is the entrance into Church membership. Other occasions which are celebrated with much ceremony cannot compare with this one in earthly and eternal significance. It should be a grand and joyful memory. The lifelong feeling about a church membership depends much on the impression which was made at the time of joining.

It must never be hurried, though the temptations are many. There may be a mass of other business; the officers' families may be impatient to get home; it may be crowded in with some other event to save a trip to the church. But tension and haste and off-handedness at such a time dishonor the Church and the Holy Spirit. It can almost be said that members should never be received just before or after a Sunday morning service.

Candidates should be brought to the meeting by officers who shield the timid from the pain of confronting a strange group. Relatives and friends may come, if such meetings are not closed. The atmosphere and use of prayer are important, but a stiff solemnity is not appropriate for so joyful an occasion. Candidates should be introduced with some friendly word about the circumstances which brought them to the church.

The questioning of candidates is serious, but it should be less an inquisition than a helpful interview. As Dr. McAfee said,

"Officers who are sticklers for fine points of doctrine or behavior ought to exercise their zeal on their fellow officers instead of on candidates." The profession of faith and the vows should be clearly separated. Churches are increasingly asking candidates to tell in their own words such things as why they seek membership or what Christ means to them or how they expect to serve Him. If this is to be done, they should be told in advance; the very inarticulate can be helped to prepare answers in writing.

Forming a new church connection is one of life's landmarks. Even when Church law does not require those who come by transfer to be received in a meeting, there is great advantage in it. They need the acquaintance with the church officers, the information about the church life, the evidence that their coming is very important and very welcome.

Ways of making this meeting memorable are important. One or two officers may give short talks, with a welcome and advice about Christian life and growth and churchmanship. Spokesmen for church activities or for stewardship may be present. Each new member may sign a roll book which has a membership covenant. A memento—a pin, a cross, a book—may be presented. The minister or officers may lay their hands on the new members' heads as they kneel for the consecrating prayer. They may adjourn to a worship place for prayer or for the Lord's Supper. Each officer can give his hand to the new members, expressing his happiness and his wish for theirs.

The meeting for reception may follow a church night dinner, with the new members the guests of honor. Some churches have the meeting on Palm Sunday afternoon, followed by a light supper at which the new members meet each other and church people.

4. The Reception in the Church Service

The occasion of first taking a public stand for Christ and coming into the eternal fellowship of believers should give the sense of its earthly and heavenly glory. The handclasp which welcomes new members joins them to a physical and spiritual succession which goes back through the forefathers and martyrs and apostles until it touches the very hand of Christ Himself—and it goes upward to the Church of the redeemed.

The observance merits careful planning and a search of all the sources of suggestions. New members can be given the sense of moving into a new world of thinking and living. Observers can have their church loyalty renewed. The congregation can be made more eager for evangelism by a service which makes receiving members seem the most joyful thing the church is doing.

If the new members rise one by one, the congregation can identify them—which is important. It helps also if their names and addresses are in the church bulletin and if some personal word is said about each one.

They may answer questions separately or as a group or read statements or repeat them after the minister, as in the marriage service. One minister has the new members at the front of the church face the congregation as they exchange promises; he stands where he can face the new members. Extra emphasis on who is to rise will spare embarrassment to visitors when the congregation rises to give its welcome and promises. The congregation's pledges may be read in unison if they are pasted in the hymnals. One church has a covenant which is read in unison by new members and old. The new members may kneel for the prayer. A stanza of a hymn of fellowship is often sung. "Blest Be the Tie" is most frequently used, though some weary of it. A small church has the reception of members near the close of a morning service so that the minister and officers can introduce them to the congregation as it files out.

White flowers are often given the new members so the church people can recognize and greet them after the service. Signing membership certificates, by the church clerk and the new members, may be a part of the ceremony. A memento, or a packet with booklets and a pledge card and devotional aids, may be presented.

There is great value in having baptism administered in the presence of the congregation. Only so can its solemnity and beauty and connection with the whole fellowship be fully expressed. People may shrink from having it known that they were not baptized earlier. There may be cases of extreme nervousness in which it is better to administer baptism in the presence of only the officers—if the Church law permits that. The end in view is the fullest Christian life, not the keeping of Church traditions. But candidates can usually be shown the value of being baptized in a church service. The sacrament must never be minimized to make it easy for the unconcerned.

5. Classes

a. Why. The love of Christ is a sublimely simple thing, but following Him in every part of life is not a simple thing at all. It requires all the guidance that can be given. It is when the Church has neglected practical pedagogy in passing on to its incoming members the truths it has been given by revelation and experience that it has been most enfeebled by vagueness, misbelief and indolence.

It is startling to recognize that many churches do more to prepare little boys to become tenderfoot scouts than they do to prepare adults to enter the eternal Church as disciples of Jesus Christ. There is another peculiar paradox—in many churches boys and girls who have been getting training in the church school are required to take special instruction before they join the Church, while older people who have had no training of any sort are taken into membership without instruction.

A Protestant Church, believing in the spiritual freedom of the individual before God, leaves a great deal to its members' private judgment. Unless it gives these members a knowledge of the Bible and a spiritual understanding, they will not be equipped to exercise their freedom. They might then be better off in a Church which would do their deciding for them.

Splendid evidence that the modern Church is rising to its evangelistic responsibility is seen in the fact that many more churches each year are providing classes for their new members. Some denominations have always required these. In others, where a decade ago communicants' classes for adults were exceptional, they are now becoming the rule.

All those coming into the Church need preparatory training. Those who come through the church school need to have what they have learned summarized and made specific; those with an outsider's knowledge of the Church and Christianity, like the vaguely informed Apollos, need instruction in "the way"; those being restored to membership obviously need something they did not have before; those transferring to a new church home need an introduction, and they often are glad to have a refreshing of their knowledge.

b. When. Most churches have the classes before the members are received. Others have them afterward, but make them seem a necessary part of the church-joining process. Some combine the recently received and the prospective members in the same classes. Those looking forward to membership are more likely to be faithful in attendance.

c. Voluntary or not. Should attendance at classes be a condition for membership? It is legally possible in denominations which do not require it; the local church may declare it to be necessary evidence of the candidates' knowledge and sincerity. The decision to join the church then includes the promise to take the course of training. The desirability of that requirement is widely debated. One unconvinced officer complained, "It's getting so it takes an act of Congress to get into this church." Others insist that those who do not care enough about the church to do so easy a thing are not ready to join.

A three-fourths attendance of new members is considered good in churches which make it voluntary. Would the total spiritual good of the other fourth have been increased if the training had been required? That is the moot point. Some churches are insisting that the requirement of classes has increased instead of restricted their receptions. Those which permit no exceptions often send someone to the homes to give the instruction to any who, because of health or occupation, are not able to come to the regular classes.

d. Hour. The Sunday-school hour is the most popular time for adult communicants' classes. Others, in what seems to be the order of popularity, have them on a week night, on Sunday evening or on Sunday afternoon. They are sometimes combined with a mid-week service. One hour is the usual length of a session.

The number of series of classes each year depends on the rate of receptions. Some large churches keep them going continuously. A small church may have them not more than twice a year. Two new members with the minister can make a splendid class. Most ministers wish there might be at least ten classes, but settle for five or six.

e. The teacher. Almost invariably the minister is the teacher. Not only is he supposed to be specially qualified, but the class builds a valuable tie between him and the new members of the church. However, a Midwestern church has one of its official boards take charge of the new member classes, with a different officer teaching each session. The minister assists each teacher until he becomes proficient in his subject. He believes that this does most both for the new members and for the officers. Many ministers invite the lay leaders of the church organizations or activities or finance to talk on those subjects.

The success or failure of the classes depends most of all on the quality of the teaching. Most ministers are not trained to be teachers, so that only by determined effort and experiment can they become adequate. Subjects that easily seem dull must be made to sparkle. A great deal must be touched on in a short time without its seeming to be a skeleton with no living flesh. Vividness and economy of words come only with hard work. The work is well invested, because the same ideas will be used again and again —with improvements each time. The natural tendency is to preach, but this is a poor way of teaching—even though gems from old sermons may have an enticing glitter.

f. The methods. The lecture method has been described as a process for transferring the contents of the teacher's notebook to the student's notebook without passing through the brain of either. On such subjects as Church history or government the teacher must do most of the talking, but he can find ways to give it variety. Outlines or diagrams on the blackboard help. He may inspire questions which let him put what he was going to say anyway in the form of answers. Audience participation makes a class more interesting but less worth while—so some reasonable compromise must be made. There may be recitation on assigned reading. In such matters as Christian behavior or difficulties in belief, discussion can be very valuable. If it begins to wander, the teacher may interrupt by saying, "That is very important! Let's hold it till we can give it more time."

Many subjects can be dramatized. The class can be taken to the church sanctuary for the instruction on public worship or Church symbolism. Going to the rooms where the various activities take place may illustrate a lecture on the whole program of the church. Dr. Cartwright tells of using Hofmann's picture of "Christ and the Rich Young Ruler" to illustrate his talk on dedication; he put the class around a table, as in the upper room, when he explained the meaning of the Lord's Supper.

Audio-visual aids are helpful. There are film strips on Church history, Christian home life, stewardship and evangelism. A full-length religious moving picture may be shown after a class.

Examinations can be stimulating—perhaps in the form of check sheets or true-or-false tests. It may be tactful to assure the class members that they can grade themselves, with no announcement made of the results.

Some teachers ask the class to bring in written statements on such subjects as, "What I believe about Jesus Christ," "How I think of God," "Why I am a Christian," "What Christ expects of me."

Definite training in Christian habits is often given to new members—usually in connection with a class. Candidates may be required to attend a stated number of Sabbath services before they are received. One pastor gives the members of his preparatory class a cross-lined sheet with dates listed down the left margin and vertical columns entitled "Bible Reading," "Private Prayer," "Public Worship," "Donations," "Serving" and "Witnessing." This record of performance is to be brought at the time for reception into membership. It is not regarded as a test but as a help in Christian habits. This combines the laboratory method with the instruction and raises immediate questions about these habits which can be discussed in the classes.

Some classes give assignments for memorizing—the Lord's Prayer, the Apostles' Creed, Bible passages, hymns, sections from the creed or catechism.

g. *Textbooks.* Some denominations supply excellent textbooks and related material for adult communicants' classes. In others, each church must discover its own books and develop its own work sheets or outlines. The paper-bound booklets published by the denominations' educational and evangelistic offices are useful for a class. These are available on most of the subjects such a class touches. The teacher should inspect as many samples as possible before he makes his selection. No one denomination has the best material on all the subjects. These booklets can be given or mailed out as an assignment of homework and a reminder of the next class. There may be a chief book with these smaller publications supplementing it.

h. Content. (This list is a sampling from many courses, not an outline for any one course.)

1. Christian beliefs, the creed, information about the Bible, a summary of the Bible's contents, how to use the Bible.

2. What the Church is, church history, the denomination's government and organization and distinctive characteristics, ecumenical Christianity.

3. The organization, activities and program of the local church, the responsibilities of membership, guidance into church activities and service, stewardship, missions, evangelism.

4. The ways of spiritual growth, how to get the most from the church services, the sacraments, what prayer is and how to pray, how to use the Sabbath, the personal knowledge of Christ.

5. Christian morality and behavior, social ideals and responsibilities, the Christian home, vocation.

i. For Inquirers. Many who have never given their hearts to Christ and the Church can be brought to do so in a communicants' class. Ideally, an Inquirers' Group (see Chapter XII) and a communicants' class should be separate. But many ministers, with limited time, are finding the combination practical. Having arranged the classes for new members, they then try to bring in all who might be interested.

6. Literature

Though classes are the liveliest and most effective method of teaching, the amount which they can cover is limited. There is no limit at all to the instruction which can be gotten through reading.

It requires a considerable effort to investigate the pamphlets and books offered by one's own and other denominations, and by independent publishers. But what is discovered will be of the utmost value for years—not only for new members but for every part of the church's work.

What is given away is usually thrown away. Getting the best of literature read is no easy matter. Simply to hand it out is usually to waste it. Therefore, strong motives must be given. Many churches get a great deal of reading done—but never without shrewd and vigorous promotion.

There are two rules: (a) Never give large quantities at once. (b) Present each item with an enthusiastic and colorful description of its value.

Here is the plan a Nebraska Presbyterian church uses (the titles refer to paper-bound booklets): (a) The pastor, at his preliminary conference gives "Twelve Rules for Christian Living" and "Our Faith." (b) Before each of the five classes, as preparation for the next one, there is given "A Brief History of the Church," "The Duties of a Church Member," "A Guide to Prayer," "The Organization of Our Church," "Christians in Society." (c) Soon after reception into the church, an officer calls at the home with a "new-member kit" which contains a booklet on stewardship, a financial pledge card, a leaflet describing the organizations and activities of the local church and a copy of a denominational magazine. He explains each of these. (d) The sponsor brings to the home a guide for Christian family life.

There are other sorts of literature which are valuable for new members:

a. A clear, readable Bible. A Bible-reading plan. An introduction to the Bible. Where to look in the Bible for special purposes.

b. A membership roll, with addresses and telephone numbers. A history of the local church. An enthusiastic description of the opportunities the church offers every age, with the hours of meetings, dates of recurring church events and the sacraments, and the names of the officers and leaders of every organization. An explanation of church finance. The importance of service in the church and the ways of serving.

c. Devotional tracts on such subjects as "what Christ means to me," "overcoming temptation," "my Church," "the life that God intended," "table blessings," "daily readings."

d. Subscriptions to Church periodicals or devotional magazines. Some churches give each new member a year's subscription.

e. Some pastors write a personal letter to each new member. Others have these letters written by church officers. In some churches, letters are written on the anniversary of reception into membership. This may come just when it is most needed to strengthen the feeling for the church.

Most churches give the paper-bound literature, and even more expensive volumes, without charge to the new members. But there are some which make at least a nominal charge, not only to take the burden from the church budget but because they believe it makes the material seem more respectable and therefore more likely to be read.

Church lending libraries have special value for new members. One minister gives six books to each six new members, with the names of all listed on the fly leaves. On the first of every month, the books are to be passed to the next one on the list. Some ministers, just in a friendly, personal way, lend their books to new members.

A display of religious books and Bibles and Bible helps at the classes for new members will get some purchasers. The most needed books for a personal library can be discussed in a class.

7. Getting New Members into the Church Family

From the earliest times, Christian living has meant being a part of the *koinonia,* of the loving fellowship of believers. A church is a home and its members are a family. They are drawn to each other by the strongest of ties—their love of Jesus Christ and their common dedication to His service.

Spectator membership in a church is a precarious fragment of the real thing. Those who attend church only as an audience attends a theater are missing some of the greatest joys it has for them. And they are missing what is essential for a Christian's health and growth. "We know that we have passed from death unto life, because we love the brethren" (I John 3:14). A new member who never gets into the love and friendships of the church is likely to be lost. This is a major reason for the modern Church's appalling record of suspensions.

In the days of the underground railroad, escaping slaves were sheltered by church groups which passed them on their way to freedom. If the church people did not shield them carefully enough, the pursuers would catch up with them and drag them back to slavery. People who join the church are pursued by old habits and associations and states of mind. Unless the church people can surround them with loving and protective care, many will be lost.

A minister who had talked to the young contractor who was remodeling his house was delighted when, as a result, the man joined the church. He attended the services and the minister thought that something great had been accomplished—but he was mistaken. The contractor dropped out; then when he reappeared, he told the minister this story.

"When I came out of the Navy, I was drinking so hard it was breaking up my home and ruining my business. When you talked to me about the Church, I thought maybe that was what I needed. But it did not do a bit of good. You would have been surprised, when you saw me some Sunday mornings, to know the state I had been in just a few hours before. So I quit. Then I got into a group called, 'Alcoholics Anonymous.' The first night I was there, one of the men said to me, 'Where are you eating lunch tomorrow? Can't we get together?' and one of the women said, 'Why don't you and your wife have dinner with us one night this week?' They really got hold of me, and I haven't had a drink for months."

The other group succeeded where the church had failed. It put its arms around the man and would not let him get away. Of course that was a specialized treatment for a special trouble. But all who join the Church have some need, some problems which require help. Unless the church is able to put its arms around them and surround them with its fellowship, it will fail them.

This is one of the most difficult parts of evangelism. It takes the most time. A decision can be gained in one call; a series of classes is soon finished. But the things a church should do to help new members form friendships and associations have to be carried on for months.

Those who have not been members often think of the church as a private club into which they cannot force themselves. People have been known to walk past a church on several Sundays before they get up their courage to go in. If they do go in and hear the call of Christ and join the church, they may still feel a great gulf between themselves and the church members. It takes more than a few official handshakes to make "those church people" seem like "we members." Often timidity will make new members seem aloof and unresponsive. Church members, thinking of themselves as an open fellowship, may not understand this social conservatism. They may be completely unrealistic in thinking that routine announcements of church functions and invitations to participate are all that should be needed. The new members may still feel that they could not presume to enter into the church life without a great deal of urging. The pain of going among a group of strangers may seem to be more than it is worth. The strain of trying to get into new groups may make the new members sensitive so that they will too easily imagine slights and drop away resentfully.

Moreover, Christian love can have a seamy side. It may make church members enjoy one anothers' company so much that they have no time for strangers. Often groups are cliquish because they have such a good time together. Not having seen each other for a week, they give newcomers a brief nod and eagerly get on with the communion of saints. Without being perpetually reminded, they will just not think to make room for others in their conversations and rows of chairs and automobiles and after-meeting gatherings.

If left to the natural laws of social life, the assimilation of new members is not likely to take place at all. Therefore, churches find it necessary to make special provisions for it.

a. The organizations. Getting new members into the fellowship groups and into church-school classes is one of the best ways of bringing them into church friendships. Those who join the church should be given information about all the groups for which they are eligible, with a glowing description of the advantages they offer and any publications they may have, such as the women's annual program. New church members' names and addresses and telephone numbers should be given to the recruitment officers of these groups. Some churches tell new members, "By virtue of your membership in the church you now belong to the ———— group which meets at ————."

The first assumption must be that impersonal invitations are useful as advertising, and never bring anyone. Announcements in public or invitations in writing can help to prepare the way. But the new members are not likely to be brought until someone says, "Can I stop by for you?" or at least, "Can I meet you there?" The group must be carefully coached in cordiality to newcomers. This is not supplied by appointing a few well-wishers to give the official handshake.

Without a definite routine for notifying the groups about new church members and for getting them started in the groups, nervous energy and new members will be lost. Nothing is more wearying than an unorganized duty.

When there are gaps in the fellowship program, so that there are no groups at all for people of some ages or temperaments, evangelism is handicapped. Sunday school classes for new members of all ages have the double evangelistic value of friendships and instruction.

Special activities—the choirs, sports, sewing, dramatics—may have great use as points of entrance into church friendships.

b. Calls. Having church members call gives a heart-warming impression of the desire of the church to be friendly, and commences acquaintanceships. Such calls should be arranged without appearing to be. A disappointed new member, telling of the "unfriendliness" of the church she had joined, said, "In this whole year, not a soul from that church has ever come to see us! Of course, the pastor and his wife have been here several times." Lay callers are necessary.

A board of deaconesses or a pastor's aid committee can arrange for this. Church officers are sometimes sent with a special purpose—to take literature for new members or communion tokens or an invitation to some church event. A Rochester church sends an elder to call on each new member with a membership packet, and a deacon calls to take a pledge card and a package of contribution envelopes. It is well if husbands and wives call in homes together. Though a call has a special purpose, social visiting and general conversation about the church are important.

c. Invitations. Nothing can show new members that they have been accepted as friends and taken into the church family as surely as can invitations into homes. It does something which no amount of cordiality at the church can do. A church member's home is not a castle that is shut against a chance to do essential Christian service. The evangelism committee can work out ways to be sure that every new member is welcomed into someone's home. Not as a substitute for lay invitations, but of great value in itself, a pastor may invite new members to his home for a social evening in which they get better acquainted with each other and with the pastor and his wife.

d. Social events. New members may be the guests of honor at some church function. If they are put at a special place or are given some designation to wear and are introduced by name, it helps the church members to get to know them. Special hosts and hostesses for each new member may be assigned. The air of welcome and celebration lets them know of the church's delight in having them.

This may be a special event, as in those churches which have a new member reception each May to honor those who have joined during the year. It may feature some regular church event—the annual congregational meeting or a church night dinner. It is interesting to have all present wear name badges which show the year in which they joined. They may be asked to rise as the year is called, with recognition for those longest in the church as well as for the newest members. As has been noted, it is a splendid idea to have a time of fellowship in connection with a meeting for the reception of members.

e. Pictures. Pictures of new members in a church publication or posted on a bulletin board can aid in their assimilation. Group pictures may be made at the communicants' class or at the time of reception or by special announcement on some Sunday.

f. Ushers. The ushers should be given the names of new members so that they can make a special effort to welcome them by name. Ushers can help them choose the section of the church in which will be their accustomed place.

8. Sponsors

Sponsors are needed because everybody's business is nobody's business. The attention and care which the whole church has promised to give its new members will not be given unless someone in particular is appointed to give it. A sponsor is a designated friend.

A sponsor (sometimes called "Fellowship Friend" or "Special Friend") is assigned to each new member. A married couple is usually assigned to sponsor a married couple. Sponsors should be in age and interests as much as possible like those they sponsor. An entire family may be appointed to sponsor another family in which there are young people of about the same ages.

Friendly people with a lively interest in the church and a strong sense of duty make the best sponsors. Sometimes, surprisingly, a person who has not been a model of church zeal will be a splendid sponsor and will get a tonic from the task. A church soon discovers who make good sponsors and whom not to ask.

A sponsor (a) Congratulates the new member. (b) Calls. (c) Greets the new member at the church and introduces others. They may come to church together or sit together for the first few Sundays. When the new member misses a service the sponsor telephones, not as a truancy officer, but to inquire whether there is illness and to express regret that they did not see each other. (d) Tries to get the new member into organizations and activities, perhaps arranging to go together or prodding an organization if it is negligent in recruiting. (e) Gives an invitation to the sponsor's home, or arranges for social occasions at the homes of other church members. (f) Discovers and tries to get use of any talents. (g) Gives such guidance in Christian habits as can tactfully be offered. (h) Watches for any signs of failure to get a good start in the church and tries to correct it—perhaps calling on other members for help and always notifying the pastor if there is real difficulty.

If the sponsor and the new church member are seeing each other frequently and a bond of friendship is developing, one or two calls or special contacts may be enough. In other cases, a great deal of attention will be required. The major part of the task should be finished in the first three to six months. But the sponsor should still keep an eye on the new member long after that. Abiding friendships often develop.

Some churches let the new member know about the sponsor. Others feel that a friendship will be more effective if it does not seem official.

Sponsoring the sponsors is essential. Human nature persists and, without some way of checking on failures and giving reminders, some new members will be sadly neglected. There may be a chairman for sponsors, who telephones them at stated intervals to find what has been done and how the new member is doing. One church gives each sponsor at the time of the assignment five dated post cards with spaces to report contacts made, whether the new member is attending services and has joined an organization, etc. These are to be mailed at monthly intervals. If such information is checked on a master list of new members, one can see at once which sponsors are negligent or which new members are not responding well. If all this seems cumbersome, the pastor can remember that it takes much less of his time than for him to give the needed attention to new members by himself—and it will probably be more effective.

The pastor or the chairman of the New Member Committee appoints the sponsors when new members are received. Consent to serve is then secured. Some denominations publish a leaflet with instructions for sponsors. Churches often mimeograph their own. It is useless to appoint sponsors without giving them specific duties. Personal information about the new members, which will be very useful for sponsors, is given to them in writing. A list of all assignments is kept at the church. If a parish is divided, the officers in charge of each zone may be the sponsors for all new members who live there—or appoint their sponsors. Sponsors can be called together for instruction, prayer, discussion and assignments.

9. Responsibilities

A new member never feels that "their church" is "my church" until some of his time and energy have been invested in it. A member never fully belongs to a church unless the church, through its work, belongs to him. Nonworking members always have the feeling of being second-class members, and this is often rationalized into resentment of those whose labors keep the church going.

For their own soul's good, the church owes it to the new members to turn them to some unselfish pursuits. It owes them a chance to get the feel of discipleship and the thrill of worth-while accomplishment. Having extracted a pledge to serve Christ and His Kingdom, the church then has the obligation to offer some way to fulfill that pledge.

The surest sign of a church's strength is not its size or building or budget—it is the average number of hours per week its members are giving to its work. Many a church with a slothful tradition, in which every attempt to stir the old members out of their half-hearted ways has failed, has found new life by bringing in new members with a different point of view.

A first improvement must often be the reorganization of a church's work. A large Eastern church found in a survey that 642 of its men were willing to accept some task. It then discovered that there was no way in its present program to use more than about 65 of them. The Church limps along on half power, doing only a fraction of the things a church ought to do, while its members are spiritually starved for lack of any function.

The inability to use many workers indicates that a church is not covering its field save for a few ruts. It is no help for a church to devise some "made work" which will be recognized as trivial and a proof that church work is not worth the time of busy people. A church will never have to try to make up jobs until it is doing all the important things for people that Christ wants done.

Those who join must be helped to see from the very first that church membership is supposed to mean an active participation. A layman in Chicago told what a shock it gave him, at the meeting when he joined the Church, to have the minister say to him, "Our church has all the members it needs and, unless you intend to take an active part, we do not want you. What part do you expect to have in the service of this church?" The man hesitantly said that his advertising experience might be useful, and right then he was assigned some work to do. He believes that his whole career as a very faithful lay worker was started at that time. Most ministers would not be able gracefully to use quite so blunt a method. But that conception of church membership must be given at the start.

The inexperienced should not be frightened by too exacting demands at the outset. There is danger of overloading new members, but there is greater danger in not loading them at all. Some are discouraged by wrong assignments. A critical task, such as teaching in the church school, should not be given to those whose qualities are untested.

It can be very useful to have new members check, on a list of all the forms of service which can be rendered in the church, those in which they have interest or ability. There will be a letdown and a sense of hurt if the proffered services are never requested. The list should match what the church wants done, not what it dreams about. It should not be put away until the new member has been brought into some service. Keeping the list in sight will prevent its being forgotten. After the lists are filed they are still used to locate workers for future tasks.

Church organizations and activities are important in connecting new members with responsibilities.

New members are often the finest evangelists. Their enthusiasm is still fresh and they know why they are grateful. They have more close contacts with those outside the Church than does the average member. A "New Member Club," for all who have joined during the year, often undertakes evangelism. A new member may be sent out with an experienced evangelistic caller, and thus trained for personal work. The obligation to share the faith should be made very clear at the time of reception, and practical guidance in how to go about it should be given. It is the surest way to stimulate a new Christian's spiritual growth.

Rev. Robert E. Graham of Altoona gives everyone who joins the church a blank decision card, with the new member's name on the back. The new member is told, as evidence of gratitude to God, to get someone's decision for Christ and then to put the signed card in the collection plate as the finest offering that can be made. The story of Andrew and Philip is applied (John 1:41 and 45).

10. Finance

Evangelism is intensely concerned with giving new members a right start in church finance, not because it is so eager for their money but because it is so eager for their hearts. The law, "Where your treasure is, there will your heart be also," has never been repealed. Every pastor knows that the giving chart is a pretty accurate spiritual health chart for his members. Those who have a weak financial relationship to the church are likely to be weak in all their other church relationships. Those who give poorly are hard to hold and hard to please.

Evangelism is not complete until people have been taught the meaning of consecration. This must be taught, not in vague generalities, but in practical terms. Without the experience of dedication and self-sacrifice there will be no Christian growth. The new member will understand the Christian meaning of vocation only as he comes to know that his day's work, through the contributions it earns, is being built into the Kingdom.

Churches fear that a too pointed emphasis on giving when members are received will seem materialistic. When people are in the glow of a new experience with Christ, an exhortation about their share of the mortgage and of the pastor's salary can seem out of place. When a church presents its pledge cards too coldly or too insistently, it invites the suspicion of a financial motive in its evangelism. The appeal must always be given in its spiritual setting. It should be made clear that the church is different from worldly organizations in that it has no fixed fees, no expulsion for unpaid dues, no public announcement of the amount of the members' contributions. But this fear of presenting financial matters in the wrong way leads many churches into the even graver danger of being so reticent that their members remain deficient in this essential branch of Christian knowledge.

New church members need to be shown: (a) The Christian idea of stewardship—with its conception of time, talents and material possessions as a trust from God to be used in His service for the benefit of all mankind. (b) The financial methods of the local church, with the reasons for making a definite pledge. (c) The reasons for giving to missions and the other benevolent causes, with a heart-warming appeal in terms of actual needs. (d) How to estimate the amount to be given. (e) What proportions of the giving should go to local church support, to Church benevolences and to charitable and religious causes outside the church.

New members can form a low opinion of a church which lets weeks slip by with no word on this subject. Those who join at Easter should not have to wait until the next fall's canvass to get their start in church support. Negligent giving may be becoming habitual by then.

Church members are often not to blame for their poor level of giving. When they joined the Church and needed some definite guidance they were told, "This is between you and God—only your conscience can tell you what to do." So they made a guess, which was a poor one, and it remained their standard from then on. Attitudes soon become fixed. Years of pleading may not lift a church member to a standard of giving which he might have readily accepted when he joined the Church.

New members are often sincerely puzzled about how much they ought to give. From its long experience with how good Christians live, the Church can certainly offer more practical help than the indefinite expressions about "according to your ability" or "proportionate giving." What proportion? The fact that tithing can be taught too legalistically or with the superstitious promise that those who tithe will prosper does not at all weigh against the teaching of tithing as the historic and honored tradition of the Church. There are no theological objections to presenting tithing as a goal, as a method which has been the source of endless blessing, as the most common standard among Christians. The Church has not yet discovered any other teaching which is better calculated to give new Church members a healthy start in their use of money. Those who recognize that Church members should be free to give more than a tenth may still permit tithing to be urged until there are more in the Church who approach at least this standard.

There are other ways of giving definite guidance. A fatherly officer can talk to a young couple in terms of his own experience—telling what he gave when he was in their situation. A new member can be shown that the things the Church is doing are worth more to him than some of his other budget items—golf club, amusements, school taxes.

Adequate instruction about giving has to be offered in three ways:

a. In writing. There are many excellent booklets and leaflets on stewardship. A church can mimeograph or print its own teaching, and a description of its financial practices.

b. In groups. At the time of reception into membership and in the new-member classes much that is helpful can be said.

c. In private conferences. A first pledge card needs to be presented and talked over in a personal way. Questions which would not be asked in a group may have to be discussed. Someone must make a call. This is a lay task; the minister's salary interest is an inescapable embarrassment, and lay members can talk to each other from the same point of view. Happy is the church which has an officer of great gentleness and tact, perhaps a man retired from business, who can call on all new members to talk with them about their giving.

Some churches make a financial pledge a condition for membership. They believe that the willingness to give a freely determined amount is essential evidence of Christian consecration, and a logical demonstration of the sincerity of the vow of church loyalty. Others feel that such a condition is sacrilegious. In any case, it is certain that instructing and starting new members in their giving is a necessary part of bringing them into the Christian life.

11. Checking Up

The time immediately after joining the church is exceedingly precarious. That is the period in which old habits and companions have the strongest hold. New ways are still not established. Many of the joys of church life have not yet been discovered. Timidity and a sense of strangeness are formidable problems.

Without some way of knowing how the new members are doing, some of them will slip away and be lost before the trouble is detected. Every week that a remedy is postponed makes its success less likely. The boy who joined the Church at Easter and attended until he went off to a summer camp, but did not return in the fall, will be back again if someone goes to see him before Christmas. After that, the connection may be broken beyond repair. The family, which joined by transfer but never got over the unhappy feeling that it was not like the church back home, may return and learn to love the church if some members go to see them; but in a few months they will have decided that the church did not really want them—and they will be permanently lost.

It is tragic that the only systematic check many churches ever make on the state of their members is a preliminary to expulsion. New members are set adrift in the church and no eye kept upon them until it is necessary to clear away the wreckage. The hit-or-miss knowledge which comes from pastoral contacts or chance observation may save a few, but many will be lost before it is noticed.

The names of all who have joined the church during the past eighteen months should be reviewed at three-month intervals in some official meeting, of a board or a committee. In that same meeting plans are made to give help where it is needed.

A health chart for new members is almost indispensable. It is very easy to arrange. Down the left border of a sheet of cross-ruled paper are the names of the new members. At the tops of the vertical columns are such headings as Date of Reception, Pastor's Call, Classes Attended, Officer's Call, Sponsor's Report (those five enable the church to check on itself; the following five enable it to check on the new members), Attending Services, Organization Joined, In Church School, Pledge Received, Task Accepted.

In many churches, information about what the new member is doing can be filled in from observation. Larger churches will need some source of knowledge. Sponsors may supply it (and getting it can be a good way to keep the sponsors active). An attendance registration of all the congregation or communion tokens will show who is missing the church services. Organization records and a general discussion in a meeting can supply more information.

The pastor will always take a keen interest in keeping this chart up-to-date. In some churches, official responsibility for it is assigned to a lay officer.

Such a chart shows at a glance which new members are not getting a good start in the church. Then immediate remedies must be devised—through the organizations, through calls, through neighbors, through a request to do some special task, through the tactful stratagems which a loving determination can devise.

A city church has a telephone check-up three months after reception. An officer calls each new member and, after referring to their meeting each other at the time of joining, has a friendly conversation in which he gets the answers to such questions as: "How are you liking the church?" "Is there anything we can be doing to make the church more useful for you?" "Has someone called with your membership certificate?" "Have you gotten into the ———— Club yet?" "Do you like to bowl?" "Are the members of your family getting started in the church all right?" The officer is checking off a mimeographed list of questions as he talks, and he mails it, with the answers, to the pastor.

The checking-up is often done in groups. One church, after an intensive three-month induction period—with classes and assigned literature and calls—has the new members meet once more for a friendly conference with a committee of the official board.

A New York church has a supper for new members each of the first three years after they join. They are asked first, "In what way has the church failed you?" then, "How have you failed the church?" They review, one by one, the vows they took when they joined. Then the conference goes to more personal matters, "Just what do you say when you pray?"

Whatever be the methods, a systematic check-up is essential. For at least the first eighteen months a pastor must at stated intervals have a careful look at how every new member of his church is doing. It is one of the most important ways of keeping that path from the front door to the back door from being so often traveled and so very short.

XV

Absent Members

A. The Inactive

At any conference on evangelism, the first question asked is likely to be, "What can we do to get back our inactive members?" No problem is more painfully on the Church's conscience. The thought of the many he has lost oppresses every pastor with the sense of failure and guilt. Those are people with whom the Church had its chance. They promised so much which they and the world so greatly needed—and never got.

The problem is grievous not only because it is so large but because it is so difficult. Second-try evangelism is the hardest sort. It is much easier to win a new member to the Church than to rewin an old one.

That fact must be weighed by those who ask, "Ought we not first to do something for the backsliders for whom we are already responsible, before we go out for new people?" The practical answer is that a church will be wise to gain competence in evangelism by seeking those who are clear outside before it attempts the far harder task of reviving its neglectful members. After the use of lay evangelistic visiting has given skill to the visitors and spiritual warmth to a church, it may then with some hope set out to rekindle the cold zeal of its inactive members.

Though it is more difficult, second-try evangelism can be richly rewarding. Like a cold motor, church interest on the first attempt may sputter out, but with continued trying it may catch and warm up into full and enthusiastic participation. Although the best place at which to prevent losses from the back door is at the front door, there can still be splendid results from back-door efforts. In any group of loyal church workers there are likely to be a surprising number of those who at one period in their lives had dropped out of the church.

A church may convince itself that it is a great evangelistic success when it is simply operating on the principle of easy come and easy go. By this it is succeeding only in doing the greatest amount of spiritual damage to the greatest number of people. The callousness with which some churches cast off their inactive members, with no warning and no attempt to revive them, is inexcusable. It amounts to premature burial when what is needed is emergency medicine.

A common reason for this is the fear of offending relatives and friends. The awful acts of excommunication and suspension are performed by the mere stroke of a pen in secret for fear of stirring up trouble.

The opposite temptation is to keep a fraudulent roll by carrying as active members those who have no living contact with the church at all. These twin sins can be escaped only by a church which gives regular attention to its roll, removing from its membership those who have no claim to it, but doing so only after the most prayerful and painstaking efforts to prevent that disaster.

1. Identifying Those Who Need Attention

Church sickness is one of those diseases which may be healed if it is caught soon enough, but with delay it tends to become incurable. Many churches get discouraged about their attempts to rewin their lapsing members because they never start the remedies until it is too late.

A roll must be reviewed at fairly frequent intervals if trouble is to be discovered in the early stages. There needs to be a schedule for this. Some official boards as a regular item of business at each monthly meeting read over a certain proportion of the names on the roll. With each name the officers speak of any needs or problems which it brings to mind. Those who should have special attention of any sort are noted, and the responsibility is assigned. Three sorts of members are listed for immediate action—the slipping, the moved and the temporarily nonresident. That section of the roll may also be a prayer list for the meeting. Some boards devote the greater part of a meeting in January and another in midsummer to reading through and praying through the entire roll. In a large church this responsibility may be given to a subcommittee which will report all cases of special concern to the entire board.

A pastor needs to make frequent reading through the church roll an administrative and devotional exercise.

Those who have been suspended from a church's list of active members are not to be banished to the outer darkness. The names of all who have been dropped in recent years should be periodically studied and fresh attempts made to bring them back or to get them into some other church. Spiritual interest often travels through a cycle and a church frequently finds to its surprise that someone who had been completely unresponsive has become ready to return.

A church attendance registration (see page 77), a zone system (see pages 273-74) and an every-member visitation can identify those who need special care.

2. Evangelistic Visitation

Visitation evangelism can be splendidly used for the rewinning of inactive members. The decision to be sought may not seem as clear-cut. The callers often are trying to strengthen a connection which is not yet broken. Some churches use a card on which renewed Christian loyalty and habits can be pledged. There may be a written promise to attend services for a stated number of Sundays, as a part of a church attendance campaign. In visiting those who have been suspended, some definite statement which can lead to the process of reception back into membership must be sought.

There is an important psychological difference between those who are clear outside the Church and those who are fellow members or have been. The latter may think that they know as much about the benefits of the Church and of the Christian life as do the callers. They will resent any implication that they are an inferior class of Christians. There must be special care to make the attitude that of sharing—not of condescension. The callers go out to kindle others by their own enthusiasm for the Church, to heal any grievances, to reason and to bring back a clinical report.

Though the warning of members before they are suspended may be a legal duty, there must be no touch of legalism in its performance. The heavy-handed sternness we find in the church records of former generations rarely does much good today. The possible separation must be shown to be a source of deep sorrow to the church. The church's share in the blame must be acknowledged. The plea can be, "If you will come back to the church, with God's help, we will all do better."

The reasons for a failure in membership which visitors discover can lead to constructive action. There may be real causes of grievance which can be remedied or misunderstandings which can be cleared up. Improvements in the church program or more tactful dealings or better ways of assimilating new members may be indicated.

Those who make calls to rewin the inactive need to be trained. The suggestions in Chapters VIII and IX may help them. Even experienced evangelistic visitors should have some special preparation for this more difficult sort of visiting.

3. Every-Member Visitation

When calls are to be made in all the church homes, in connection with a communion service or for some other reason, special attention can be given those whose church participation is weak. If a list of these is prepared in advance, the callers can be told where such attention is needed. Or there may be a group of callers who deal only with such cases. Those who are visited as a part of an every-member program do not feel that they have been set apart as black sheep, and the callers do not have to wonder what reason they will give for coming.

4. A Church Attendance Campaign

One of the best reasons for a special church attendance campaign is the chance it gives to recommence the habit of churchgoing when it has been broken. Those who come on the stated Sundays to fulfill a promise are likely to keep on coming. Most backsliding is not due to any grievance or change of heart, but simply to carelessness. It can be cured by bracing too weak good intentions with a framework of definite duties. One of the Loyalty Sundays may well have a sermon on the value of regular public worship.

A church attendance campaign offers an ideal occasion for calls on the inactive. It gives the callers a natural reason to talk about church loyalty. The written promise to attend the services saves the calls from vagueness by giving them a key objective and a definite result. Conversation about the value of the church and the need for Christian living and the reasons for regular church attendance all come logically into a presenting of the purposes of the loyalty campaign. When all church homes are being visited in such an effort, the visitors will need special training in what to say to the minority who decline to sign the loyalty card. They may find some help in the suggestions in Chapter IX on "What to Say."

5. A Task

Every church has at least a few of the sort of activists who will be unfailing in their performance of any task they are given, and never come near the church at any other time. That is a weakness, but it is a weakness with which the church must reckon by seeing that such people are kept busy—at least until they acquire other motives for church loyalty.

Many who have drifted away from the church will return if they are given some responsibility. The church must not imperil its work by giving those of dubious spiritual insight such a task as the guidance of its youth or the formulation of its policies. But those who are losing interest will feel that they are needed and that their place is in the church if they are given some share in its work. One pastor declares that the best of all ways to reclaim an inactive member is to give him the name of another whom he is supposed to bring back. Not only does he have a ready-made rapport with the one on whom he is working but, as a fellow conspirator with the pastor, he feels he has to set a good example.

6. Evangelism through Fellowship

The organized groups may be the best bridge, not only to the unchurched, but to the dechurched. Those whom a direct approach cannot reclaim may be brought back through the drama group or the men's club. Those in charge of the church organizations or activities may be given the names of lapsed church members and asked to try to rewin them.

Friends or neighbors can be enlisted in a stratagem to rewin a slipping member of the church.

7. Special Meetings

Special evangelistic services may be able to revive and rewin lapsed and lapsing members. Particular attention should be given to getting them to attend.

8. Mail

A personal letter or an attractive advertisement of what the church is doing or a leaflet on church loyalty may have some effect. The danger is that, having used the mail, a church will feel that it has done its duty. Mail has real value as preparation for a personal contact; without that contact its accomplishment is small. Mailings to all the members—a church paper, enthusiastic announcements of church affairs, pastoral letters—are useful in keeping the unstable from forgetting about the church. A printed statement of the reasons for suspending members may prevent those, who must be warned of this, from feeling that it is a personal affront.

9. Special Attentions

By winning the appreciation of inactive members through some extra attentions, a pastor may renew their attachment for the church. There are special days which people like to have remembered—birthdays, wedding anniversaries, the anniversaries of joining the Church. The pastor may keep on the watch for news of a promotion or a graduation or an engagement or some achievement by one of the family. A phone call or a brief note or a personal visit at such a time may stir a grateful feeling of friendship for the pastor and the consciousness of being important in the church.

B. *The Out-of-town*

The new evangelism has developed some splendid ways of dealing with the problem of moving members.

Ours is a nation on the move. It has been estimated that most Americans move to a new community on an average of once each decade. A Christian's growth, therefore, is the responsibility, not of one church, but of an assembly line, as members are passed along a succession of churches through the years. Church life must be designed for this sort of ministry. Newcomers must be quickly reached, made to feel at home, lovingly cared for, and passed on to a new home without delay.

Church methods have been too largely based on the classical conception of a congregation as a fixed fellowship. But it is not that at all. It is a procession. An important section of the typical church moves every year. In a decade its membership will be decidedly different. Like a frustrated mother hen which has hatched out duck eggs, the Church has not been psychologically equipped to care for the members of its flock who migrate. The loss in transit exposes one of the Church's most deplorable inefficiencies. The breaking of all church connections by members who move is the largest single source of losses from the rolls. The shocking situation is revealed in every neighborhood census, which shows that a large part of any community is made up of former Church members who left the Church of Christ when they changed their addresses.

It is said that half of the members of rural churches and three-fourths of those in cities have come by transfer. The life and power of the Church depends on its success in getting memberships transferred.

It is the younger section of the population which is doing most of the moving. To lose it is to make the Church an aging and dying institution.

Whether we like it or not, the old one-church technique for perfecting the saints is out of date for many people. Churches must learn to be stages in an assembly line which takes care of Christian growth by passing members from one to the next.

1. An Understanding of the Church

In order to prepare them to survive the crisis which will come if they move, church members must be made to feel that their loyalty belongs, not to a parish, but to the great Church of Jesus Christ. When the Hebrew exiles were first away from their homeland they thought that they could not worship God any more; they had left Him back in Palestine—"How shall we sing the Lord's song in a strange land?" Many modern church members have been allowed to have something of that primitive conception of God and of His Church. They are limited to one local church in their appreciation of fellowship and worship. It is "the church" for them and they never find their place in any other. Evangelism is incomplete until its converts have come to feel that the world-wide Church is their spiritual home.

Those who join must be shown that the local congregation is merely a door through which they are entering the Christian Church. They can be told that in a very real sense they have joined all the other Christian churches in the neighborhood, and in the nation, and in the world. In the preparatory talks to them and in the forms for their reception they can be given the sense of having come into a close fellowship which goes far beyond the local parish.

Some churches wisely include in the vows for new members the promise to transfer without delay to another congregation if they move away.

The members of the church can be kept conscious of the duty of finding a new church home as soon as they leave the present one. Paragraphs on that can be put from time to time in the church bulletin or paper. Sermons can refer to it. When members are received by transfer, something can be said in commendation of their having done what good members are always supposed to do. News of members who have transferred to some other church can include an expression of joy at their having so soon found a place in which to continue their Christian growth and service. One advantage of invitations from the pulpit is the opportunity they give to tell, in the hearing of the present members, why membership should be transferred.

Keeping before the church reminders of denominational and ecumenical matters gives members a tie to something greater than the local group. This is one of the benefits of getting members to subscribe to a Church paper.

We are inclined to blame the sad losses on the provincialism of members who thought when they joined the great Christian Church that they had merely joined a little home-town institution. But what shall we say of the worse provincialism of the pastors and officers who seem to think that their responsibility for the spiritual welfare of their members ends when the members can no longer be a part of the local group? There is many a church in which not a hand is turned to help moving members to continue in a church relationship except as the last act before striking them from the roll, by which time it is usually too late. There are not a few churches which deliberately try to hold on to their moved members so that they may keep their contributions. Such a church might have a legitimate claim upon benevolent support. But an organization has lost its claim to be a church when it puts its financial interests above the spiritual welfare of its members.

2. Parting Words

As soon as a pastor hears that a member is about to leave, he should find an occasion, in person or by telephone, to express his regret and good wishes, and at the same time give strong advice about the necessity of finding a new church home. He must make it clear that he and the church members will be complimented by the desire to keep an active church connection uninterrupted. He may be able to find out something about churches near the new address and give definite advice about where to go.

Many pastors give a letter of introduction (which must be carefully distinguished from a letter of transfer). If this says complimentary things about the members, they will be the more anxious to give it to some church. A printed Certificate of Introduction may be given: "This will introduce to you——, (name) well loved in the membership of our church and now commended to your fellowship and interest." This may be joined at a perforated line to a form, addressed to the home church, requesting a letter of transfer.

A "Service of Godspeed" has become a valuable institution in many churches. At a church service, not long before members leave, they are given an affectionate farewell. Something is said of the church's gratitude for them and of its hope that they may soon find a happy church connection. There is a prayer for God's blessing in their new home. It is made to seem something like a reversal of the service for reception, so that the members will feel that their active attachment to the church has come to a happy, but quite definite, termination. A letter or certificate of introduction may be presented. This ceremony reminds all present of what they are expected to do when they move. If it is made known that members who intend to move are supposed to notify the church, it will save them from feeling hurt if this service is not held for them.

3. Letters to Moved Members

Delay is dangerous. As Dr. Walter E. Woodbury reminds us, when plants are moved the longer the roots are in the air the less chance there is for the transplanting to succeed. Nonchurch habits in a new community are quickly formed. The period of transition soon passes. Correct addresses become hard to get.

First letter

Dear ———:

It has meant a great deal to this church to have you in its membership, and you will always be a part of its love and friendships. But now that you are too far away to have an active part in our church life, we are anxious for you to have the blessings of a church home where you are.

When you transfer your membership you will not have left us, for we will all be members of the great Church of Christ. We will be complimented to know that you are anxious to find soon again what you enjoyed with us here.

The longer you wait to get settled in a new church home, the more you will be missing. Christ wants all of His followers to keep constantly in the fellowship of believers. You will need to feel that a church is a part of your life now—with its services and its friendships—not as an outsider but as one who belongs.

If you have not yet decided which church to join, I hope you will get that settled soon. We will send your letter of transfer at once to whatever church you designate. We will feel closer to you when we know that you are active in the Church. The love and prayers of this church are with you, wherever you go.

Very sincerely,

As soon as members move they should receive a warmly personal letter, without the stereotypes of business correspondence, expressing the church's affection and urging them to find a church home. The Church law on the subject may be quoted, with care to keep it from sounding peremptory. A printed leaflet on the reasons for transferring may be enclosed.

Fatal delay in writing to moved members can best be avoided by a frequent check of the entire church roll. When this is done in an open meeting there are more sources of information about removals. When there is a general mailing to all the members the Post Office, for a fee, will supply information of changed addresses. Cards, on which to report any changed addresses, may be sent out with a mailing and bring news from some whose mail is being forwarded.

It is a good practice for a pastor to write all of the nonresident members four weeks before Easter, advising them to place their membership in some church at Eastertime.

Urgent letter

Dear ————:

We have greatly valued your membership in this church. But now that you are gone from this community we cannot realistically count you as an "active" member. Our Church law says that when members have been absent for two years without asking to be transferred to another church, they are to be placed on the suspended roll.

We should greatly regret having to do that with you. It would mean that you are no longer a regular member of any church at all. But it is not right for us to continue long to count as active members those who are too far away to have any part in our church life here.

We are anxious to have you keep an active church connection. Every follower of Christ needs a church home near his own home. He needs its services and its friendships and a part in its work. He needs the fellowship of those who share his faith—not as an outsider but as one of them.

Will you not write soon for the transfer of your membership to some congregation near you? You will not be leaving us, for we will still be together in the one great Church of Jesus Christ. And we will be rejoicing to know that you are still finding what you were seeking when you came to us.

Very sincerely,
For the ———— Church

P. S. If you have already formed a new church connection, please notify us.

There is another sort of letter which is written to those who have been absent for a considerable time without transferring their membership. The tone of this letter will be more urgent—though threats and denunciations will do no good. It may speak plainly of duty and of the needs of the Christian life and tell with sorrow of the necessity of suspending from active membership those who for too long have had no active participation in any church. A stamped, addressed envelope for reply should be enclosed. There will be more answers if these letters go by registered mail.

4. A Letter to Another Church

As soon as a member moves the pastor should write to a church near the new address, with a request that this church try to bring the member into its fellowship. Personal information, which can help in understanding the situation and in making a friendly connection, should be included. It will make the task of the other church much easier if this letter is sent soon. It is important that the address given be accurate; it is well to telephone some friend or relative to be sure of this before writing. Church people are properly irritated when they are asked to waste their time running to wrong addresses or trying to interest those who have been neglected until the time has come to drop them from the roll.

When a letter is written to a moved member, it is a good idea to send a carbon copy of it to a near-by church.

When it is difficult to be sure what church is nearest, the letter may be sent to some likely church with a request for forwarding if there is another nearer. Or it may go to a denominational or church-federation office with a request for forwarding. If there is no church of the same denomination near, another minister may be asked to suggest a church of his or her denomination.

5. The Church on the Receiving End

A church which receives a request to give attention to a member who has moved to its neighborhood has an obligation of the most pressing sort. A golden opportunity to add to its strength has been presented. The church life or death of the member may depend on what is done soon.

All the enlistment forces of the church should at once be set in motion. The pastor and neighbors call. Invitations and notices are sent through the mail. Representatives of the church groups and activities try to bring the various members of the family into their fellowship. Lay evangelistic callers come with a definite invitation into the membership (See pages 145-48).

The failure to make a report to the church which sends a name is a flagrant breach of courtesy and good churchmanship.

6. Denominational Help

Some denominations have begun requesting their congregations to send the names and addresses of the out-of-town members with the annual reports. Blanks for this purpose are sent to each church with the report forms. When the names are received, a denominational office makes out a slip for each one, giving the local church membership and present address, and sends it to the nearest church, with a request for attention and for a report. In cases of doubt, as in most large cities, the names are sent to a local denominational officer with a request for forwarding to the proper church. A denominational magazine has its circulation department stamp each changed address on a card, to be sent out as above.

7. Temporarily Nonresident Members

Members away at school, those in the armed services, and those whose employment prevents settled church contacts require a special ministry from their church—personal letters, the church paper or bulletins, devotional helps. Whenever they can be back at the home church, a special effort to welcome them and let their friends celebrate their presence is useful. The minister can write to chaplains or to college pastors asking for attention to his absent members.

XVI

Out Beyond the Walls

1. Outposts

Religiously the frontier is still here. The need for pioneering has never ended. Outposts, reaching beyond the settled areas of church life, must be the growing edge of the Christian Church.

The gospel cannot be confined behind walls of brick and stone. The Church will never reach America by shutting up evangelism within its buildings. There are hundreds of thousands of people who will never find the Church until the Church goes to them.

There are city slums and rural slums and across-the-tracks sections of small towns which are not being adequately reached by any church. The people there may be completely unresponsive to any effort to bring them into an established congregation.

Many thousands of migrant farm laborers live all through the year in settlements which are out of reach of any church. They are too transient to maintain churches of their own.

Those in infirmaries, penal institutions, orphanages, homes for the aged and mental hospitals cannot be ministered to in the churches, but their spiritual needs are a direct responsibility of Church people. They test a church's evangelistic sincerity for they offer it no inducement save the satisfaction of reaching those who need Christ.

An outpost Sunday school or a weekday church school can accomplish much. A neighborhood chapel or neighborhood evangelistic meetings can reach those who would never be won inside a church. A community center may introduce wholesome activities where they are greatly needed and be a first step toward a church.

Outposts in underprivileged neighborhoods can be a bridge into Church membership. Those who find the social or cultural distance too great to be crossed in one step can be brought into the Church, first through a contact in their own communities, then into regular participation in the parent church. Or the outpost may be a permanent branch of an established church, permitting members to have some of their church life at the outpost, and some of it at the parent church.

The gospel must be taken to people in new housing areas where churches have not yet been built. An outpost may be the first stage in the building of a church.

A church with vision will keep an eye on the area around it to see where it might meet religious needs by some sort of outpost. The pastor will have this on his heart. The official board will discuss it, from time to time.

Some outpost work is best done by a single church, some by persuading an association of churches or a mission board to undertake it.

Misplaced sentiment and zeal are often back of unrealistic projects. It is well to consult specialists in that sort of situation, neighborhood surveys and the intended beneficiaries.

When the desired program is laid out, provision for housing and materials and financial maintenance must be secured. Workers must be engaged. The minister will be a guiding and inspiring spirit in the enterprise. But much of its work is likely to come at the very hours when he is most confined by other tasks. The service of lay members must therefore be assured.

2. New Churches

In the census decade from 1960 to 1970 the population of this country increased by 23,892,123—13.3 percent. It is still increasing, but from 1965 to 1971 the amount spent on new church buildings decreased by almost a third from $1,207,000,000 to $813,000,000. Inflation makes this decrease 30 percent greater.

The problem of being underchurched would thus be bad enough if the population had been sitting still during these years. But the fact is that this has been a period of mass shifting around on an unprecedented scale. Frontier days have come back, not with the old movement from East to West, but with a back-and-forth movement which has put new settlements in many states and frontiers around old cities. There are today more Americans living in communities which have no churches than ever before.

Materialism is becoming the pattern of life in whole areas because they are cut off from religious influences. There are many new communities where former church members are settling into habits of godlessness because there is no church near them.

Evangelism is frustrated by the lack of churches. Countless numbers of those who are ready to be won will not be because there is no church or church school near enough to reach them. Many ministers are saying, "I would like to do more about evangelism, but there is no use. We do not have room for the members we already have." Some of these, by such devices as multiple services, might stretch their facilities. Some do not seem desperate enough in their rebellion against having their churches kept from being true churches of the saving Christ because of barriers of brick and plaster. But it is still true that millions of children are kept from knowing their Saviour and countless people for whom Christ might be a daily presence are living with little thought of Him because the gospel is imprisoned by our too-tight church walls.

Much that has to be done is financial—with Christians empowering the church-building agencies of their denominations. But there is much that congregations can do directly.

This direct action should not be taken impetuously. Many a church has been started in the wrong place because zeal has outrun investigation. The religious complexion of neighborhoods and the direction of probable population growth must be investigated.

Other churches' plans and their present ability to serve must be found out and scrupulously considered. Interdenominational committees for "comity" in building plans must be consulted, and their recommendations observed. Disagreement with such recommendations can be expressed by educating or changing the committee— but never by the anarchy which throws all Christian planning into confusion. The urge to get an elbow into a neighborhood ahead of some other denomination has great money-raising power. Church loyalty is one of the most convenient windows through which the vices Christians have thrown out the door come sneaking back.

Once the right spot is determined, then lay workers are needed to make calls which will announce plans and arouse support, to teach in a Sunday school or to conduct worship services. These are lay duties because they largely come at times when pastors must be in their churches. The meetings often start in a home or an empty store or a school building or a firehouse.

There is a saying that a big church's killing power is wider than its saving power. When its members move so far that it can no longer serve them properly, it can still keep them from joining other churches; and it can still keep needed churches from being started. By this it may guard its strength for one generation, but at the expense of the Kingdom and of the children of its widely scattered members.

The happy contrast to this is the great thing many large churches are doing in putting out colonies. It requires courage for a church to detach a portion of its members, who are living in an under-churched area, so that they may be the nucleus of a new congregation. It is an inspiring evidence of devotion when a church gives away a generous section of its finances to help such a congregation get a building and survive for the first few years. Yet that is just what is being done with increasing frequency. In most of these cases the parent churches are not trying to maintain their proud statistics by keeping the new churches in permanent affiliation. They give them the chance for a healthy life of their own.

3. Pastorless Churches

In many areas there is a shortage of ministers. Some churches, which are the only spiritual centers for the people living around them, are unable to maintain or to share pastors.

The adult Bible classes of a Missouri church are regularly providing Sabbath services for five Ozark churches. A group of ministers helped a rural Pennsylvania church by being teammates for its few laymen in a week of evangelistic visitation. As a result the church, which had not had regular services for a long while, gained enough in membership to be able to carry its share of a two-point ministry. A California minister helped his officers conduct services in two small churches; he talked over their plans with them and gave them books of sermons and prayers until they no longer needed assistance. Many churches supply the leadership for Sunday schools in pastorless churches.

4. Industrial Evangelism

The tendency of the larger denominations to be the Churches of the middle class is sadly obvious. Their failure to reach large numbers of those in industry must be a source of shame and self-examination. Many of the finest Church members are, and intend to remain, industrial workers. But the great mass of those completely untouched by any Church is one of the most pressing evangelistic responsibilities.

The fate of other countries, where the failure of the Church to reach the workers has resulted in their becoming almost solidly secular or Marxist, is often cited as a warning to us. But the essential drive in evangelism will not come from a desire to save institutions but from a desire to save people who are living and dying without knowing Jesus Christ. It is not prudence but a burning pity which will drive minds to the fierce intensity of thought which will find the solutions.

Important things are being done. By such devices as labor-management conferences, by its social pronouncements and by courses in union leadership the Church is demonstrating that it is concerned with the problems of industry and is relevant to them.

Modern evangelism is searching for ways of taking the Church's ministry directly to industrial workers or bringing them more largely into its present congregations. Home mission agencies maintain some highly successful centers for church and community life at places where factories or mines have brought an overcrowding of workers, with inadequate facilities for wholesome living.

The industrial internships, which require ministers to spend some time as industrial workers, have helped them understand the problems and viewpoints of those they hope to serve.

Some of the denominations are conducting institutes on "the church and industry" for ministers from factory and mine communities. These give courses on labor and management problems and offer instruction by those who are specialists in this sort of ministry.

At a great many places, services are being held for the workers in shops or factories. Usually half the time these require, on one day a week, is given by the employees from their lunchtime or at the end of a shift, and half is given by the management from working time. The pastor comes early and stays afterward to give a chance for conversation and discussion of private problems. Not every good minister has the knack of easy personal contacts with the workers or of holding services which will meet their needs. Those who do have this gift can use it to increase their ministry in a deeply significant way.

In Kansas City such services have been a permanent part of the program of the Church Federation. In New Jersey the ministers of one denomination have established them in such numbers that a pastor has been employed who will make the arranging of these meetings and the securing of leadership his full-time work. It is well to have the plan for such services presented first to the workers and then to their employers. Workers often have a bias against provisions their employers make for their religious welfare.

Services held outside factory gates between shifts have some evangelistic value. A sound truck with several helpers can win an intent hearing for the messages and the music. The helpers pass out pamphlets and encourage interviews. A denominational agency in Philadelphia has a sound truck which has a regular schedule of meetings outside large plants. The workers know when to expect the meetings and many make it a point to bring their friends. The helpers are pastors of churches, with a leader for whom this work is a part-time employment.

The chapel truck or trailer has a wide usefulness in evangelism. A well-equipped one will have a loudspeaker, record player, portable organ, motion-picture and film-strip projectors, hymn books or song sheets and folding chairs. It may also have liturgical furnishings. This equipment is useful for meetings in streets or vacant lots. It can provide for children's story hours or Bible schools. It reaches rural centers and migrant workers' settlements and new housing developments. It can go to fairs or be used at a courthouse square on Saturdays. Catchy music or a moving picture may assemble the crowds for a gospel message.

A French Protestant evangelistic group has made an interesting use of moving pictures in industrial areas where there is such hostility to the Church that a direct attempt to give its message would be violently resented. A secular film is shown, one whose plot raises questions of morality or ideals. At its close the leader asks the audience to stay for a discussion. Into this discussion he brings the statement of what the Christian philosophy of life has to say about such questions.

The great weakness in most of the industrial evangelism which has so far been attempted is that it is left hanging in mid-air. The workers are met apart from their homes and families. They are not related to any lasting Christian fellowship which can make helpful impressions become a permanent pattern for life. Few of them will have even a factory service for more than a brief period in their lives. Much of the benefit will pass unless they are related to a church. Since those in any factory usually come from all sections of a city, that is difficult.

We do not have to take a stand on whether or not *extra Ecclesiam nulla salus* in order to recognize that apart from established churches no satisfactory form of evangelism has yet appeared. Industrial evangelism is no exception. The final answers are likely to be found in some sort of church fellowship in the neighborhoods in which the workers live.

XVII

Using the Means of Mass
Communication

"Neither do men light a candle, and put it under a bushel, but on a candlestick" (Matthew 5:15). Modern methods of mass communication offer the Church unprecedented opportunities to let its light shine before men.

1. Advertising

A church needs a publicity committee. Many laymen know a great deal more about advertising than do their ministers. They have contacts which enable them to secure publicity for their church. Members who are not easy to enlist for other sorts of church work may be greatly interested in this.

a. Newspapers and Magazines

Paid advertisements have the minimum value of keeping the public reminded that churches are important, and giving a directory of hours and places. At their best they can also proclaim Christian truth.

The queer ideas about the Church held by those who are ignorant of it are a sort of folklore. Many know nothing about the Church which gives it any significance for them.

Some churches are using paid advertising to dispel these misconceptions and to explain themselves in the most appealing way. Under a provocative heading, perhaps with a picture or an eye-catching make-up, one paragraph can answer such questions as, "Who started the Church?" "How do people join the Church?" "Why did God make men?" "What has the Church for you?"

For financial and psychological reasons, this may better be undertaken by a combination of churches, through a federation or a denomination. The addresses and hours of service of the participating churches may be set at the margin. A state or county lay organization may make this a project.

By far the best example of how to do this has been given by the Knights of Columbus. They pay for the space they use, not coming to the editors as mendicants. They employ highly skilled advertising counsel. Such advertising does a great deal more good if it leads to further contacts. The Knights of Columbus reported that within two months 41,239 persons wrote in response to their advertisements. To them went pamphlets, personal letters, the offer of a course of religious instruction by mail and, when the way was open, a visit from a local priest.

Any church which frequently uses advertising should have professional help. The layout proposed by a newspaper cannot be distinctive.

Excellent broadcast material for local stations is offered by denominational and ecumenical agencies. This can be brief spots, dramas, panels, or talks. The "Religion in American Life" campaign is donated by an association of the largest advertising agencies, guided by a laymen's committeee. For one month each year it puts expensive and beautifully designed material on billboards, car cards, newspapers, radio and television. Information about how a community can make the most of this can be secured from Religion in American Life, 475 Fifth Avenue, New York, N.Y. 10017.

Advertising intended for secular readers should not be on the church page.

Pessimists often cite the sermon reviews in the Monday papers as proof that the Church is about done for. How can congregations long endure such empty platitudes? The error, of course, comes from expecting to find live flesh on skeletons. Many ministers feel obliged to put an outline of the entire sermon into one paragraph. A reporter will do the same. Thus the reader is informed that the minister believes prayer, Bible reading and faith to be desirable. Nothing of the why or how gets in.

Sermon reports can have evangelistic value if the minister will send the newspaper one living paragraph. Let him use the space so generously given for one illustration or one striking statement of truth, so fully put that it can count as literature not as a bill of lading. Visiting dignitaries can be asked in advance to prepare such paragraphs for the reporter.

Newspapermen are often indignant over the churches' failure to report matters of real interest and requests that the dullest sort of announcements be printed as news. They want colorful facts about people, the dramatic features of events, topics which will strike the public's interest. Names make news. What will happen is usually more newsworthy than what has happened. Arrestingly worded sermon titles are important. Paragraphs should open with brief and mind-catching sentences. Material should be sent to the newspapers early, typewritten, double spaced, on one side of the sheet, with initials and spelling correct. It should answer the five well-known news questions: Who? What? When? Where? Why?— all in the first paragraph, if possible. Pictures are valuable and should be in a form which can be reproduced attractively on newsprint.

A famous American minister learned the important lesson that information for the newspapers should not be submitted orally when he saw his sermon given a big play under the headline: DR. ———— SAYS AMERICAN WOMEN SLAVES OF PASSION. The word he had used was "Fashion." It is because of such slips that newspapers do not like to take information over the telephone.

A letter of thanks to an editor for printing a requested item, or for any sort of helpful religious material he has used, will have a good influence on his future attitude.

b. Church Printing

A parish paper serves in many ways. Personal news about members builds the family feeling in a congregation. An announcement of events builds attendance. A paper is a weekly visitor to their homes which draws the less ardent members closer to the church and keeps the insecure from drifting. It is a tie to those who must be absent for a time—to those in the armed services or away at school. Its editorials can do effective teaching. It has evangelistic value as a communication to prospective members. Recognition through it encourages workers.

Such a paper does not have to be expensive. Neat mimeographing can be done. The paper may be combined with the Sunday bulletin, to save typesetting costs. Some beautifully designed church papers are inexpensive and some which are costly are among the worst examples of printing. It is a good idea to collect papers from as many churches as possible and imitate the best ones. Plagiarism is evidence of humility, and humility is a great Christian virtue.

An attractively printed folder or card can splendidly serve evangelism by carrying a warmhearted invitation to the church, a description of what it offers and a list of the hours and places of its meetings. It can be enclosed with letters, slipped under doors or in mailboxes, carried by visitors, given by church members to their friends, handed to newcomers at the church. Professional artists or layout experts will often give their help. Colored ink and paper, drawings or photographs, unusual folds and attractive lettering can be important.

c. The Church Building

An illuminated cross or a beautiful window which can be lighted from the inside can help incline people to the church. Some neon signs for churches have too close a family resemblance to those on taverns.

An outdoor bulletin board can offer more than names and obscure sermon titles. A slogan can reveal the church's quality. "A Friendly Church With A Welcome For All" or "How Will You Spend Eternity?" would disclose how a congregation sees its mission. Texts and epigrams can be evangelistic. People who pass a church every day can feel drawn toward it by what it says to them.

d. Mailings

The postman can never do the churchman's work—and expecting him to is a common weakness. Mailed invitations never bring anyone. But mailings can be useful in preparing for personal contacts. Personal letters, printed messages, appealing notices about the church or its activities and cordial invitations to participate can make people interested and receptive when callers see them.

2. Literature

By far the best way for a Christian to help others accept what he believes is for him to tell about it in his own words. He cannot escape the responsibility for doing this by handing out tracts. But a printed message can be a valuable supplement to what is said. It can be pondered later, as a spoken word can not. It can say some things which cannot be said in person. It can tell more, with more vivid phrasing and illustration, than can a conversation. It can go where personal contacts cannot go. And it may offer a chance to get a conversation started.

Most denominations publish, in brief, paper-bound form, cards and leaflets and booklets for such use. These must be carefully chosen. Many of those from the tract-producing organizations are excellent in their quick appeal, but some are not very satisfying for thoughtful seekers. Those from the denominations are well thought out, but are often too heavy in style to be read by those who do not have a ready-made interest in the subject. A minister will do well to examine what is offered by a variety of denominations and publishers.

Church members need to know how to use such literature and where to get it. A pamphlet may say just what they have been wishing to tell someone. It should be given as one shares an interesting book with a friend whose opinion is valued—not condescendingly. To talk over a piece of literature may be the best way to bring a conversation to subjects which it has seemed difficult to approach. Bible portions can be used for this purpose. Church members in their private correspondence, or churches in their mailings to prospective members, can make good use of evangelistic literature.

A literature rack can splendidly serve a church's ministry of comfort, inspiration, education and evangelism. Church members and visitors can be urged to read its booklets and to take them to others. Literature racks are common vestibule atrocities. A church which cannot have a rack which will match its furnishings, or cannot find anyone who will keep it neat, will be better off without one.

Racks in public places may get a Christian message to those who need it. This is unattached evangelism, and therefore likely to make only a passing impression. But there are accounts of people who have received great blessing from something picked up at a hospital or a bus station.

3. Radio and Television

Radio and television offer the Church the most powerful medium of mass communication it has ever had. The greatest preaching evangelists in the past counted their hearers in thousands, but radio audiences can be numbered in millions. Never before has the Church had access to the minds of the sort of people the air waves reach. By television the minister goes to places where no representative of the Church was ever seen before. People to whom the inside of a church is as unfamiliar as the North Pole now sit before the pulpit or watch the choir.

Moreover, the mood of this medium is suited to evangelism. The experts say that radio and television are best used by those whose manner is very personal and intimate. The listeners should feel that they are hearing from a good friend. The speaker should imagine that he is talking to just one person, who is sitting right across the table from him.

Other methods of evangelism can reach only that small minority of people who some way have gotten on a church's list of prospects. Radio can reach those who should be on such a list and are not. In this country it has 130 million listeners.

Radio and television impose some strict disciplines which speakers for the Church have to learn. The switch is within quick reach, so the first sentence has to make people want to hear more. The attention span is limited, so only a genius can hope to keep attention beyond about thirteen uninterrupted minutes. For radio an interesting voice must make up for the lack of facial expression and gestures. The theme must be repeated for those who tune in late. Action words and picture words and those whose sound suggests their meaning are most effective. The vocabulary and ideas must be within the range of those who have no church background. The sort of listeners and the state of mind of the audience will vary with the time of day. Music which sets a mood or tells a story, dramatic skits or a variety of voices can help evangelism give its message. The Church is still searching out the best ways to use the air waves, but a great deal has been discovered.

A sampling of listener reactions has brought surprises. Church-goers much prefer the sort of services they are used to—choir music, prayers, great sermons by great preachers. Nonchurchgoers dislike that sort of programs, but they will listen to unusual presentations of religion—to group discussions, questions and answers, dramatic episodes. Sermons which Church people enthusiastically considered exactly right for evangelism were often rated by those outside the Church as entirely unintelligible and uninteresting.

Splendid recorded religious programs, some of them strongly evangelistic, are available from various producers. Some supply the expensive instrumental and choir music and other parts of a service, leaving an open time for a local speaker to give his message.

Many independent religious broadcasts give such a discreditable impression of Christianity that it is urgently necessary for the Churches to offer a better one. Millions whose only knowledge of religious bodies comes by radio and television will be repelled from the Christian faith and from the Church unless there are programs which give them a truer conception.

The most common failure in the Church's use of broadcasting is that it leads to nothing. Broadcasting should be breadcasting, but bread which is cast upon the radio waves is unlikely to be found again unless it is tied to something. Radio religion is too likely to go off into the ether with no result for the unchurched beyond the brief impression of a good idea. It is a strange thing that many ministers on the radio never give the slightest hint that anything more than radio religion is necessary.

If the Church does not believe in itself, it has been adequately represented by its radio spokesmen. But if it believes that discipleship cannot be complete or normal or obedient or secure outside the Christian fellowship, if it believes that God put the Church on earth to give blessings which cannot be had without it, then it has been shamefully wasting this opportunity to draw people to itself. The typical denominational or interdenominational broadcast goes to the wandering sheep with a comforting pat and a handful of feed—and then leaves them where they were.

Stations have no restrictions which prevent a minister from preaching about the Church and the benefits of Christian fellowship. He may advise his hearers to seek out a minister or a church. If the program invites correspondence or offers something by mail, the names and addresses of those who write can be relayed to the nearest church. This does not require any loss of the opportunity to help people with their immediate needs. Most of the splendid sermons which are given over the radio could lead straight into counsel about definite discipleship. What a preacher can effect in those few minutes may be small, but what he can commence is limitless.

XVIII

Organizing for Evangelism

1. The Evangelism Committee of the Official Board

The modern church is freeing itself from the conception of evangelism as a special activity for special people at special times and is making it a normal activity for all the church people all the time. This conception needs to be reflected in the organizational structure of a church. Hit and miss evangelism can set up a temporary organization for its spasmodic performances. But an adequate evangelism requires permanent leadership from the highest governing body of a church.

The Committee on Evangelism should be the most important one for a church's officers. Their meetings should give the business of this committee a large place. This committee can resist the natural tendency to let evangelism slip. It keeps in good repair the wide range of activities which a church's evangelism requires.

2. The Evangelism Council

Evangelism is an orderly and linked process, involving Contact, Cultivation, Commitment and Conservation. Every church group has some part in it. Through an Evangelism Council they can all share in its planning and operation. An Evangelism Council is a fifth wheel in the same sense that a steering wheel is. It offers the least cumbersome way of caring for duties which no church can escape. It avoids inefficiencies and wasted effort.

Representatives of all the organizations, with the pastor and the Evangelism Committee of the Official Board, make up the Council. Its most important meeting comes in the early fall, when methods and materials are considered and the evangelistic activities for the whole year are determined. This meeting is so important that

272

many churches make it a retreat—all day or overnight. The Council needs to meet at intervals throughout the year.

Churches differ in how they divide the responsibilities between the Official Board and the Evangelism Council. This whole book is an inadequate outline of what they have to do. There is enough to keep them busy! They plan how to make a church spiritually able to evangelize. They design the evangelistic activities of the whole church and stimulate those of the separate groups. They co-ordinate dates. They pool information about prospective members. They see to the care of new members, and in their meetings check up on how each one is doing. They see lacks which no one would notice in the provision for evangelism—a church-school bus, an outpost Sunday school, a junior choir. They are a prayer fellowship for evangelism.

3. The Zone System

By dividing its parish into zones, with lay leaders, a church can greatly increase its evangelistic power. This is sometimes called the "Sub-Parish" or the "Under Shepherd" plan. Some churches name the zones after the twelve tribes of Israel or the thirteen American colonies. Most churches just give them numbers.

Each zone is cared for by its shepherd, who may be a church officer or specially chosen for that task. A man and a woman may be co-leaders. These leaders are given the names of all the church members and prospective members in their zones, with useful information about them.

The zone plan beautifully gives a large church the intimacy and the personal concern of the members for each other which small congregations enjoy. It saves small churches from that impossible situation in which the minister is expected to do everything which needs to be done for everyone. It carries out the principle which Jethro persuaded Moses to adopt—and for much the same reason (Exodus 18:13-26).

The under shepherds make periodic calls at all their homes. There may be a special purpose for these seasonal visits—to deliver attendance tokens, to take a church opinion poll, to tell about a church project, to ask about prospective members. The leaders may make telephone contacts between visits. A ten-call-ten telephone plan, with lists kept by lieutenants and sublieutenants, makes it possible to get information rapidly to every home in the parish.

An occasional zone social, in the home of one of the members, can increase church friendships. There may be devotions or study or discussion of some church problem. These meetings can be highly useful for evangelism—giving nonmembers who are invited a desire for the church, helping new members to grow in church friendships and knowledge, reactivating inactive members, discussing prospective members.

Evangelistic visiting and calls on new members can be arranged through the zone leaders.

4. The Church's Individuality

Every church has a distinct individuality, just as plainly as does a person. No two are alike. Churches are old-fashioned or frivolous or contentious or serene or friendly or austere. Some are far more attractive than others. This distinctive quality is of the utmost importance for evangelism.

Like a strangely pervasive aroma, the sources of this quality may seem mysterious—but they can be traced. Some of them lie in the traditions of the church, and traditions can be changed. The spirit of the minister and of the lay leaders radiates through a church. If church members are remote from each other they will have little appeal for outsiders—and a loving church family can be developed by arranging opportunities for the members to learn to like and enjoy each other. Strife in a church will poison the atmosphere. The enthusiasm of church members for their church makes it attractive to others.

The appearance of the building can make a church seem pleasant or unpleasant. Some buildings look as though the members love them—and some do not. The most expensive may be the most unkempt, and some very appealing ones have modest budgets. Familiarity makes members blind to eyesores which strike visitors at once—the broken-down table, the grimy poster, the rusty wire which held up the Christmas lights.

Church members must be trained to be cordial to strangers. This requires both the sincere desire and continual reminders not to forget. Members with a naturally friendly manner should be assigned to greet visitors as they come and leave, without making the greetings seem to be assigned. There are occasionally criticisms of a too intrusive cordiality, but complaints of too little friendliness are much more numerous. The mood of the service may make effusiveness afterward inappropriate, but a friendly contact is never out of place when Christians gather. The old rule is a good one, "Before the service we speak to God; in the service God speaks to us; after the service we speak to each other."

The ushers are the church to strangers. It is the ushers whom they are most likely to meet and to observe. The ushers can be trained to seem what the church would like to seem—friendly, considerate, reverent, neat. One manual says, "An usher should 'smile with his eyes' rather than mechanically smiling with his mouth." Ushers need to meet for training and self-criticism. There is reason for the saying, "Better an untrained choir than an untrained group of ushers."

"I know thy works" is the evaluation by which outsiders judge a church. They will admire a church which is interested in youth, helping the unfortunate. Many moderns become conscious of social sin and their need of a Saviour from it before they become troubled by their personal sin. When they discover Christianity as a power for social righteousness, and find themselves joined with Christians in the struggle for reform, they can be led deeper until they discover the faith from which the Christian's social passion springs.

Today's evangelism is escaping from the old alienation of the hot gospelers and the social gospelers. The churches which are really doing most about social ills are found to be keen for evangelism, and the ardently evangelistic are showing a lively social concern.

5. The Denomination

The Communion of Saints can be experienced as a communion of labor—the joining of a vast number of hands and minds and souls in some great enterprise for God. The guidance of the Holy Spirit is communicated not only vertically but horizontally, as the insights which have been granted to one congregation are shared with all.

A denomination's evangelistic organization is a clearinghouse through which the best ideas and methods which have been worked out anywhere are made available. Through its employed leaders and its area and district evangelism committees a vast amount of help can be transmitted to the local churches. Its schools and conferences provide in-service training for ministers in a field in which few have a chance to become expert. It educates the constantly changing lay leaders. It supplies printed and audio-visual tools for evangelism.

A denominational evangelistic program can stir all the congregations with the sense of being part of a glorious nation-wide or world-wide movement. Those who would dismiss their pastor's suggestions as impractical will accept those same proposals when the authority of the whole denomination is behind them. Slow-moving churches, which would never by themselves get around to setting the dates or making the plans for an evangelistic effort, may do so when the dates and plans are given to them through a co-operative program.

Though there may sometimes be reason to suspect that a highly publicized program has had its source more in official activism than in prophetic vision, it always deserves a thoughtful appraisal before it is rejected. The composite wisdom of a denomination's leaders is usually worth considering. Such a program usually offers new inspiration and better methods for doing what, one way or another, has to be done.

The evangelistic agencies of the denominations share each others' literature and leaders and ideas. The professors of evangelism from theological seminaries come together annually to keep abreast of scholarly and practical developments. Our shrinking earth makes the winning of people to Christ increasingly an international enterprise, with inspirations and methods going from one land to another. Today's evangelism is worldwide. In it the churches find the reality of the universal church as they labor together to make disciples of all nations and experience together the truth of the promise, "Lo, I am with you always, even to the end of the world."

A List of Books on Evangelism

BASIC THINKING

Bloesch, Donald. *The Crisis of Piety*. Grand Rapids: Wm. B. Eerdmans, 1968. 159 pp. Investigates spirituality and faith as the sources of evangelism.

Brown, Fred. *Secular Evangelism*. London: SCM Press, 1970. 117 pp. Why churches are meaningless and religion is real to most people today. British.

The Church of England. *Towards the Conversion of England*. London: The Church and Publications Board, 1945. 156 pp. A famous, wide-ranging, profound, beautifully drafted Commission report.

Ford, Leighton. *The Christian Persuader*. New York: Harper & Row, 1966. 149 pp. A Billy Graham associate surveys today's special needs for faith.

Green Bryan. *The Practice of Evangelism*. New York: Charles Scribner's Sons, 1951. 258 pp. A calm powerful Anglican evangelist's intelligent views on preaching, counsel, goals. British.

Hunter, George G., ed. *Rethinking Evangelism*. Nashville: Tidings, 1971. 94 pp. Six authors write on the goals, the present situation, and the methods.

Hyde, Douglas. *Dedication and Leadership*. Notre Dame, Ind.: University of Notre Dame Press, 1968. 157 pp. A Christian ex-Communist finds models in Communist evangelism.

Jones, E. Stanley. *A Song of Ascents*. Nashville: Abingdon Press, 1968. 400 pp. The autobiography of a famed evangelist has many insights on evangelism.

Kelley, Dean M. *Why Conservative Churches Are Growing*. New York: Harper & Row, 1972. 179 pp. A tolerant minister-sociologist explains why tolerant churches lack evangelistic force.

Niles, Daniel T. *That They May Have Life*. New York: Harper & Row, 1951. 120 pp. A forceful call for evangelism by "heroic service and humble kindness."

Sangster, W. E. *Let Me Commend*. Nashville: Abingdon Press, 1948. 140 pp. Sparkling thoughts and illustrations on purposes, message, preaching. British.

Stott, John R. W. *Our Guilty Silence*. London: Hodder & Stoughton, 1967. 118 pp. Our neglect seen against the urgency and message of evangelism. British.

Webster, Douglas. *What Is Evangelism?* London: Highway Press, 1959. 192 pp. On Baptism, conversion, why churches miss some social groups. Biblical. British.

ON WORLD MISSIONS WITH INSIGHTS FOR CONGREGATIONS

Blauw, Johannes. *The Missionary Nature of the Church*. London: Lutterworth Press, 1962. 136 pp. Asks on a world scale, "Does everyone need Jesus Christ?"

McGavran, Donald. *Understanding Church Growth*. Grand Rapids: Wm. B. Eerdmans, 1970. 369 pp. The factors that make churches grow or diminish in many lands.

Stowe, David M. *Ecumenicity and Evangelism*. Grand Rapids: Wm. B. Eerdmans, 1970. 78 pp. New strategies in world missions. Recent criticisms of evangelism.

METHODS

Baker, Gordon Pratt, and Ferguson, Edward, ed. *A Year of Evangelism in the Local Church*. Nashville: Tidings, 1960. 210 pp. Twenty-eight writers describe various evangelistic activities.

Barclay, William. *Fishers of Men*. Philadelphia: Westminister Press, 1936. 113 pp. The noted commentary author describes evangelism by public and private teaching.

Chafin, Kenneth L. *The Reluctant Witness*. Nashville: Broadman Press, 1974. 143 pp. How lay people can share their faith. Pastoral, practical, down-to-life.

Coleman, Robert E. *The Master Plan of Evangelism*. Old Tappan: Fleming H. Revell, 1963. 126 pp. Learning from Jesus the essential principles and strategy.

Drummond, Lewis A. *Evangelism: The Counter-revolution*. London: Marshall, Morgan & Scott, 1972. 192 pp. The pastor's leadership, theology, strategy, preaching, obstacles, resources.

———. *Leading Your Church in Evangelism*. Nashville: Broadman Press, 1975. 165 pp. Foundation principles and guidelines for local church evangelism.

Gage, Albert H. *Increasing Church School Attendance*. Grand Rapids: Zondervan, 1939. 130 pp. An old classic. Said to be "the book that made the Baptists big."

Little, Paul E. *How To Give Away Your Faith*. Downers Grove: Inter-Varsity Press, 1962. 131 pp. How lay people can share their faith. How to start. What to say.

Little, Sara. *Youth, World and Church*. Richmond: John Knox Press, 1968. 201 pp. Evangelism through church work with youth.

Mallough, Don. *Grassroots Evangelism*. Grand Rapids: Baker Book House, 1971. 143 pp. How lay people can share their faith. Dwight L. Moody would approve.

O'Brien, J. A., ed. *Winning Converts*. New York: P. J. Kenedy & Sons, 1948. 248 pp. Eighteen Catholic priests and Mrs. Luce describe interesting methods and settings.

Southard, Samuel. *Pastoral Evangelism*. Nashville: Broadman Press, 1962. 185 pp. On the old evangelism, conversion, child evangelism, pastoral revivalism.

Turnbull, Ralph G., ed. *Evangelism Now*. Grand Rapids: Baker Book House, 1972. 109 pp. Ten authors offer basic insights and methods.

Woodson, Leslie. *Evangelism For Today's Church*. Grand Rapids: Zondervan, 1973. 159 pp. On "Meaning, Motivation, Method, Mobilization." On recent controversial thinking.

PREACHING

Coleman, Robert E. *Dry Bones Can Live Again*. Old Tappan: Fleming H. Revell, 1969. 127 pp. On renewal and evangelism through revival meetings. How to conduct them.

Dodd, C. H. *The Apostolic Preaching and Its Development*. New York: Harper & Row, 1936. 92 pp. The British scholar says that "to preach" in the Bible means to Evangelize.

Soper, Donald. *The Advocacy of the Gospel*. London: Hodder & Stoughton, 1961, 119 pp. Sparkling counsel and illustrations from a gifted English preacher.

Stewart, James S. *A Faith To Proclaim*. New York: Charles Scribner's Sons, 1953. 160 pp. The Yale Lectures. On presenting the gospel convincingly by preaching.

THE LAY MISSION

Archibald, A. C. *New Testament Evangelism*. Philadelphia: The Judson Press, 1946. 149 pp. Gives incentives for lay evangelism and a program for home visiting.

Chafin, Kenneth L. *Help, I'm A Layman*. Waco: Word Books, 1966. 131 pp. How lay people get into the ministries to which Christ calls them.

Gibbs, Mark, and Morton, Ralph. *God's Frozen People*. Philadelphia: Westminster Press, 1964. 192 pp. Many British and European illustrations of work by "ordinary Christians."

FOR SEEKERS

Gordon, Ernest, and Funk, Peter. *Guidebook for the New Christian*. New York: Harper & Row, 1972. 145 pp. For private reading or new member classes. Interesting bibliography.

Shoemaker, Samuel M. *How To Become A Christian*. New York: Harper & Row, 1953. 158 pp. For seekers, but also tells evangelists what steps to suggest.

HISTORY AND SOCIAL ACTION

Green, Michael. *Evangelism in the Early Church*. Grand Rapids: Wm. B. Eerdmans, 1970. 268 pp. A scholarly and careful survey by a British professor.

Smith, Timothy L. *Revivalism and Social Reform*. Nashville: Abingdon Press, 1957. 253 pp. Shows the strong social gospel in the great revival movements.

Sweet, Wm. Warren. *Revivalism in America*. New York: Charles Scribner's Sons, 1944. 192 pp. A standard history of the colonial and later revivals.

Wirt, Sherwood. *The Social Conscience of an Evangelical*. New York: Harper & Row, 1968. 177 pp. Calls evangelicals to the social action that should be their heritage.

THEOLOGY

Baillie, John. *Baptism and Conversion*. New York: Charles Scribner's Sons, 1964. 121 pp. Clear, scholarly, brief, biblical.

Barclay, William. *Turning to God*. London: The Epworth Press, 1963. 103 pp. What conversion is and what it requires of the convert and the church. Biblical.

Barth, Karl. *Church Dogmatics,* IV:3 (2nd half-Reconciliation). Edinburgh: T. & T. Clark, 1950. On vocation, the Holy Spirit, the Christian Community, the Christian hope.

de Jong, Pieter. *Evangelism and Contemporary Theology*. Nashville: Tidings, 1962. 112 pp. On Reinhold Niebuhr, Tillich, Bonhoeffer, Brunner, Barth, Bultmann.

Division of Studies, World Council of Churches. *A Theological Reflection On the Work Of Evangelism*. Geneva: The Bulletin, 1959. 45

pp. The report of a Consultation. Rambling, but some luminous thoughts.

Documents of Vatican II. New York: Herder & Herder, 1966. 792 pp. See especially the sections on "Laity" and "Missions."

Hoekendijk, J. C. *The Church Inside Out*. Philadelphia: Westminster Press, 1966. 212 pp. A call to evangelize, not by bringing outsiders in, but by sending insiders out.

Kantonen, T. A. *Theology of Evangelism*. Philadelphia: Muhlenberg Press, 1954. 98 pp. Heavy. For students. Sees evangelism at the heart of all church activities.

Kraemer, Henrik. *The Communication of the Christian Faith*. Philadelphia: Westminster Press, 1956. 120 pp.

——. *A Theology of the Laity*. Philadelphia: Westminster Press, 1958. 191 pp. A decisive study which has had great influence.

Stott, John R. W. *Fundamentalism and Evangelism*. Grand Rapids: Wm. B. Eerdmans, 1959. 80 pp. Fundamentalism's bearing to evangelism from a British viewpoint.

Index